P9-CCV-284

JESSE JAMES WAS HIS NAME

JESSE JAMES

WAS HIS NAME

OR, FACT AND FICTION CONCERNING
THE CAREERS OF THE NOTORIOUS
JAMES BROTHERS OF MISSOURI

by William A. Settle, Jr.

COLUMBIA, MISSOURI
UNIVERSITY OF MISSOURI PRESS

To Marjorie

Acknowledgments

M<small>Y</small> INTEREST in the Jesse James legend has extended over a period of more than twenty-five years. It has brought me into contact with countless people who share this interest, and almost without exception they have generously given their knowledge and their materials. The aid and advice of the staffs of the several libraries, including those of newspapers, in which I have worked were invaluable. To all the people who have helped me in any way I gratefully acknowledge my indebtedness. I am especially indebted for assistance in research to Professor Homer C. Clevenger of Lindenwood College; Mr. Elmer Pigg of Orrick, Missouri; Mr. Harry Fleenor of Topeka, Kansas; the late Martin E. Ismert of Kansas City, Missouri; the late Robert F. James and Mrs. James of Excelsior Springs, Missouri; Dr. Floyd C. Shoemaker and his successor Dr. Richard S. Brownlee and their staffs at the State Historical Society of Missouri; and the University of Tulsa for research grants that twice enabled me to devote summers to writing. Secretaries in my department, especially Freda Disch and Leta Nunn, have rendered valuable assistance in addition to their typing.

Dean W. Francis English, President Elmer Ellis, and Professor Lewis E. Atherton of the University of Missouri and Dr. Richard S. Brownlee have at various times read portions of manuscript and have offered helpful suggestions and criticisms. My debt of gratitude to President Ellis and Professor Atherton is second only to that I owe my wife Marjorie for her aid in research and typing and for her encouragement. She and our children Bill and Carol have often freed me from other responsibilities in order that I could, as they said, "work on Jesse."

W. A. S.

December, 1965

Contents

H. M. Belden, ed., *Ballads and Songs Collected by the Missouri Folklore Society*, 2d ed. (University of Missouri Studies, Vol. XV, No. 1; Columbia, 1955), 402–404.

Illustrations

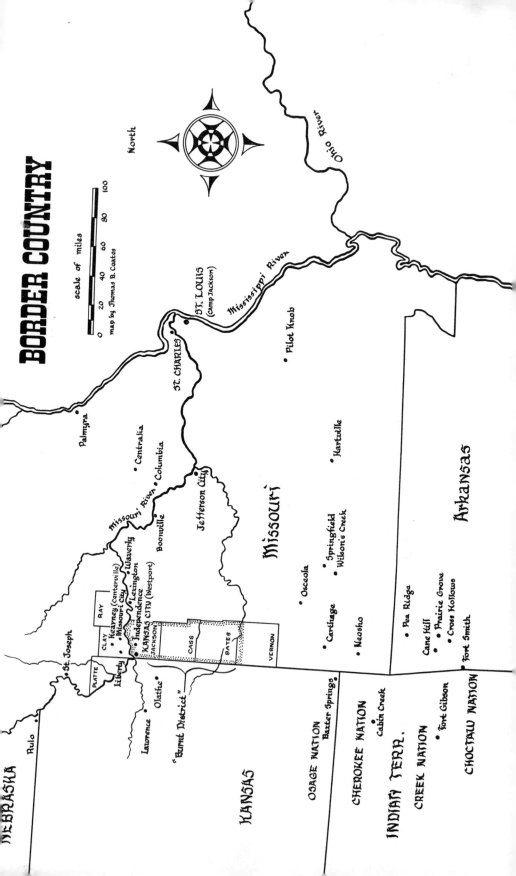

I

Jesse James was one of his names,
Another it was Howard.
He robbed the rich of every stitch.
You bet, he was no coward.

"Greatness," said Mark Twain, "may be classed as the ability to win recognition. Some time ago I was making a purchase in a small town store in Missouri. A man walked in and, seeing me, came over with out-stretched hand and said, 'You're Mark Twain, ain't you?'

"I nodded.

"'Guess you and I are 'bout the greatest in our line,' he remarked. To this I couldn't nod, but I began to wonder as to what throne of greatness he held.

"'What is your name?' I inquired.

"'Jesse James,' he replied, gathering up his packages." [1]

Greatest in his line! Jesse was not alone in this estimate of himself. Carl Sandburg has said, "Jesse James is the only American bandit who is classical, who is to this country what Robin Hood or Dick Turpin is to England, whose exploits are so close to the mythical and apocryphal." [2]

The man who can be likened to both Robin Hood and to Dick Turpin certainly showed two faces to the world; the legends that have grown up around Jesse James reflect these opposite characters. One blood-and-thunder biographer of Jesse James declared that he was "superior in audacity and rashness, courage and hellishness to all other romantic scoundrels"; he despaired because no language contained "enough lurid words, wild synonyms, ensanguinary adjectives and murderous verbs to do justice to this horrible monster." [3] But the writer of another paperback thriller described Jesse as a modern Robin Hood who robbed the rich and gave to the poor, who took human life only to defend his own, who used liquor, tobacco, and bad language sparingly, who loved his mother devotedly, and who manifested the same easy grace when robbing trains and banks that he did when protecting helpless women and children.[4] Badman or Robin Hood — take your choice!

Whichever form of the legend you favor, both are based on fact. No other bandits in American history match the record of Frank and Jesse James for evasion of the law. For sixteen years after the first bank robbery by a band of which they later became the acknowledged leaders, they went unapprehended. Even then, officers of the law did not capture them. Jesse was shot from behind by a traitor in his own band; Frank voluntarily handed his gun to the governor of Missouri. Their exploits were indeed real; their crimes are of public record.

The legend, however, is a different matter. In it fact and fiction are so entwined that it is difficult — at times, impossible — to untangle them. And of the two faces presented by "the greatest in his line" — the merciless, murdering robber and the dashing Robin Hood — it is the latter that appears more frequently as the years pass. Books, ballads, dime novels, newspapers, magazines, motion pictures, radio, television, and the tellers of the tales that comprise American folklore — all have, sometimes unwittingly, conspired to build this legend. In the legend Frank shares equally with Jesse their title, "The American Outlaws," but it is Jesse — Jesse of the alliterative name — who lives on as King of Bandits.

Jesse James has been front-page news since 1869. As late as 1927 a Kansas City lawyer created a national sensation by suggesting, as part of a scheme to promote a motion picture, the erection of a monument to Jesse James. Letters of protest and of approval deluged editors the country over.[5] In March of 1950, when one J. Frank Dalton — surely the last man to claim that he is Jesse James — asked the court at Union, Missouri, to change his name to Jesse James, newspapers throughout the United States and abroad reported the legal proceedings, and newsreel cameras recorded the scene.

How did these cold-eyed bandits who gunned down unarmed men and terrorized the countryside become heroes? How did their robbing and murdering become the stuff of legend? The answers lie in the motives and attitudes of Americans who, according to one theory, find Jesse James fascinating because, through reliving his exploits, they release vicariously something of their own outlaw spirit and their suppressed rebellion against the restrictions of modern society. Obviously, in the motives of the society that sustains the legend there is much to account for its creation. But these motives are many and complex — too much so to be examined here.

While there is no one simple explanation of the making of the James legend, the James band's career of lawlessness and the growth of the legend around it are deeply rooted in and inextricably bound to the events of the Civil War and its aftermath. The nature of the war in Missouri, a border state, produced bands of guerrillas from which many of the postwar outlaws came. The feeling that developed toward the Missouri bushwhacker, favorable or unfavorable, was probably more intense than that toward any other participant in the war. Political developments in the state during the war and the subsequent years of rule by the Radical Republicans fueled the flames of hatred between ex-Confederate and ex-Union groups. In such an environment acts of banditry by men who had served the Lost Cause as irregular warriors easily acquired political meanings that brought forth defenders who glorified the men who committed the depredations. Thus was laid the foundation for the legend.

The Grangers' resentment of the practices of railroads and banks, the East's contempt for the West, the economic rivalry between Chicago and the cities in Missouri, and the long-exercised proclivity of the press to exploit the sensational are all ingredients of the James saga. Under these influences, misrepresentation of facts was inevitable. The numerous histories of the James band that began to appear even before the organization broke up and the dime novels that utilized themes based on the James boys' escapades for over twenty years tended to transform the brigands from real to mythical characters. Today's media of entertainment extend the legend with every money-making repetition of it.

Thus, the James legend is a significant part of American political and social history, produced and sustained by powerful forces that have left their marks in countless other ways on the course of American development.

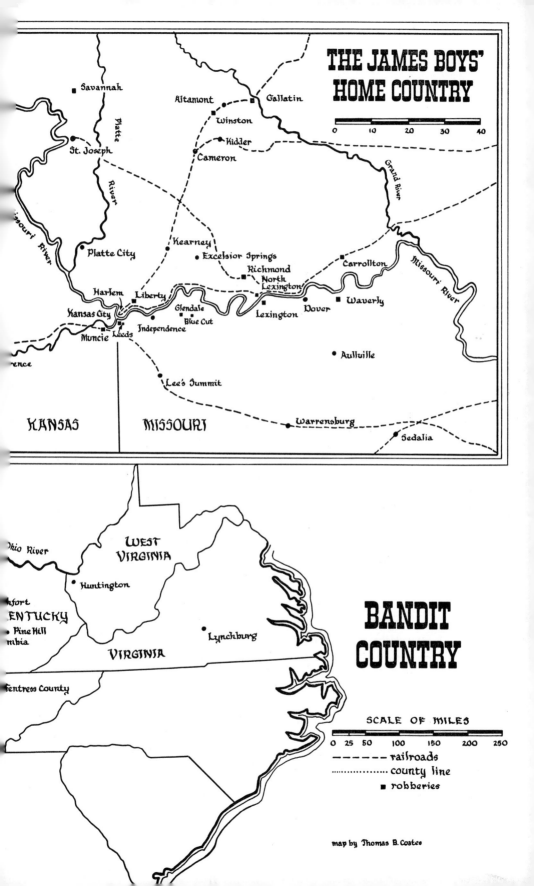

THE JAMES BOYS'
HOME COUNTRY

Savannah

Platte River

Altamont

Gallatin

Winston

Kidder

Cameron

St. Joseph

Grand River

Missouri River

Kearney

Platte City

Excelsior Springs

Richmond

Carrollton

Missouri River

Harlem

Liberty

North Lexington

Glendale

Blue Cut

Lexington

Dover

Waverly

Kansas City

Independence

Muncie Leeds

Aullville

KANSAS

MISSOURI

Lee's Summit

Warrensburg

Sedalia

Ohio River

WEST
VIRGINIA

Huntington

BANDIT
COUNTRY

kfort

ENTUCKY

Pine Hill

mbia

Lynchburg

VIRGINIA

Fentress County

SCALE OF MILES

0 25 50   100   150   200   250

- - - - - railroads
.... county line
■ robberies

map by Thomas B. Coates

His mother she was elderly,
His father was a preacher,
Though some do say, I can't gainsay,
His mother was his teacher.

Through accident of time and place of their birth, Frank and Jesse James entered life in the midst of great events in the making. Yet there was nothing in their circumstances by which one could foretell that these two sons of a Baptist minister and his young wife were to become a national legend. Frank, christened Alexander Franklin James on the day of his birth, January 10, 1843, and Jesse Woodson James, born September 5, 1847,[1] were the sons of Robert James and Zerelda Cole James, who had migrated from Kentucky to western Missouri in 1842. The courtship of this couple had started when Robert was a ministerial student at Georgetown College and Zerelda was attending school at a Roman Catholic convent in Lexington where her guardian James M. Lindsay had placed her. They were married on December 28, 1841, after Lindsay had given written authorization to county officials and after James and a friend had posted bond of fifty pounds of tobacco to guarantee his fulfillment of the marriage agreement.

In their first year of marriage, Robert and Zerelda traveled to Clay County, Missouri, to visit her mother, who was living there with her second husband Robert Thomason. Here the young couple decided to settle. Soon James acquired land and took over the pastorate of the nearby New Hope Baptist Church. Things went well for this forceful frontier preacher. The church was reorganized; its membership grew;

6

and in 1844 it joined the North Liberty Baptist Association, which James helped found. He is credited with organizing two other congregations, and there is no doubt that he gave unstintingly of his material means, his time, and his energy for the work of his Lord.[2]

That the Reverend Robert James was a man with intellectual interests is indicated by an inventory of his estate, filed in Clay County Probate Court in 1851. It listed in his library fifty-one books dealing with mathematics, chemistry, philosophy, theology, astronomy, grammar, history, literature, Greek, Latin, public speaking, and other subjects. He was a leader in the founding of William Jewell College, sturdy Baptist school, at nearby Liberty, and he served on the college's first board of trustees.

James prospered. By 1850 he held unencumbered title to the 275 acres of land that he farmed and on which he had built a modest home. On the farm were thirty sheep, six head of cattle, three horses, and a yoke of oxen; in addition, James owned seven slaves.[3] Besides Frank and Jesse, two other children were born into the family — Robert, on July 19, 1845, and Susan Lavenia, on November 25, 1849. Robert died in infancy.[4]

As sudden and as inexplicable as some of his sons' later actions was James's decision to leave his established farm to accompany a party of gold seekers to California. Susan was less than a year old, Jesse not yet three, and Frank just past seven when this man of God, about whom a contemporary said, "No better man than Robert James ever lived," left his family to go West.

In later years those who sought to explain his action found an answer in the personality of his wife, strong-willed and determined. Although devoutly religious in her own way, Zerelda did not share Robert's enthusiasm for the ministry, according to Robert's brother. Her emphatic objections to his absence from home for revivals so annoyed the Reverend Mr. James, goes the explanation, that he determined to leave for California to minister to the searchers for gold. He planned to return after an absence of about twelve months, and he hoped to find that his wife's disposition had mellowed a bit in his absence.[5]

Another explanation was James's desire to provide more abundantly for his family. According to one writer, he almost lost his nerve to the point of giving up the trip when little Jesse, clinging to his father's legs and crying, looked up and begged him not to go. But Robert had given his word to the others in the party, and a man could not go back on his word.[6]

One of these explanations or the two combined may account for his going, but in Clay County the old-timers still whisper gossip handed down through the years of serious trouble between Robert and Zerelda.

"She wasn't straight"; too many men shared with Robert James her affections; Jesse was not his son, but the bastard offspring of a local doctor, and James, who could stand the humiliation no longer, was leaving her for good! [7]

No evidence to support this charge against Zerelda James has been found. The canard that her spouse was saying goodby to her forever in 1850 because of her unfaithfulness is destroyed completely by two letters he wrote to her on his way to California and one he wrote after reaching his destination.[8] These letters, manifestly written by a devoted husband to his cherished wife, are concerned mainly with details of travel and the condition of his companions. None express anticipation of riches at the end of the journey. A letter dated July 19, 1850, five days after reaching the diggings, tells of his washing one pan of dirt; he had spent the remainder of the time in efforts to find Clay Countians who had preceded him. No hint that he had left an untrustworthy wife appears in these communications. A letter "from old Fort Carney April 14th 1850" urges Zerelda "to train up your children in the nurture and admonition of the Lord and live a christian life your self." The closing sentence directs her to "Give my love to all inquiring friends and take a portion of it to yourself and kiss Jesse for me and tell Franklin to be a good boy and learn fast."

In his next letter, written on his knee in a tent at "Grand Island 1 mile from New Fort Carney on our way May 1, 1850," Robert James expressed a longing "to see you and the children." But, knowing "that it will be 12 or 18 months," he found consolation that through the art of writing he could converse "as if face to face." To his wife, children, and friends he again sent his love and asked Zerelda to "pray for me that if no more [we] meet in this world we can meet in Glory."

A few weeks after arriving in California, Robert James, then thirty-two years of age, became ill, died, and was buried in an unmarked grave.[9] It is interesting to speculate on the effect this man might have had on the lives of his sons had he lived and returned to guide them in their developing years.

Zerelda James married twice after Robert's death. Her second union, with Benjamin Simms, was of short duration. A few months after their marriage, they separated, and Simms died a short time later. One explanation for the brevity of this marriage is that the boys tormented Simms, older than Zerelda by a number of years, until he left the family. The tradition in the James family is that Zerelda left Simms because he was mean to her sons.[10]

In September, 1855, Zerelda married Dr. Reuben Samuel, presumably a physician, who devoted most of his energies to farming, and they made their home on the James farm northeast of Kearney, in Clay County. Samuel was quiet and self-denying, whereas his wife was stormy and self-assertive. Somehow they got along — possibly, because he let her have her way and because he was good to the boys. To Dr. and Mrs. Samuel four children were born — Archie, John, Sallie, and Fannie.[11]

Actually, little is known or can be learned of Frank's and Jesse's boyhood. After they attained notoriety as bandits, the writers of the cheap paperback books spun many stories to show that their savagery as guerrillas and outlaws was inherent and had been manifested in childhood. One anonymous author declared that "of the milk of human kindness they had none," for they had "drunk in from their earliest days only bitterness and malice." They hated "with the hatred of the most remorseless cruelty." He described their pleasure in torturing dumb animals, cutting off the ears and tails of dogs and cats and removing the wings of birds, for the "pitiful cries of the dumb suffering things was a sort of music they delighted in." [12] The same writer reported that rifles and pistols were common playthings for the James boys and that as children they became expert in their use. Such tales of the cruel and lethal sport of these youngsters were printed repeatedly.

There is no evidence to show that Frank and Jesse were any better or any worse than normal boys of their time and circumstance. However, these were crucial as well as rough times, and undoubtedly the great events that were happening on the Jameses' doorstep left their mark upon the boys. Clay County, in which the family lived, is separated from the western boundary of Missouri by only one county, Platte, which nestles in the great eastward bend of the Missouri River above Kansas City. South of Clay County and across the Missouri River lies Jackson County, on the Missouri-Kansas border and containing the towns of Kansas City and Independence. The three counties that extend south of Jackson County along the Kansas border are Cass, Bates, and Vernon, in that order. Clay County is bordered on the east by Ray County, with Richmond as its county seat, and south of Ray and across the Missouri lies Lafayette County. Liberty, the county seat of Clay County, is fifteen miles northeast of present-day downtown Kansas City, and Kearney (sometimes called Centerville), near the James farm, is twelve miles northeast of Liberty.

The western border of Missouri had, after the second decade of the century, been the frontier of settlement and the jumping-off place for travelers headed for the Spanish Southwest, California, and Oregon. To the west of Missouri lay the Territory of Kansas, occupied mainly by resettled tribes of Indians from the East and denied to land-hungry whites. The Missouri Compromise had prohibited slavery there, and

9

on this issue organization of the territory had foundered. But in 1854 Congress opened Kansas and Nebraska to settlement and authorized the people to determine for themselves whether slavery should be permitted or prohibited in the territory.

Slaves made up only 9 per cent of the population of Missouri, but three-fourths of the people had slave-state backgrounds. Most Missourians had favored opening the Kansas Territory without restriction on slavery, but even the proslavery men were satisfied with the arrangement made in 1854, under the presumption that Kansas would be slave and Nebraska free. Soon, however, the formation in the North of organizations to assist the migration of antislavery settlers to Kansas aroused proslavery Missourians to feverish opposition. If Kansas were a free state, they reasoned, slave property in western Missouri would not be safe.

All hell broke loose on the border. Newspapers along the border quickly suggested the use of force to keep Northerners out of Kansas. At Liberty, only fifteen miles from the Samuel farm, the *Democratic Platform* shouted: "Let every man that owns a Negro go to Kansas and settle and our Northern brethren will be compelled to hunt further north for a location." Kansas must be a slave state if half the citizens of Missouri had to emigrate there with musket in hand, prepared to die for the cause. "Shall we allow such cutthroats and murderers . . . to settle in the territory adjoining our own state? No! If popular opinion will not keep them back, we should see what virtue there is in favor of arms." [13]

Missourians now crossed over into Kansas, some to reside, others to influence elections, and all to intimidate the emigrant from the North who opposed slavery. Jackson, Clay, Lafayette, and nearby counties were the marshaling points for these activities. Prominent citizens of this region and even some of Missouri's most important political leaders led the forays.

Soon the nation was hearing of "Bleeding Kansas," as the newly formed Republican party and the antislavery forces in the North propagandized events in Kansas for their own purposes. No doubt the violence was exaggerated and the issue of slavery overemphasized in contemporary and subsequent accounts of happenings along the Missouri-Kansas border from 1855 to 1860, but old John Brown was there, Missouri's "Border Ruffians" did raid into Kansas, and Kansans retaliated. Competition for land and conflict over claims probably caused as much violence as the slavery question. Political intrigue and rivalry for patronage in the new territory were involved, too. Anarchy prevailed, and crimes of violence — murder, theft, burning of homes, and other out-

10

rages — were common to the region. Never more than a small segment of Missouri's population was involved, but the years of lawlessness on the Missouri-Kansas frontier left bitter hatreds that influenced the nature of the irregular warfare that was to agitate Missouri from 1861 to 1865.[14]

The James boys' mother was a Southerner, and she owned slaves. Her sympathies and those of her family were with the forces fighting to preserve slavery. It is likely that her young sons did indeed hang John Brown and other abolitionists in their play. Children could not have been so close to these violent events without being affected. Soon, even greater forces engulfed the James family and their contemporaries as civil war swept over the land.

III

My Jesse dear, your mother here
Has taught more than she ought ter.

The "border ruffians," as they were named in the Eastern press, who battled with Kansans in the 1850's were not truly representative of Missourians, although many people in the North and East believed they were. The state's vote in the presidential election of 1860 was a vote for moderation; Douglas and Bell together attracted nearly 71 per cent of the popular vote, while Breckinridge and Lincoln, representing the two political extremes, received barely 29 per cent. No doubt most Missourians hoped that moderation would resolve the growing discord between North and South and prevent the threatened division of the Union.

The question of what Missouri would do should the Southern states secede was not answered by this election, however. Unconditional Union men and radical secessionists were only a small part of the state's population, but since three-fourths of the citizenry were of Southern origin, there was in the state widespread acceptance of the view that if a breakup of the Union came, the seceding states should be permitted to withdraw peaceably. In his farewell address in January of 1861, outgoing Governor Robert M. Steward excoriated abolitionists and secessionists equally, but urged the state to take a position of armed neutrality in case of war. Steward's successor, Claiborne F. Jackson, whose pro-Southern views had long been known, had openly supported Douglas in 1860, but in his inaugural address he advised Missouri, in case the Union was dissolved, to go with the South.

As the secession movement gathered strength in states of the lower

South during the winter of 1860–1861, the Missouri legislature, in a move strongly supported by Jackson and by other Southern sympathizers, called a convention to consider Missouri's relation with the Union, but specified that any ordinance of secession had to be approved by Missourians at the polls. The election of delegates on February 18 gave pro-Union men an overwhelming majority, and when the convention met, it resolved that "at present, there is no adequate cause to impel Missouri to dissolve her connection with the Federal Union." This was the wording devised by the Conditional Union men, who maintained something of a wait-and-see attitude. The convention adjourned on March 22 after granting a committee of eight members authority to convene it at any time before the third Monday in December, 1861.

Governor Jackson, however, was not restrained by the action of the convention, for in response to the Secretary of War's call for troops after the firing on Fort Sumter, he answered that Missouri would not provide a man for an "unholy crusade" to coerce the seceded states. While saying openly that he was defending the state's right to remain neutral, the Governor was soon taking steps for Missouri's active support of the Confederacy by raising and arming a state force. He called the legislature into special session and ordered the State Guard into summer encampments.

Frank P. Blair, General John C. Frémont, Captain Nathaniel P. Lyon who had been ordered from Fort Riley, Kansas, with a small unit of troops, and other leaders in St. Louis were now determined that Missouri should participate in the war against the seceded states. The first armed clash between this group and Jackson's forces occurred on May 10 at Camp Jackson on the outskirts of St. Louis, where about eight hundred members of the State Guard had been encamped for a week. The Confederate government had secretly supplied siege guns to the camp, and plans were in the making for storming the Federal arsenal in St. Louis.

Blair, distrusting Jackson, had used his influence with the Lincoln Administration to have General W. S. Harney, commander of the Federal forces in St. Louis, replaced by Captain Lyon, who quickly transferred most of the arms and ammunition in the arsenal to Alton, Illinois. On May 10 Lyon's and Blair's regular and volunteer forces surrounded Camp Jackson and peaceably obtained the surrender of the entire body there. As the camp's garrison was being marched away under guard, the nature of the proceedings was altered suddenly by a shot from the crowd that had gathered to witness the surrender. The Federal forces retaliated for the killing of one of their men, and in the brief fight that followed, twenty-eight people died.

Before another month had passed, Jackson had obtained from the legislature an appropriation to arm the state and had issued a call for fifty thousand men to resist invasion. He conferred the rank of major general on Sterling Price, a former governor of the state and a hero of the Mexican War, and appointed him commanding officer of the State Guard. At the same time Lyon and Blair, with influential connections in Washington, determined to save Missouri for the Union with Federal troops. The issue was now drawn.[1]

The James family was already caught up in events. Mrs. Samuel was outspokenly pro-Southern; probably most of the people in Clay County favored the South in the early part of the war. The first blow struck by either side in the state fell on April 20 with the seizure, by residents of Clay and Jackson counties, of fifteen hundred stands of arms and four small cannon from the Federal arsenal at Liberty. These weapons, in time, made their way to the forces of Price and Jackson.[2] Meanwhile, communities in the county had begun to form companies of local militia or "Home Guards." On May 4 a company was organized at Centerville, later called Kearney, a few miles from the Samuel farm, and one of its members was Private Franklin James, then eighteen years old.

Resolutions adopted at the organizational meeting of this company of Home Guards stated the Clay Countians' allegiance. They declared that Missouri should hold her soil against invasion from any quarter, and they endorsed Governor Jackson's refusal to supply troops to the Union. The Home Guards took their stand: "Secession is a remedy for no evil; but if we are reduced to the necessity of engaging in the present war and strife, then we will stand by and co-operate with our Southern brethren." Interestingly, the Liberty *Tribune*, edited by Robert H. Miller, former Whig and later a strong Union man, approved the formation of these military companies and commented that they were composed of the best men in the county.[3]

Clay County units were among those that answered Jackson's call for fifty thousand men, but from the entire state not over one-tenth of that number responded. The Governor and General Price, in command of state forces, evacuated Jefferson City, the capital; it was quickly occupied by Federal troops commanded by Lyon, now a brigadier general. After a preliminary skirmish at Boonville, which gave the Federal forces control of the Missouri River at that point, both armies concentrated in southwest Missouri. Minor engagements of regular forces occurred throughout the state, but the major battle of 1861 in Missouri was the Battle of Wilson's Creek, fought near Springfield on August 10. There, Price's Missourians and Brigadier General Benjamin McCulloch's Arkansans defeated the Federal army commanded by Lyon, who was killed. It was a bloody fight, resulting in long casualty lists for both sides.

With new recruits who rallied to his banner after the victory at Wilson's Creek, Price moved northward and captured the Federal garrison at Lexington on the Missouri River. The massing of Union soldiers soon made this position untenable, and he retired again to southwest Missouri. Price's withdrawal reflected the effectiveness of Lyon's command, for Federal forces had seized control of the Missouri River and all important railroads in the state before the General's death at Wilson's Creek. North Missouri was now secure for the Union.

The state convention had reconvened on July 20 and summarily deposed the governor and lieutenant governor, abolished the legislature, established a provisional government with Hamilton R. Gamble at its head, and prescribed an oath of allegiance to the United States and the provisional government that, in time, all state and county officials and all voters were required to take. The provisional government ruled the state until 1865.

Governor Jackson, safely behind Price's lines, called a session of the legislature to meet at Neosho in October, 1861. This body, without a quorum and in violation of the law that called the state convention, passed an ordinance of secession and elected two senators and eight representatives to the Congress of the Confederate States of America, which in November admitted Missouri to the Confederacy. But political identity brought no military advantages. Reinforcements called for by Price did not appear in the numbers he anticipated and needed. With telling effectiveness Federal patrols obstructed his recruiters in central and north Missouri from reaching him with men so that, in early 1862, he was forced to retreat into Arkansas. In March the forces of Price, McCulloch, and sundry other units, all under the command of Major General Earl Van Dorn, were defeated in the Battle of Pea Ridge by an army less than half as large as theirs under Major General Samuel R. Curtis. McCulloch was killed. Federal forces, it became evident, would hold Missouri for the Union. The provisional government continued to function within the state, and the Confederate government of Missouri was forced into exile.

With a force of about four thousand men Price crossed Arkansas into Mississippi and entered the Confederate service. Many of his men returned to Missouri, some to act as recruiting agents for the Confederacy, but no major engagements between regular armies occurred in Missouri until Price invaded the state in the fall of 1864.

One of Missouri's most gallant Confederate heroes, later a staunch friend of Frank James, led a contingent of men that crossed Arkansas to Mississippi with "Old Pap" Price in 1862. This man was Joseph O. Shelby who, by the war's end, held the rank of brigadier general and who bears the distinction of being the only Confederate general who never surrendered. A native Kentuckian, Shelby was a young and prosperous landowner, stockman, and rope manufacturer at Waverly in Lafayette County in the middle 1850's. With Claiborne F. Jackson and David R. Atchison, powerful political figures, he had led some of the earliest forays of Missourians across the border into Kansas and had done his part in sustaining the bloody border warfare.[4] By coincidence he was in St. Louis on May 10, 1861, the day that Camp Jackson capitulated to the forces of Blair and Lyon. Blair, a cousin of Shelby, had sent for him in the hope of getting him to accept a commission in the Federal army. But Shelby's real mission in St. Louis was the purchase of 100,000 musket caps. These were shipped in flowerpots to Lexington, Kentucky, for the use of John Morgan, organizer of the famous "Morgan's Raiders," against Federal forces. Instead of joining Blair, Shelby returned to his plantation and waited a few weeks until his second son was born to his young and delicate wife Betty. Thus he missed the Battle of Boonville, but immediately afterward he joined the Lafayette County Cavalry. Minor engagements and the Battle of Carthage on July 5, a preliminary to Wilson's Creek, plus a recruiting ride to his home county engaged him until the victory at Wilson's Creek. From that time to 1865 he worked and fought tirelessly for the Confederacy as recruiter and raider.[5]

Joining Shelby in 1862 and chronicling his exploits through most of the war was the man who probably contributed more than any other to making the James legend. This was Major John Newman Edwards, formerly Shelby's fishing and hunting companion, now his adjutant. Edwards, born on January 4, 1839, at Front Royal, Virginia, had come to Lexington in the mid-1850's and soon was working as a printer on the local newspaper, the *Expositor*. Before the end of the decade he was the paper's editor and for over twenty years following the war, ranked among the greatest of Missouri's newspapermen. In the war years, his and Shelby's paths crossed those of notorious guerrilla fighters. Both the General and his adjutant admired these irregulars for their recklessness and dash and valued their power to confuse the Federal forces. More important, Shelby's and Edwards' warborn loyalty to them was never to be shaken by the guerrillas' postwar careers of crime.[6]

Nothing has ever been witnessed in American life like the horror, terrorism, bloodshed, and disregard for human life that Southern guerrillas wreaked upon large areas of Missouri between the fall of 1861 and the spring of 1865. Since Federal troops in the area were also guilty of acts of unbelievable brutality, residents of the state endured the worst of an irregular war from both sides.

General Price was, to a degree, responsible for the beginning of this irregular warfare, for, in desperation, in the fall of 1861 he sent recruiting officers into central and northern Missouri, behind Union lines. Obviously irritated that less than five thousand men had answered Governor Jackson's call for fifty thousand, he was determined to raise an army by one means or another. He also instigated a plan to destroy the Union rail and telegraphic communications, hoping so to divert the enemy that recruits could get through the lines. Few men were added to the Confederate ranks, but the burning of railroad bridges, firing on and wrecking of trains, and cutting of telegraph wires brought the vengeance of Federal forces down upon Confederates caught behind the lines and also on civilians.[7]

Major General Henry W. Halleck, now in command of the Department of the West, decreed on December 22, 1861, that anyone caught in these acts of sabotage would be immediately shot. Trial by military commission and punishment by death if found guilty were ordered for those accused of, although not caught in, such an act.[8] Halleck followed this order on January 1 with another that made clear the distinction between the guerrilla bands who had no rights and the regular military units that were, if captured, entitled to treatment as prisoners of war.[9] Halleck thus prescribed the treatment of guerrilla prisoners; numerous later orders reiterated his position. Since guerrillas were to receive no quarter, they would give none. Their depredations continued.[10]

Guerrilla fighting behind enemy lines cannot be carried on successfully without a sympathetic civil population to sustain it with shelter, subsistence, information, and men. Starting with a small group of active pro-Southern sympathizers in 1861, the number of persons who had cause, or thought they had cause, to lend assistance to these independent bands grew with events of the war. No small factor was the behavior of Union troops composed of men from other states and of the state militia maintained by the provisional government. The state was under martial law from August, 1861, to March, 1865. Admittedly, Union commanders in Missouri were faced with problems that only the most competent officers could have handled. But from the beginning to the end of hostilities there were ineptness, misunderstanding, political maneuvering, frustration, bitterness, vicious desperation, lack of discipline, and utter stupidity in the actions of Union officers and their men. Their own official reports, especially those for 1861 and 1862, are filled with ample evidence.[11]

Interference with unoffending citizens, arbitrary arrest and imprisonment of men and women, illegal requisitioning of supplies by irresponsible citizens, robbery, pillage, arson, and murder by Federal and state troops were perhaps inevitable in the circumstances, but they created an environment conducive to the most desperate measures of reprisal. Many young men "went to the brush" because of the indignities and injustices suffered by themselves and their families. Unable to reach regular Confederate units, they joined the guerrilla bands, which offered their only refuge and their quickest opportunity to strike back.

While partisans sent out by Price brought guerrilla warfare to northern Missouri, the civil population in the counties along the Missouri-Kansas border south of the Missouri River was preyed upon mercilessly by pro-Union troops commanded by three veterans of earlier Kansas conflicts: James H. Lane, Charles R. Jennison, and James Montgomery. Once "Lane's Brigade" had crossed the state line, everyone in its path was assumed to be disloyal, and Lane's outfit, composed of some of the most desperate and dangerous men ever brought together in a legally constituted army, turned to indiscriminate looting and stealing. Property of Union sympathizers was seized as ruthlessly as that of Southerners.

On September 23, 1861, Lane's Kansans almost totally destroyed Osceola, the county seat of St. Clair County, which had for a time been a supply base for Price's army. Everything in the town that could be loaded into stolen wagons was hauled away by stolen teams. Only three buildings were spared from burning. The forces of these three zealots, Lane, Jennison, and Montgomery, raided the Missouri countryside, burning farmhouses and laying waste everything in their path. Pressures exerted in Washington by Union men in Missouri to bring these Kansas troops under control were of little effect, for Jim Lane, while serving in the Senate, had become a power in Washington.[12] In March, General Halleck wrote George B. McClellan that authorities in Washington did not understand conditions in Missouri and that the conduct of Federal troops, especially those of Lane and Jennison, had "turned against us many thousands who were formerly Union men." [13]

Early in the war, the thieving, pillage, and killing by the hated Kansans brought no immediate retaliation, but by December of 1861 the band of William Clarke Quantrill, which was to wreak vengeance beyond calculation on Kansans, was taking form. Quantrill had, as a youth, begun to show the characteristics that in 1862 and 1863 made his the most feared name on the border. This man, who was known to his followers as Charley or Charles W. "Quantrell," was born in Canal

Dover, Ohio, in 1837, and had come to Kansas twenty years later when the border troubles were at their worst. He had soon gone west to Utah, but had returned to Kansas in 1859. In Kansas, where he was known as Charley Hart, he was an antislavery Jayhawker and horse thief. After teaching a term of school and after experiencing several brushes with the law he joined five young Quakers in December, 1860, in a slave-stealing raid at the farm of Morgan Walker in Jackson County, Missouri. There he betrayed his companions and led them into an ambush in which three were shot and killed. Quantrill then invented a fantastic tale to gain the trust of his new allies, who had no natural love for a traitor. He told them he was born in Maryland and had come to Kansas to join an elder brother on a trip to California, but they were waylaid by Montgomery's men; his brother was killed, and he was left for dead. He recovered, joined a band of Kansans, and had been avenging his brother's death by killing the murderers one at a time: the Quakers he had betrayed were some of them. His wartime followers accepted the fable without question.

Quantrill spent the winter of 1860–1861 in Jackson County, but is believed to have gone to the Cherokee Nation in present northeastern Oklahoma in the spring of 1861 and to have joined his Cherokee friends in the Battle of Wilson's Creek. There is evidence that he went from there with Price to Lexington, but left the General as he retreated southward. By Christmas of 1861 Quantrill was the leader of ten young Jackson County men, around whom his pro-Confederate guerrilla organization grew. William H. Gregg and George Todd, who soon had reputations of their own, were among them. The Seventh Kansas Cavalry, led by Jennison, was harassing Jackson County in December and providing incentive for retaliatory measures by the guerrillas.[14]

Through the early months of 1862 Quantrill's band accelerated its activities, committing one act of wanton violence after another against Union troops and sympathizers. The pattern was to ambush, rob, kill. The band knew the area, could ride wildly, shoot accurately, and disperse quickly, and they had sympathetic supportive friends in the countryside.

Wild and reckless youths who saw an opportunity for adventure and some who saw a chance for pillage and plunder were attracted to Quantrill by the band's daring exploits. Also, the policies of Union forces alluded to earlier and the determination of Union leaders that there be no neutrality played into the hands of Quantrill and his lieutenants. When Price and Jackson failed to hold Missouri for the Confederacy, many who had joined their forces and other Confederate units returned to their homes under amnesty offers made by the provisional government through the military authorities. One such order, issued by Major General Henry W. Halleck on February 14, 1862, and published widely, gave those not accused of violating the laws of war and those not recognized as "notoriously bad and dangerous men" an opportunity to take an oath of loyalty to the government upon giving bond with good security for their conduct.[15] A considerable number of Missourians who had served with Confederate forces surrendered and were paroled under terms of this proclamation.

But surrender and parole did not kill a man's commitment to the Confederate cause. Hence, bitter resentment was aroused when the provisional government, on July 22, 1862, ordered every man of military age to enroll in the state militia, subject to call for service by the commanding officer of the Department of Missouri.[16] Parolees considered the order a violation of the parole bargain; they were noncombatants who should not bear arms against the agents of a government for which they previously had fought. Many took to the brush rather than enroll.

Halleck's order may have influenced Frank James to go to Quantrill. According to tradition, Frank's Clay County company joined the forces of Sterling Price in the summer of 1861 and fought in the Battle of Wilson's Creek. Undoubtedly this tradition is correct.[17] He was also among those men who accepted the amnesty offered in the spring of 1862. The Liberty *Tribune* of May 2, 1862, lists him as one of several who, the week before, had taken the oath of allegiance and had given bond of $1,000 for future good behavior to Colonel William R. Penick in Liberty. But Frank's whereabouts in the winter of 1861–1862 are a matter of conjecture. One story is that he was with Price until the latter's retreat from Springfield in February, 1862, and was left behind because he was sick with the measles. He subsequently fell into the hands of Federal soldiers, who permitted him to go home.[18]

There is no record of the date and circumstances of Frank James's entrance into a guerrilla band. The oral tradition, later reported in many written accounts, is that he was arrested for violating his parole and that he escaped from jail and went straight to the brush.[19] The writings of Major John N. Edwards, often unreliable, place Frank with Quantrill in the fall of 1862, and this could well be true.

In 1862 one Confederate general believed strongly in the military value of irregular outfits like that of Quantrill and was willing to give them official approval and to use them at every opportunity. This was General Thomas C. Hindman, who by July of 1862 commanded the Confederate District of Arkansas. On April 21, 1862, the Congress of the Confederate States of America had passed the Partisan Ranger Act, authorizing President Jefferson Davis to commission officers to form bands of partisan rangers. As interpreted by the War Department, Confederate departmental commanders would pass on all applications for such commissions. Taking advantage of this provision, Hindman in July made his own rules for guerrilla warfare and soon selected several Confederate officers to go to Missouri to start guerrilla activities. Included were Colonel Upton Hays, Colonel Joseph C. Porter, and Captain Joseph O. Shelby. These agents of Hindman came into Missouri at a time when Union forces were carrying out the "extermination policy" toward guerrillas with grim determination.

Joe Porter picked up enough recruits to bring a reign of terror to northern Missouri. He also fought open battles with Federal troops, a type of action that guerrillas avoid if possible, and his departure from the guerrilla methods proved disastrous for him. He was killed in early January near Marshfield. But the desperation to which he drove Federal officers is illustrated by what Southern men in Missouri call the "Palmyra Massacre."

An elderly Union man named Andrew Allsman had disappeared from Palmyra and was believed to have been killed by Porter's forces. The Federal officers issued a public proclamation giving Porter ten days to return Allsman safely, else ten prisoners from Porter's command would be executed. Allsman was not returned; ten men were selected from among the prisoners, and they died before a firing squad.[20]

Less drastic measures generally enabled regular Union troops to deal effectively with the guerrillas in northeast and central Missouri, but not along the Kansas border, where at least six of the officers sent by Hindman united their efforts with those of the guerrilla bands. A savage attack was made on the Union forces of Lieutenant Colonel James T. Buel at Independence on August 11. Buel and those survivors who had not run away surrendered and were paroled. The Union forces' well-planned but poorly executed retaliatory strategy resulted in a fierce and bloody battle at Lone Jack on August 16, in which the guerrillas attacked and defeated the command of Major Emory Foster. After Foster's surrender, guerrillas hastily moved southward and were joined by men Jo Shelby had recruited, for Union troops were massing.[21]

Quantrill missed the Battle of Lone Jack, and he and Hays did not move south with the others. On August 14, Colonel Gideon W. Thompson swore Quantrill and his men into the Confederate service as partisan rangers. The men then elected Quantrill as their captain, William Haller as their first lieutenant, George Todd as second lieutenant, and William H. Gregg, third lieutenant. On September 6 Quantrill looted the town of Olathe, Kansas, and for weeks he moved about freely in Jackson County and the region south. But by November, Colonel E. C. Catherwood's Union forces at Harrisonville were making it so hot for him that Quantrill took his men into Kansas and headed south along the Fort Scott–Fort Gibson road through the Osage Nation in southern Kansas. In mid-November he joined Brigadier General John S. Marmaduke, the cavalry commander for the District of Arkansas. Marmaduke later was governor of Missouri when the last charges against Frank James for crimes committed in Missouri were dismissed, following his surrender.[22]

Quantrill and about 150 men were assigned to Jo Shelby's brigade at Cross Hollows, Arkansas. Tom Hindman, demoted because of his government's dissatisfaction with his ambitious plans, including the guerrilla attacks in Missouri that Jefferson Davis did not approve, was commanding the army in northwest Arkansas. He was pleased to have Quantrill's group in the area.[23]

Quantrill soon was absent, but his men, led by Lieutenant William H. Gregg, in the next two and a half months participated in battles at Cane Hill and Prairie Grove, Arkansas, and at Springfield and Hartville, Missouri. During this time Quantrill went to Richmond, Virginia, to seek a commission and official approval of his guerrilla band. No record of the commission exists, but there are evidences in the *Official Records* that Quantrill displayed a commission, authorized by Jefferson Davis, when he was in conflict with Confederate officers later in Texas.[24]

Was Frank James one of Quantrill's men in Shelby's command in November and December, 1862? According to legend he was, and he is credited with being in the small group commanded by John Jarrette that rescued Shelby from death or capture by Major James M. Hubbard on the eve of the Battle of Prairie Grove. As far as Shelby was concerned, these guerrillas saved his life, and he was never to forget it.[25]

Notwithstanding the certainty with which some writers have placed Frank James at Prairie Grove, evidence exists that casts doubt upon the claim. The anonymous author of *History of Clay and Platte Counties, Missouri,* published in 1885, stated that in the spring of 1863 Frank joined the bushwhackers under Fernando Scott, who was making a raid on Missouri City.[26] The Liberty *Tribune* of May 22, 1863, listed "James of Clay" as one of Scott's band that had just attacked Missouri City.

John McCorkle, who had served in the State Guard as Frank James had, joined the guerrillas in 1862 and lived through three years of wartime violence. He was at Prairie Grove, and in his *Three Years With Quantrill: A True Story* he wrote of witnessing the incident in which Major Hubbard was prevented from killing Shelby. Later in his account

McCorkle told of the return to Missouri in late April of 1863, his activities upon his return, and his brother Jabez' accidentally shooting himself while the two were on a hunt for Federals. Jabez died "after lingering for some time." McCorkle's book does not give dates, but records that soon after Jabez died, "Frank James, Capt. Scott and Tom Harris" came up. This, according to McCorkle, was the first time he met Frank James.[27] Either McCorkle's memory was untrustworthy, or Frank James was not at Prairie Grove to help save Shelby from death or capture.

In passing, one other news item about Frank James in 1863 should be noted. On August 7, 1863, the Liberty *Tribune* reported that "Franklin James" was one of the "Three Southern Men in Search of their Rights" who the day before had robbed a man named David Mitchell of $125, his pocket knife, and a pass from the Provost Marshal permitting him to cross the plains.

Another Quantrill man whose name figured heavily among postwar outlaws was no doubt in Shelby's command in Arkansas. This was Thomas Coleman Younger, overgrown son of a wealthy Jackson and Cass County landowner and staunch pro-Union man, Henry W. Younger. Cole was in Quantrill's band by the spring of 1862.[28] His father's livery stable in Harrisonville had been looted in the summer of 1861 by Kansas troops that took wagons and carriages worth four thousand dollars and forty saddle horses.[29] After Cole joined the guerrillas, Henry Younger was robbed and murdered by Federal militiamen commanded by a Captain James Walley. Cole attributed his entrance into Quantrill's band to earlier troubles with Walley. His prominence as a guerrilla caused his mother's house to be burned and brought other harsh treatment to her and her family at the hands of Union men during the war.[30] Cole's brother James fought as a guerrilla in 1864, but Robert and John, of importance later, were not old enough to participate in the war.

Quantrill was back in the saddle in 1863, and Cole Younger and Frank James rode with him. Many were the band's deeds of violence, but the bloodiest slaughter was done during Quantrill's raid on Lawrence, Kansas, on August 21. Leaving Shelby's command in late April, Quantrill's men were in Lafayette County, Missouri, before Union forces detected them. It was the old story. Houses of Union men were set afire, mail and telegraph communications were disrupted, patrols were ambushed, bridges were burned, and fear gripped the countryside. Through a hurried reorganization of the military forces, General James G. Blunt in Kansas and Brigadier General Thomas C. Ewing at Kansas City were given responsibility for stopping the guerrillas.

Ewing decided the first step was to eliminate or render ineffective the sympathetic pro-Southern population; he began arresting and jailing wives, mothers, and sisters of well-known Quantrill men. The arrests enraged the guerrillas. For lack of adequate prison space Ewing planned and sought authorization for the banishment of the families of Quantrill's men from the region. Tragedy intervened before Ewing's banishment policy could be carried out.

On August 14, a three-story building in Kansas City that was being used as a prison for these women collapsed. Four girls were crushed to death, another was fatally injured, and others were badly hurt. A sister of Bill Anderson, who was soon to be known as "Bloody Bill," was killed, and another injured. Christie McCorkle Kerr, whose brother John McCorkle and husband were with Quantrill, was killed. Other victims were sisters and cousins of men in Quantrill's band. Soon the rumor was circulated that Ewing had ordered his men to weaken the structure to cause the collapse and had thus deliberately murdered the prisoners. This incredible charge was believed by the men in the brush, and they became savage with rage.

Four days after this tragedy Ewing issued General Order Number Ten, approved by General John M. Schofield, which set into operation machinery for banishing from the state the families of guerrillas and others who aided them. This order may also have influenced the decision of Quantrill's band to raid Lawrence, home of the hated Jim Lane and long a target for these men.[31]

The lieutenants of Quantrill — Bill Anderson, Cole Younger, George Todd, and others — assembled their bands in Johnson County, Missouri, and united under Quantrill for the assault on Lawrence. About 450 men rode for Lawrence. During the two days they bore toward the doomed town they pressed farmers into service as guides, some of whom the raiders shot when they had served the band's purpose. At dawn on August 21 they were poised and ready to spring upon the unsuspecting town of three thousand people, and a few minutes later the most fiendish massacre of the Civil War was under way.

In the next two hours at least 150 defenseless victims — mostly men, but also a few boys — died at the hands of the raiders from Missouri. No women were harmed, but many of them and their children were forced to witness the cold-blooded slaying of husbands and fathers. Houses and buildings were looted and burned, sometimes with occupants hiding inside. Senator Lane escaped; upon hearing the rebel yell he made for a cornfield in his nightshirt and was not found. Quantrill had planned to take Lane back to Missouri for a humiliating execution — a public hanging or burning at the stake. Many of the guerrillas celebrated their victory by getting drunk on the loot of saloons. At nine o'clock the reported approach of Union troops stopped the orgy and put the raiders to flight toward Missouri. Their only casualty in Lawrence was a man too drunk to ride away with his fellows.

The flight was a running battle back to Missouri, but the guerrillas suffered few losses. With thousands of Union troops in eastern Kansas and western Missouri joining in the hunt, it was expedient to disband and disperse, once Missouri was reached. Only a few guerrillas were caught, and they were quickly executed.[32]

The military and political reverberations of the Lawrence raid extended from the border to Washington. Senator Lane was informed that United States troops would block an invasion of Missouri by Kansans. Nevertheless, Lane, who blamed Ewing above all others for the fate of Lawrence, forced the General to carry out his banishment policy through issuance and execution of his famed General Order Number Eleven of August 25. The order gave all persons living in Jackson, Cass, Bates, and half of Vernon counties, Missouri, except those within one mile of the principal towns, fifteen days to leave their homes. Those who could prove their loyalty to the nearest military commander were permitted to take up residence at military stations; others were forced to find refuge outside the proscribed area.

The stunned evacuees had little chance to take even a small part of their movable possessions while prodded by troops who looted and then burned what was left. Murder and arson laid desolate a huge area that came to be known as the "Burnt District." The pitiable condition of these banished people, as witnessed by an Unconditional Union man and army officer, the artist George Caleb Bingham, inspired his painting, "Order No. 11," depicting the execution of the order. These and other incidents of 1863 left a legacy of hatred on both sides of the border.[33]

In October about four hundred guerrillas reported to Quantrill in Johnson County, formed into four companies commanded by William Gregg, George Todd, Bill Anderson, and David Pool, and hastily moved south to Texas. Near Baxter Springs, Kansas, the only skirmish of the trip occurred when they met a train of ten wagons convoying General James G. Blunt, guarded by a one-hundred-man cavalry unit, to Fort Gibson in Indian Territory. Most of the Union force escaped, but the Missourians mistakenly thought Blunt was among those they killed. From the wagons they obtained needed supplies. Except for approbation for the routing of Blunt, the reception of Quantrill's gory crew by regular Confederate officers in Texas was not very cordial. During the winter of 1863–1864, which they spent in the region of Bonham, Denison, and Sherman, demoralization of the band set in. Lawrence had been too much for some of them.[34]

Frank James was with Quantrill at Lawrence, where he had slaughtered ruthlessly,[35] but Jesse James had not yet joined a guerrilla band. The exact time of his initiation into guerrilla warfare has not been determined. Some evidence indicates that it was the fall of 1863, and in that case he would have spent the winter in Texas. Other information points to his joining a group led by Fletcher Taylor, a lieutenant of Anderson, in the early summer of 1864 after the guerrillas rode back from Texas. In either instance his record of bloody action began in 1864 when he, a seventeen-year-old boy, rode with Bill Anderson's band.[36]

The oral tradition, which made its way into print after the James band became notorious, holds that rough treatment of his family by militiamen caused Jesse to go to the brush. No records exist to substantiate the details of the tradition, but they are consistent with verifiable events in other families. No one who could have known the truth openly questioned this tradition.

Mrs. Samuel is the central figure in the story at this point. It was not in her nature to hide her sentiments, and once Frank became active in the war she, too, was a participant. Presently, she and Jesse were under surveillance of the local militia for carrying messages and serving as lookouts for guerrillas. In time the militia visited the Samuel farm. Finding Dr. Samuel first, they tied a rope around his neck, threw it over the limb of a tree, and yanked him up four times in an unsuccessful attempt to make him talk. Next, they abused and insulted Mrs. Samuel, who was pregnant. Still failing to get information, they sought Jesse in a field where he was plowing and there administered a sound lashing to his back as he ran through the corn rows trying to escape. After maltreating the family, the militia left.

A few weeks later Mrs. Samuel was arrested, and with one or more of her children she was held prisoner in the jail at St. Joseph for a brief time. These happenings, usually dated in the summer of 1863, are said to have hardened Jesse's determination to join his brother Frank in the guerrilla bands.[37]

Frank was in Texas during the winter encampment of 1863–1864 and saw Quantrill lose control over his men, many of whom quit the raiders for all time. Some of Quantrill's men transferred to the regular forces: William H. Gregg entered the regular Confederate service with Shelby's brigade in Louisiana; Cole Younger also joined the regular army, and was assigned to a recruiting expedition to New Mexico that failed. By the end of 1864 Younger was in California, where he stayed until after the end of the war.[38] Others of Quantrill's men rallied to the banner of Bill Anderson, who had broken with Quantrill. Those men who stayed with Quantrill now saw him virtually replaced by George

Todd as head of the band. Todd and Anderson were the real guerrilla leaders in Missouri in 1864, and they were the ones who led two separate columns from Texas to the counties on the Missouri River in early summer, 1864. There they caught the Union military unaware, and they struck Federal garrisons and patrols and Missouri towns with unbelievable force and viciousness.[39]

During the late summer and fall the guerrilla fighting of Todd and Anderson was co-ordinated with the raid General Price led into the state; the guerrillas were to divert Union strength from a concerted attack on Price's columns. Price entered southeast Missouri, fought a battle at Pilot Knob, passed by Jefferson City, and finally met decisive defeat in the Battle of Westport (now within the boundaries of Kansas City) on October 23. From there he retreated to Arkansas. Marmaduke and Shelby had come into Missouri with Price, and for a time Todd's guerrillas were a part of Shelby's command.[40]

The reminiscences of old guerrillas indicate that Jesse James was with bloodthirsty Bill Anderson through the summer and early fall of 1864. Of him, Bill is said to have remarked, "Not to have any beard, he is the keenest and cleanest fighter in the command." In activities near the Ray-Carroll county line on August 12 or 13 Jesse sustained a severe wound on the right side of his chest. Although not expected to survive, he responded quickly to care given him at the home of John A. Rudd in Carroll County, but the wound left a permanent scar. He was able to ride again with Bill Anderson by mid-September and to take part in the most horrifying guerrilla action of the year—the Centralia massacre and the subsequent rout and slaughter of the company of Major A. V. E. Johnson.

On the night of September 26 followers of Todd and Anderson to the number of 225 encamped on the Singleton farm, four miles south of the Boone County town of Centralia and only fifteen miles from the university town of Columbia. Early the next morning Bill Anderson took thirty of his men and rode into Centralia to terrorize the residents. For three hours Bloody Bill's men had a high time, and they even set fire to the railroad depot. Then the Columbia stage arrived, providing a load of victims for the robbers. One of the passengers in the stage was a member of Congress from Columbia, James S. Rollins, whose distinguished efforts for higher education in the state later earned him the title, "Father of the University of Missouri." Wisely, he used neither his correct name nor the title of his office on this occasion.

About noon the train from St. Charles approached the station, but was stopped by ties that Anderson's men had piled across the track. Amid random discharge of revolvers, its passengers were forced from the cars; among them were twenty-five unarmed Union soldiers on furlough. These defenseless men were forced to line up and strip to their underclothing, for Union uniforms were now being used as disguise by the guerrillas. Upon questioning, one of the soldiers, Thomas Goodman, admitted that he was an officer (although only a sergeant), and Anderson ordered him out of line. Arch Clement, who delighted in bloody acts, was told casually to "muster out" the soldiers. He began shooting point-blank at the helpless men, and the rest of the guard quickly joined in the slaughter. Only Tom Goodman was spared. Anderson and his men then returned to Singleton's, taking Goodman with them.

That afternoon Major Johnson and his mounted infantry arrived at Centralia. Upon learning what had happened, Johnson left part of his command in the town and rode out to find Anderson. When he did locate him, Johnson made the mistake of ordering his men to dismount; the guerrillas quickly mounted and charged on horseback, all but annihilating the Union force. Only those men who were holding horses in the rear escaped. Over one hundred soldiers were killed by the guerrillas, who lost three men, one of them Frank Shepherd, who rode next to Frank James; after the carnage, James discovered that Shepherd's brains and blood were splattered over his leg. In time, seventeen-year-old Jesse was publicly identified as the man who fired the shot that killed Major Johnson; his brother Frank stated in an interview for a Columbia newspaper a number of years later that Jesse shot Johnson.

One month later Bill Anderson was killed when the forces of Major S. P. Cox led the guerrillas into an ambush in southern Ray County. Jesse James was with Anderson's men, but escaped. George Todd had been killed five days earlier near Independence. Time was running out for the men in the brush.[41]

of being treated as Confederate partisans. These roving groups of irregular fighters had lost their reason for being and presently degenerated into bands of outlaws.[2]

Jesse James is believed to have been among a group led by George Shepherd to Texas and to have remained there through the winter.[3] He certainly was with the men who returned to Missouri in the spring of 1865. Some of them rode back from Texas, ignorant of Appomattox. Their leaders included Dave Pool, whom John N. Edwards once called "a daredevil . . . as pitiless as a famished Bengal tiger," little Arch Clement, and Jim Anderson, brother of Bloody Bill. The suddenly detected presence of this outfit in central Missouri shocked the Federal and state forces. But once the guerrillas learned the war had ended, many of them were ready to give themselves up, provided they would be treated as prisoners of war.[4]

What was to be the status of these irregular fighters to whom the rules of war and amnesty did not apply? General Grenville M. Dodge, on May 7, sent instructions to Colonel Chester Harding, into whose military district Pool, Clement, and Anderson had moved: "You can say to all such who lay down their arms and surrender and obey the laws that the military law will not take any further action against them, but that we cannot protect them against the civil law should it deem best to take cognizance of their cases." [5] This offer was enough for Dave Pool, who surrendered forty members of his band at Lexington and then acted as an agent to bring in others. At least two hundred irregulars came in, but there were many, including Jim Anderson and Arch Clement, who chose to remain outside the law.[6] Nor is there any record that Jesse James ever surrendered. While most of the guerrillas could return to their prewar homes and ways of life, the James brothers remained rootless. In early 1865, Jesse's stepfather Dr. Reuben Samuel and his family, along with six other families, had been banished from Clay County. The Samuels found a home in Rulo, Nebraska, across the river from Missouri's farthest northwest county,[7] but the family, as well as its grown sons, felt displaced from their true home.

There is an often repeated story that in May or June of 1865 Jesse James, having returned from Texas, started with a group into Lexington to surrender and receive parole. In spite of the white flag the men carried, Union soldiers fired on them. Jesse was wounded, a bullet penetrating his chest a short distance from the scar of the wound of August, 1864. Two soldiers followed the fleeing Jesse into the woods, but gave up the pursuit when their quarry shot one of their horses. That night Jesse lay in the bed of a creek to soothe his fever; the next day he dragged himself to a field, where he was found by a plowman.

When he had recovered strength enough to travel, friends helped him to his mother's new home in Nebraska; Major J. B. Rogers, in command at Lexington, is said to have paid for his transportation.[8]

Whatever the truth of this story, it is certain that Jesse suffered a serious wound at about this time. The scars from this wound and the earlier one, in addition to the tipless middle finger on his left hand, were to serve as identifying marks when he was killed. The finger tip probably was lost in June of 1864 in a battle in which two Clay Countians named Bigelow were killed by the Jameses and others, commanded by Fletcher Taylor. But Jesse's loss of a finger tip has also been credited variously to the marksmanship of soldiers of the Second Colorado Cavalry; to that of a prominent lawyer and Union soldier of Columbia, Missouri, named Carey H. Gordon; and to the accidental firing of Jesse's own gun.[9]

Tradition has it that Jesse stayed with his mother in Nebraska for about eight weeks. Making little, if any, progress toward recovery, he grew despondent and begged his mother to return to Missouri so he might not die in a "Northern" state. Mrs. Samuel brought him by boat down the Missouri River to Harlem, now North Kansas City. There they stopped at the boardinghouse home of his uncle John Mimms. Until late fall Jesse was nursed by his cousin Zerelda Mimms, or Zee as she was called. Still unable to walk, Jesse was taken by wagon to the farm near Kearney, where he slowly regained his strength. Before he left the Mimms household, Jesse and Zee were betrothed, but many years were to elapse before they would exchange vows.[10]

How hostile was the environment in Missouri to which the wartime guerrillas, or even Confederate soldiers, returned in 1865 and later? In most communities, it was as hostile as the men themselves made it. There were instances of wartime acts being avenged, certainly, but almost everywhere, if the returned belligerents became peaceful, law-abiding citizens, they were unharmed. This was true in spite of the ugly bitterness that was engendered by the kind of war that had been fought in Missouri.

The first five years after Appomattox were undoubtedly trying years for Confederate sympathizers in Missouri. The Radical Republicans had gained control of the provisional government and in 1865 had adopted a state constitution that disfranchised everyone who had aided the Confederacy. It also forbade their engaging in the principal professions. Understandably, resentment of this proscription lingered long with the proscribed. Moreover, economic recovery from the effects of the war was slow. Times were hard for several years and added economic stress to the political strains of the postwar period.

Considering the strong feelings that guerrilla warfare had generated, parole of the irregulars after an oath of loyalty was extremely lenient treatment at the hands of military officers who could have shot them without a trial. The ex-guerrillas, however, were never free of the fear of prosecution by the state. The Missouri Constitution of 1865 provided that no person should be prosecuted in any civil or criminal proceeding for acts done after January 1, 1861, in military service of the United States or of the state, or in pursuance of orders issued by persons in either the state or national military services. No amnesty was provided for persons acting under orders of the Confederacy.

As the war closed Frank and Jesse James were not notorious. Neither had attained leadership among the bushwhackers. Their names were not those that had attracted public or official attention. Hence, one wonders if their later notoriety may not have caused their guerrilla comrades to exaggerate their wartime deeds. Among these men Jesse had acquired a nickname that stayed with him: Dingus. He had used the word as an exclamation one time when part of his equipment pinched him painfully, and he was immediately dubbed with it. Frank James was "Buck" to his intimates.

For over four years after the end of the war the James boys lived at their mother's home and came and went as they pleased. They apparently cultivated the farm when they were there and got along with their neighbors without serious difficulty in spite of their participation in the most immediate violence of the war in Missouri. During this time Jesse joined the Baptist Church in Kearney and was baptized. Had he and Frank never become involved in postwar banditry, they could, without any question, have lived peaceably at home. Examples are numerous of former Quantrill men who lived in peace and prospered quietly after the war.[11]

*Many of the wartime irregulars, however, instead of settling down, continued to harass the countryside. As late as 1867 the problem of lawlessness was so serious in Clay County and in Ray County, immediately east of Clay, that local committees of safety were formed by the citizenry. At times the state militia was entrusted with the administration of the law, but it was frequently charged with greater lawlessness than the people in the areas it was supposed to control. Violence in the form of stealing, robbing, and killing was widespread and frequent.

In this setting former guerrillas found a new outlet for their unruly natures — bank robbing. In all probability, boredom and inability to adjust to the calm of postwar life drove them to crime, though their defenders assert that they were avenging wrongs inflicted by rapacious bankers. However, the outlaws' indiscriminate robbing and killing of innocent people to avenge mistreatment by others manifest a desire less for justice than for marauding and murder.

The extent to which Frank and Jesse James were involved in the several bank robberies that occurred in the area in 1866, 1867, and 1868 is difficult to determine. No contemporary evidence has been found to indicate they were even suspected in the earliest of these, but their known friends were involved, and in time Frank and Jesse came to be acknowledged as the leaders of the band that started its depredations at Liberty, Missouri, on February 13, 1866.

On that afternoon a band of ten to twelve men rode into Liberty and posted themselves at strategic places. Two of them, dressed in blue soldiers' overcoats, walked into the Clay County Savings Bank where Cashier Greenup Bird and his son William were at their desks, working on the bank's records. One of the customers stopped beside a stove as if to warm himself, while the other walked to the counter and asked change for a bill. As William Bird stepped toward the counter to make the transaction, he faced a revolver. Instinctively, young Bird backed toward his desk; the man holding the revolver jumped on and over the counter, as did his companion. Instantly each banker faced a pistol; each was warned that if he made any noise he would be shot. The customers wanted all the money of the bank and wanted it quick. William Bird, stunned by the suddenness of the attack, did not move until one of the robbers hit him in the back with his pistol, shoved him into the open vault, and forced him to transfer the contents of the vault shelves to a cotton wheat sack. The other bandit gathered the bank's paper currency and government bonds from a tin box on a table, and his accomplice put them also in the sack. The senior Mr. Bird now was ordered to join his son in the vault, whereupon, Bird reported, "I hesitated and began to parley. He told me that if I did not go in instantly he would shoot me down. I went in."

The bandits closed the vault door on their victims, but the lock failed to catch, so the two "Birds" were not so securely caged as the highwaymen had intended. In the few moments it took the prisoners to discover this and to release themselves, the bandits had left, bearing the laden wheat sack. It contained nearly $60,000 in greenbacks and national currency, government bonds, and gold and silver coin belonging to the bank, plus three bags of gold and silver owned by individuals who had left them at the bank for safe keeping.

The raiders attracted no attention while the robbery was taking place, but as they prepared to ride away, one of the men who had been in the bank suspected a passerby, S. H. Holmes, and George Wymore, a student at William Jewell College who chanced to be on the street, of attempting to raise an alarm, and he began shooting at them. Holmes was unharmed, but Wymore was killed. Then the band, all firing wildly into the air, rode out of town and south toward the Missouri River. They crossed the river on a ferry, ahead of the posse of townsmen that soon formed and pursued them. By the time the posse could get across the stream a blinding snowstorm had obliterated all tracks. The victimized bank and its competitor in Liberty made common cause against the bandits and together offered rewards totaling $10,000 for the capture of the robbers and return of the money.[12]

The plunder of the Clay County Savings Bank seems to have been the first daylight bank robbery in America in peacetime, although a daylight raid on the banks at St. Albans, Vermont, by Confederate soldiers in civilian clothes antedated it more than a year.

Other robberies on the Liberty pattern occurred subsequently. At noon on October 30, 1866, Cashier J. L. Thomas of the banking house of Alexander Mitchell and Company in Lexington, Missouri, was alone and busy at his desk when two young men entered. One of them presented a "7:50 $50 bill" and with a laugh asked the "discount" on it. Thomas, not liking the manner of the request, replied that the bank was not buying that kind of funds. By the time Thomas had finished speaking, two other men had entered the bank and were pointing pistols at his heart. Quickly, the intruders removed $2,011.50 from the cash drawer, but the contents of the cash drawer was not all that the bank's visitors sought. They threatened to kill Thomas if he did not "disgorge" $100,000 they believed the bank vault contained. Thomas denied that the bank held that much money. The robbers searched his pockets, but did not find the key to the vault. Thomas remained defiant, and when he declared that killing him would not produce the key the robbers walked out and mounted their horses, hitched in a nearby alley.

Dave Pool and his brother John, also a former Quantrill guerrilla, led the posse that pursued the bandits. Once, they came in sight of the brigands, who now numbered five, but could not overtake their fleet horses. One suspects that the chase may have been a hoax, undertaken to prevent a more effective pursuit of the gang. The bank offered no reward, and the local newspaper commented that the thieves were no doubt "Kansas red-leg robbers." [13]

The next attempt on a bank failed completely. On March 2, 1867, Judge John McClain refused the demand of six robbers to give up the keys to the vault of his private banking house in Savannah, Missouri. The bandits shot him, though not fatally, and fled without any of the bank's money.[14]

34

Less than three months later, robbers attacked another bank. An estimated dozen men rode into Richmond, Missouri, on May 22, 1867, approaching the town by different routes that converged in front of the Hughes and Wasson Bank on the public square. Four dismounted and entered the bank. Their demands, enforced by threats with army revolvers, netted them $4,000. But outside the bank several citizens, suspecting a robbery, resisted the gang. Mayor John B. Shaw, running toward the bank with his pistol drawn, was shot fatally in the chest. Young Frank S. Griffin, sheltered behind a tree in the courthouse yard, opened fire on the robbers with a cavalry rifle; a shot from one of the robbers struck him in the forehead, killing him almost instantly. B. G. Griffin, upon seeing his son fall, ran toward the bank; one of the bandits placed a pistol at his head and fired; for good measure he shot the old man again after he had fallen. A posse overtook the fleeing bandits about sundown, but after a brief skirmish the robbers left the road for the woods and escaped.[15]

The next robbery on the list of crimes usually attributed to the Missouri outlaws was in a different locale, Russellville, Kentucky, on March 20, 1868. Five bandits, led by a man who had previously visited the bank of Nimrod Long and Company posing as a cattle dealer, escaped with a sum reported to be as high as $12,000. Long, who refused to obey the robbers' orders, suffered a scalp wound when a bullet grazed his head. After a tussle, he escaped to the street where the men on guard outside fired at him without effect. The wheat sack, a regular accessory in all the Missouri robberies, was used to carry away the loot.[16]

In a few years, when the Jameses and the Youngers had become notorious for robbing banks and trains, many writers stated that their careers started at Liberty, and they attributed the series of holdups from Liberty to Russellville to the Jameses. Others stated merely that the Jameses were suspected of the crimes. And there are those "authorities" who can tell you exactly who committed each daring act. Actually, identification of the bandits is not simple. Those insiders who knew the facts talked little, and what they said was not always reported exactly. Moreover, people who could remember the events and who talked about them did not always have firsthand information. Contemporary newspapers openly accused other individuals of the crimes, but no instance of their directing suspicion to the James or Younger boys has been found.

From the start, however, these crimes were charged to former bushwhackers, several of whom had been associates of Frank and Jesse in the war. The Liberty *Tribune*'s account of the robbery in that town commented, "The murderers and robbers are believed . . . to be . . . old bushwhacker desperadoes" who should be "swung up in the most summary manner." This paper refrained from naming suspects, but other papers were not so cautious. Of nine men said to have been recognized among the bandits at Liberty, six had served with Quantrill, as Frank James had. These were Oliver Shepherd, Bud Pence, Donny Pence, Frank Gregg, James Wilkerson, and Joab Perry. Others accused were Red Monkus, Ben Cooper, and Bill Wilkerson.[17] The Pences were relatives of the James brothers. Strangely, it seems now, warrants were issued for the arrest of William Easter, Aaron Book, and James Couch. Couch was arrested, but the prosecution failed to make a case against him.[18]

Three persons, R. McDaniels, Robert Pope, and "a certain Fitzgerald" were listed as suspects in the robbery at Savannah,[19] but none of these were mentioned in connection with the holdup at Lexington.

In the tragedy at Richmond there were several suspects, and some of them, when apprehended, were dealt with summarily. Two nights after the robbery, Felix Bradley, a criminal with a long record including horse thievery, was removed from the Richmond jail by a small mob and hanged from the limb of a tree at the edge of town. His offense was telling his fellow prisoners on the morning of the robbery that before the day was over the bank would be robbed.[20]

Newspapers reported the issuance of warrants for the arrest of Dick Burns, Payne Jones, one Flannery, Andy McGuire, and Allen Parmer, all of whom were Quantrill men, and James and John White. Jones, McGuire, and Parmer had surrendered and been paroled in Kentucky with Frank James. Parmer, who later married Susan James, sister of Frank and Jesse, immediately after the crimes at Richmond published a statement, corroborated by his employer, that he was at work in St. Louis at the time of the robbery. Marshal P. J. Miserez of Kansas City and his posse located Payne Jones at the home of his father near Independence, but Jones escaped after killing a member of the posse and a small girl who got in the line of fire. Another posseman, who became separated from the others, met and was disarmed by Dick Burns.[21] Jones and Burns were both murdered in the next few months, and at the time of Burns's death the Richmond *Conservator* referred to him as the "red-handed murderer, who did such terrible execution here when the bank was robbed last summer." [22]

Meanwhile, another Quantrill guerrilla, Thomas Little, had been arrested late in May and lodged in the Johnson County jail at Warrensburg. Complicity in the murders and robbery at Richmond was one of several charges against him. When an alibi was presented in the form of affidavits of prominent Lafayette County citizens, swearing he was at

Dover at the time of the crime, Little was given a mock trial and executed by a mob.[23]

Late in 1867, Andy McGuire, a Quantrill man who stayed with his leader to the last battle in Kentucky, was arrested in St. Louis, where he was honeymooning under the assumed name of James Cloud. Lodged in the Richmond jail, he was joined there in February of 1868 by James M. Devers, who had been arrested in Kentucky. Both were charged with the robbery, but were never tried, for on the night of March 17 a party of about fifteen men removed them from the jail and hanged them. This mob action was motivated by a rumor that plans were afoot to rescue them.[24]

The summary vengeance of Missouri towns alarmed communities in other areas. In the summer, Bud Pence, who had been reportedly recognized as a member of the gang during the robbery at Liberty, was arrested in Kentucky on the request of Richmond authorities, and Deputy Sheriff John W. Francis went east to bring him back. But the Kentucky sheriff who held Pence seems deliberately to have let him escape. The Louisville *Courier*, with great show of indignation, advised the governor of Kentucky not to honor a requisition, if Pence should be apprehended, unless Missouri would guarantee a fair trial. The hanging of Devers was evidence that a fair trial of Pence was not intended.[25]

Bud Pence had lived in the Jameses' neighborhood in Clay County and had been with both Frank and Jesse at times during the war. The Pences, including Bud's brother Donny, now lived in Nelson County, Kentucky, where there were other relatives of the James family. Donny later became sheriff of that county, and the homes of the Pence family were refuges for Frank and Jesse when later they were fugitives from the law.

The treatment in Missouri of bandits who were recognized in the acts of robbing and murdering or who were merely suspected of such crimes certainly showed at this time a determination to rid the area of these lawless men. That Missouri was an unhealthy climate for them and that bank robbery might be easier in Kentucky may account for the gang's decision to rob the bank at Russellville.

In Missouri the accusations of complicity in the bank robberies in the area had come close to the Jameses. When a Louisville detective, D. G. Bligh, went to work on the Russellville case suspicion drew closer to Frank and Jesse. Descriptions of the bandits and information furnished by Bligh led officers of Jackson County, Missouri, to attempt the arrest of Oliver Shepherd, a suspect in the Missouri robberies who had been away from home when the Kentucky bank was looted. They found him at the home of his father and killed him when he resisted arrest. Oliver's brother George, under whose leadership Jesse James had made his last trip to Texas during the war, was arrested in Kentucky, found guilty, and given three years in prison.

Bligh had no doubts about the Jameses' involvement in the crime at Russellville. Some years later, in 1875, he wrote the governor of Missouri that on the day of the robbery the James brothers were at a hotel in Chaplin, more than a hundred miles distant from Russellville, incapacitated by wounds. It was significant, in his view, that the party that robbed the bank at Russellville started from Chaplin and returned there.[26] March of 1868 was a late date for wartime wounds to be troubling Frank and Jesse, and possibly the injuries that kept them at Chaplin had resulted from bullets shot at bandits.

Three of the participants in the robbery as named by Bligh were Cole Younger, John Jarret [Jarrette], and another man believed to be a McCoy of Missouri. Jarrette had commanded the unit that was credited with saving the life of Jo Shelby at Prairie Grove in 1862; an Arthur McCoy had ridden through practically all the war with Shelby. Of those named by Bligh, including Cole Younger, none except the Shepherds had, before the crime at Russellville, been publicly linked with the robberies, nor were they immediately afterward, even by Bligh.

Later, when it was generally accepted that the Jameses were implicated in the robbery at Russellville, a pathetic motive for the crime was circulated. According to this story, the bank's money was needed to send Jesse to a sunnier climate, where he could have a better chance to regain his health; subsequently, he went by sea to California.[27]

If the James brothers did not yet have reputations as highwaymen, such questionable renown was theirs very soon after the robbery of the Daviess County Savings Bank at Gallatin, Missouri, on December 7, 1869. This crime produced tangible evidence on which to base charges against them, and from that time their names were associated with bandit raids in Missouri and elsewhere.

The robbery of the Gallatin bank was committed by two men. One of them entered alone and asked Captain John W. Sheets, cashier and principal owner of the bank, to change a $100 bill. Sheets turned to the safe for the money; the second bandit entered and, according to the contemporary newspapers, said, "If you will write out a receipt, I will pay you that bill." As the banker sat down and started writing, the man drew his gun and shot him through the head and heart before his body slumped to the floor.

The bandits then turned to William A. McDowell, bank clerk, and fired twice at him as he sought to escape. One bullet caught McDowell in the fleshy part of one arm, but he reached the street, where he cried out that Captain Sheets had been killed. Almost instantly townsmen opened fire on the robbers, who had now emerged from the bank, carrying several hundred dollars. They ran to their waiting horses, but the man who had killed Sheets was unable to mount his excited mare and was dragged thirty to forty feet before he could disentangle his foot from the stirrup. He then jumped up behind his comrade, who had halted to assist him, and the horse galloped away, bearing the two men. Outside the town the fugitives stole the horse of a farmer, Daniel Smoot, and that night they forced another local resident named Helm to guide them around the town of Kidder and to the tracks of the Hannibal and St. Joseph Railroad. They eluded their would-be captors, but that they retreated into Clay County was well known.[28]

Feeling ran high in Gallatin at the wanton slaying of Sheets, and rewards reportedly totaling $3,000 were offered by his widow, the bank, local citizens, the county, and the state. The prevailing sentiment was expressed in these terms: "Should the miscreants be overtaken it is not probable that a jury will be required to try them. They will be shot down in their tracks."[29]

The first accounts of the murder and robbery did not name suspects, but one newspaper commented, "The scoundrels were thoroughly identified, and it seems scarcely possible they can escape."[30] Several people had seen the bandits clearly, and the fine horse they abandoned in town served as a definite clue. Soon the kind of knowledge that could identify a fine horse within fifty miles of its home pointed to Jesse James as owner, so immediately it was assumed that he and Frank were the robbers.

Two well-armed citizens of Gallatin now rode over to Liberty and were joined by Deputy Sheriff John S. Thomason and his son Oscar in a raid on the Samuel farm, where they hoped to find the murderers. Contemporary accounts of what took place vary, as do the many later versions. The report in the Kansas City *Times* is perhaps as nearly correct as any. According to the *Times*, the men from Gallatin, upon arrival at the Samuel farm, slyly took positions in the woods behind the house, and the Thomasons dismounted at the front gate and walked deliberately up to the door. As they neared the door a little Negro boy ran past them toward the stable, and when he got there, the stable door opened, and out dashed two horses ridden by Frank and Jesse, who carried pistols in their hands. The horses took the barn-lot fence in a swinging gallop. The Gallatin men opened fire, as did the Thomasons. The brothers returned the fire as they dashed away. The raiders mounted, but only the elder Thomason's horse would take the fence,

39

so he pursued the fleeing men alone while the others got down to remove the top fence rails.

A short distance down the road Thomason reined up, dismounted, took deliberate aim, fired, and missed. His frightened horse broke loose and dashed on, caught up with the fugitives, and ran even with their mounts for a distance; then one of the brothers reached out with a pistol and shot the animal dead. The Jameses easily outdistanced their pursuers and escaped. Thomason returned to the Samuel farm, where he was forced to borrow a horse from Mrs. Samuel in order to get back to town.[31]

The ruthless slaying of Sheets aroused speculation as to the murderers' motive. That the killers thought Sheets was someone else is a frequently repeated explanation. The bandits are said to have whispered something to each other just before one of them shot Sheets. According to this theory of mistaken identity, the robbers had suddenly decided that the man before them was Major S. P. Cox, whose troops had ended Bloody Bill Anderson's career in 1864. Sheets did resemble Cox, who also lived in Gallatin. Impulsively, with the motive of avenging Anderson's death, the bandit shot him.[32] Contemporary reports, however, indicate that the killers recognized Sheets and thought that he had in some way been a party to Cox's killing of Anderson. In describing the crime, McDowell the bank clerk said the outlaw remarked with an oath, as he fired, that Sheets and Cox had been the cause of the death of his brother Bill Anderson and that he was bound to have revenge. One of the robbers told Helm, the man whom they forced to guide them around Kidder, that they had killed Captain Sheets and a Mr. Cox in revenge for the death of a brother, thereby implicating Jim Anderson, brother of Bill, in the crime.[33]

Newspaper comments on the James boys at this time show clearly that the name of Jesse James was not notorious. The Kansas City *Times* simply reported that the horse left at Gallatin "was identified as belonging to a young man named James. . . . The man with him was his brother, and both are very desperate and determined men, having had much experience in horse and revolver work." [34] This description of the Jameses' activities could well refer to their wartime record. Indeed, the Liberty *Tribune* remarked, "The James were noted bushwhackers during the war, and are regarded as desperate men." Nothing in these accounts indicated a suspicion that the Jameses had been involved in earlier postwar crimes, and the *Tribune*'s editor expressed the thought that "if innocent of the crime charged against them, they acted very foolishly in resisting the Sheriff." [35] But in view of the clues to their guilt, the attitude of the aroused Daviess County citizenry, and the fate of the men who were arrested for the Richmond robbery and murders, the Jameses did not act very foolishly in resisting arrest and escaping into the brush.

Every effort was made to capture them. Governor Joseph W. McClurg wired the sheriffs in counties bordering Clay to organize and hold in readiness militia units to assist in the capture or killing of the hunted men.[36] Even this measure was unavailing, for, as the *Times* had suggested, "They know every foot-path and by-road . . . and . . . they are cool, determined, desperate men, well mounted and well armed." [37]

And now began a practice that was to continue until the Jameses' careers as outlaws ended. A letter purporting to come from Jesse James was published in the Kansas City *Times*, which was edited by John Newman Edwards. Edwards had accompanied General Jo Shelby when Shelby, refusing to surrender, led a large contingent of his men to Mexico. Shelby could have joined forces with Juarez, but instead chose the more romantic and disastrous course of supporting the Emperor Maximilian. Thus his stay in Mexico was brief. In 1867, Edwards' *Shelby and His Men* was published. This book, an account of the exploits and adversities of Shelby's command in the war, was characterized by the author's stubborn defense of the Confederate cause and by his unqualified praise for all who had supported it, including the guerrillas who, he said, "like the gladiators under Spartacus, only shouted 'Kill, kill!' upon the bodies of their persecutors." Edwards, after a brief stint as a reporter on the St. Louis *Missouri Republican*, joined John C. Moore and R. B. Drury in 1868 in founding the Kansas City *Times*. The *Times* and other papers with which he was associated through the years were the mediums for publication of most of the letters alleged to have come from Jesse James, only a few of these documents appearing in other papers. Whether Jesse really wrote any of the letters is not known, but Edwards' connection with them is established.

The pattern of the succeeding letters was set in this first one. Jesse denied guilt of Sheets's murder. He had not been at Gallatin; he could not surrender without risk of being mobbed as other bushwhackers, Thomas Little for example, had been; he would give up as soon as he thought he could get a fair trial, "But I never will surrender to be mobbed by a set of bloodthirsty poltroons. It is true that during the war I was a Confederate soldier, and fought under the black flag, but since then I have lived a peaceable citizen, and obeyed the laws of the United States to the best of my knowledge." [38]

A second letter, addressed to Governor McClurg, appeared in the *Times* a few weeks later. It promised to prove an alibi "to let those men know who accused me of the Gallatin murder and robbery that they have tried to swear away the life of an innocent man." [39]

Subsequently, the *Times* published affidavits of Clay County citizens to support Jesse's alibi. Their content is of interest: John S. Groom, later sheriff of Clay County, had known Jesse since 1866 and had known his character to be good; James M. Gow, who had known Jesse from childhood, said he had always acted honorably in all their dealings; Alfred R. McGinnis had never known Jesse "to act dishonest in any way." Groom and Gow swore that Jesse was in their stores at Kearney late on December 6, the day before the robbery, and McGinnis had seen him at the home of a Mrs. Fox on the day after the robbery. Dr. Samuel, Mrs. Samuel, and Susan James stated under oath that the mare that had dragged one of the escaping robbers and that was known to be the property of the Jameses had been sold on Sunday, December 5, for $500 to a man who had said he was from Topeka, Kansas. The three members of the family swore that Jesse was at home all day on December 7. Franklin Graves, the justice before whom all the statements were sworn, stated that although Jesse had participated in the rebellion, he knew of no instance of his violating the law since hostilities had ceased.[40]

This alibi caused little comment. It was weak in that only members of the immediate family swore to Jesse's whereabouts on the day of the crime, and Frank James was not included in the denials of guilt. The trip to Gallatin, about forty miles away, and return would not have been impossible in the time unaccounted for in the testimony of outsiders, but the writer of the Kearney news in the Liberty *Tribune* was probably right in his comment, "Those who have read Jesse James' defense generally believe him innocent — at least all I have heard speak of it." [41]

That affidavits that expressed respect for the James boys could be obtained from citizens of standing disproves any claim that the James boys had been driven into banditry before this time.

No guarantee of a fair trial for the Jameses was forthcoming. But efforts to catch them must now have been few and weak, for the Kearney correspondent of the Liberty *Tribune* reported in the issue of August 5, 1870, "We have no news. We are very dry and suffering from want of rain. The James brothers were in our town this week. They were heavily armed, and well mounted. They soon left."

From the day of the robbery at Gallatin to the end of their bandit careers Frank and Jesse James were outlaws with a price on their heads.

V

Jesse James was a lad
That killed many a man.

N EARLY A YEAR passed before the James boys were heard from again. Their whereabouts during this year of inaction is unknown, but probably they remained in Missouri and possibly right at home. No other robberies were added to the list of charges against them until June 3, 1871, when four men robbed the Ocobock Brothers' Bank at Corydon, Iowa, of $6,000.[1]

The robbery was committed with little hazard to anyone, for nearly every man in town was at the Methodist Church to hear the noted orator Henry Clay Dean discuss the merits of a proposed railroad for Corydon. The bandits, on entering the bank, found the cashier alone, quietly forced him to give them the money, tied him securely, then rode to the meeting at the church, where their leader interrupted the speaker to announce that the bank had been robbed. The crowd, judging the interruption a hoax to break up the speaking, was slow to believe the leader's announcement, and the brigands rode out of town, unchallenged. Several minutes elapsed before the townsmen realized the situation and sent a posse in pursuit of the bandits.

The trail of the robbers led into Missouri and toward the home of the James boys, which was about 120 miles southwest of Corydon. Once, their pursuers drew close enough to exchange shots with them, but the bandits escaped. Descriptions of the men indicated that they were the James boys and their companions Cole Younger and a Kearney youth named Clell Miller. Their apparent familiarity with the Missouri territory into which they retreated strengthened suspicions of their identity.[2]

The Kansas City *Times* soon published a letter from Jesse, denying that he and Frank had anything to do with the robbery at Corydon or that they had ever defied the civil authorities; he and Frank were reluctant to surrender for trial because they believed that "degraded Radicals" would mob them.[3] The James boys went unapprehended, but Clell Miller was arrested by a detective who decoyed him into a fictitious horse-stealing expedition. Miller stood trial and was acquitted when Missouri witnesses swore to his presence elsewhere on the day of the robbery.[4]

At a time when the gang's funds were probably running low, April 29, 1872, five men dashed into Columbia, Kentucky. Three dismounted, but only two entered the Deposit Bank. The cashier, R. A. C. Martin, sensed immediately what was happening and courageously shouted, "Bank robbers!" He was shot dead. Two customers jumped out the windows, and a third escaped through the door after a scuffle with one of the bandits. This resistance upset the time schedule; the robbers picked up $600 that lay in sight and escaped. They outwitted a huge posse by riding straight away for several miles and then circling the town. Their identity was never established, but Detective Bligh of Louisville was convinced that Cole Younger was the leader of the gang and that Frank and Jesse James were two of the members. Men believed to be these three had been in the area for more than a week, posing as stock buyers.[5]

Frank James, according to one story, had lodged in the days preceding the robbery at the home of a well-to-do farmer and had ingratiated himself with the grandmother of the household by many attentions. He expressed great interest in her Bible and in her copy of *Pilgrim's Progress*. The latter he borrowed, and the bookmark indicated that he had nearly finished reading it when he returned it just before his departure. A man of such courtesy and such reading habits, the grandmother believed, could not have been one of the desperadoes.[6]

But the gang, in extending its enterprises into a neighboring state, did not neglect its home area. Back in Missouri, the Kansas City fair was drawing large crowds. On September 26, 1872, three mounted men rode up to the gate in the midst of an estimated ten thousand people. A report written several years later romanticized what happened: One of the riders dismounted and approached the cashier, to whom he said, "What if I was to say I was Jesse James, and told you to hand out that tin box of money — what would you say?"

"I'd say I'd see you in h—l first," was the tempestuous reply.

"Well, that's just who I am — Jesse James — and you had better hand it out pretty d—d quick or ——"

The levelling of a navy revolver finished the sentence, and out came the box.[7]

Contemporary reports described the robbery differently. According to them, one of the bandits walked up to the cashier and, without any bold talk, seized the tin cashbox, hurriedly pocketed its contents, and threw it away. Ben Wallace, the ticket seller, ran out of the booth and grappled with the robber, but a confederate opened fire, and Wallace released his grip. A bullet intended for Wallace inflicted a severe flesh wound in the leg of a small girl in the crowd. The man with the money mounted his horse and with his two comrades dashed away from the fairgrounds and into the woods. Their daring yielded a mere $978; only a few minutes before the robbery several thousand dollars had been sent to the bank.[8] The lives of a helpless crowd had been endangered and an innocent child injured for a relatively small sum of money.

Yet there was one who saw the event in a different light — John N. Edwards. In his report on the front page of the *Times*, he termed the incident "a deed so high-handed, so diabolically daring and so utterly in contempt of fear that we are bound to admire it and revere its perpetrators." He denounced the act as a crime, but praised the actors — men "who can so coolly and calmly plan and so quietly and daringly execute a scheme . . . in the light of day, in the face of the authorities, and in the very teeth of the most immense multitude of people that was ever in our city deserve at least admiration for their bravery and nerve."[9]

Two days later, in an editorial titled "The Chivalry of Crime," Edwards expressed his esteem for the Civil War guerrillas now accused of lawlessness. They were to him as chivalrous as any character created by Sir Walter Scott; their way of life was "chivalric; poetic; superb." He wrote:

There are men in Jackson, Cass, and Clay — a few there are left — who learned to dare when there was no such word as quarter in the dictionary of the Border. Men who have carried their lives in their hands so long that they do not know how to commit them over into the keeping of the laws and regulations that exist now, and these men sometimes rob. But it is always in the glare of day and in the teeth of the multitude. With them booty is but the second thought; the wild drama of the adventure first. These men never go upon the highway in lonesome places to plunder the pilgrim. That they leave to the ignobler pack of jackals. But they ride at midday into the county seat, while court is sitting, take the cash out of the vault and put the cashier in and ride out of town to the music of cracking pistols. These men are bad citizens but they are bad because they live out of their time. The nineteenth century with its Sybaric civilization is not the social soil for men who might have sat with *Arthur* at the Round Table, ridden at

45

tourney with Sir Launcelot or won the colors of *Guinevere*; men who might have shattered the casque of *Brian de Bois Guilbert*, shivered a lance with *Ivanhoe* or won the smile of the Hebrew maiden; and men who could have met *Turpin* and *Duval* and robbed them of their illgotten booty on Hounslow Heath.

Such as these are they who awed the multitude on Thursday. . . . What they did we condemn. But the way they did it we cannot help admiring. . . . It was as though three bandits had come to us from the storied Odenwald, with the halo of medieval chivalry upon their garments and shown us how the things were done that poets sing of. No where else in the United States or in the civilized world, probably, could this thing have been done. It was done here, not because the protectors of person and property were less efficient but because the bandits were more dashing and skillful; not because honest Missourians have less nerve but because freebooting Missourians have more.[10]

Although Edwards' editorial on the robbery at the fair did not refer specifically to Frank and Jesse James, it showed his attitude toward the band of outlaws of which they were said to be members. Soon he was denying their guilt while at the same time justifying their crimes and lauding their bravery and valor. His effusive defense and glorification of the James band continued until his death in 1889 and constituted a major influence in transforming Jesse James's public image from a ruthless robber and murderer into a modern Robin Hood. Many of the "facts" of the lives of members of the band were first made known by Edwards' pen, to be repeated by other writers unquestioningly. By 1872 Edwards had made the cause of the James band his own, and he found willing ears among the sons of the South in Missouri who remembered not only the years of the war but also the years of proscription that followed.[11]

Edwards' admiration for the robbers at Kansas City was not shared by the rival press. The *Daily Journal of Commerce* commented, "More audacious villains than the perpetrators of this robbery, or those more deserving of hanging to a limb do not exist at this moment."[12]

Soon Edwards' *Times* printed a communication, allegedly from the robbers, but seemingly from Sherwood Forest. In the letter the bandits boasted of the exploit, offered to pay the injured child's doctor bill, and suggested that they were more moral than members of Grant's party, who "can steal millions, and it is all right." The letter set forth two claims that became part of the tradition accepted by the Jameses' defenders: "We kill only in self-defense," and "We rob the rich and give to the poor." The signatures were JACK SHEPHERD, DICK TURPIN, CLAUDE DUVAL.[13]

Rumors that Frank and Jesse James were involved in the robbery brought forth Jesse's usual letter of denial and his routine charge that prisoners could not expect a fair trial. He stated that a resident of Independence was the source of the information that John Younger, Cole Younger, and Jesse had committed the holdup.[14] This the man from Independence promptly denied.[15]

On May 27, 1873, four men robbed a bank at Ste. Genevieve, Missouri, of nearly $4,000. The two robbers who entered the bank forced the cashier to serve as their shield as they hurried from the bank to the place where two comrades with four horses awaited them. As they were mounting, one of the horses bolted, but the bandits forced a farmer, who was driving past in a wagon, to recover the animal. The men then took the hapless cashier's watch, mounted the horses, and rode out of town crying, "Hurrah for Hildebrand!" [16] Sam Hildebrand was a widely known and much feared bushwhacker who operated independently against the Federal forces in southeast Missouri and northern Arkansas during the Civil War. His home was less than thirty miles west of Ste. Genevieve, in St. Francois County, and the bandits evidently were aware that he was a hero to local ex-Confederates. The first newspaper accounts did not accuse the Jameses of the robbery, but soon their names appeared in connection with it. The *Journal of Commerce* chided the *Times* with the suggestion that it had "a splendid chance now to talk about IVANHOE, Sir LANCELOT and other knights of the middle ages" and warned its readers to expect the *Times*'s "effusion on the subject." [17]

Soon afterwards, the James boys were charged with a new type of brigandage — train robbery. They did not invent train robbery, as is sometimes claimed; the Reno gang of Indiana seems to have originated this particular technique.[18] Nevertheless, the Jameses became adept at this application of crime to the newest mode of travel.

At dusk on July 21, 1873, a band of five to seven men loosened a rail at a blind curve on the Chicago, Rock Island and Pacific Railroad near Council Bluffs, Iowa. They attached a heavy cord to the end of the iron rail, and when the train approached the curve late at night they pulled the cord to draw the rail out of line. Engineer John Rafferty had slowed for the curve, and he saw the rail move from its place. Quickly he reversed his lever so that only the engine went through the break. The engine toppled slowly over on its side, crushing John Rafferty. The bandits quickly took charge of the train and removed an amount reported to be $2,000 from the express company's safe. Obviously, they were disappointed, and they had reason to be. They had missed by a few hours a train that was transporting a heavy shipment of gold from the West. Disgusted and furious, the bandits collected money and valuables from passengers, then, waving their hats and shouting farewell, they rode into the woods.[19] The bandits were masked as Ku Klux Klansmen, but other features led to the belief that they were former Missouri bushwhackers.

The trail of the outlaws again led their pursuers southward into Missouri, toward the homes of the Jameses and Youngers. Descriptions by persons who saw strange men in the area of the crime a few days before it happened and by those who supposedly saw the robbers on their retreat into Missouri matched each other precisely and resembled vaguely the persons of Frank and Jesse James. It was determined, too, that the man in command during the robbery looked more like Jesse James than Frank, and for the first time public opinion accused Jesse of being the chief of the band. Indeed, one reporter commented, "This Jesse James is known to be the chief of a gang of robbers which is a terror from their headquarters in Clay County to Sherman, Texas." And he added that the chase was usually abandoned when it was known that the James gang committed the depredation.[20]

The chase was not abandoned this time, however, for determined efforts to capture the murderers of Rafferty were continued by Iowa officers and detectives. Few doubted that the Jameses, Youngers, and their associates had committed the crime. The Leavenworth, Kansas, *Times* chimed, "The 'storied Odenwald' of the Kansas City *Times* . . . will be the first to claim that none but Missourians could have devised such a grand scheme of audacious murder and plunder." [21] There was common agreement with this statement.

Some time intervened between the crime and Jesse's customary denial, but in early January of 1874 a letter from him, dated December 20, 1873, at Deer Lodge, Montana Territory, was widely reprinted from the St. Louis *Dispatch*, which had first received it. (Of interest here is the circumstance that Major John N. Edwards had joined the staff of the *Dispatch* in August of 1873.) Jesse's letter reviewed the accusations against the James boys and then proposed that if Governor Woodson "will guarantee me a fair trial, and Frank also, and protect us from a mob, or from a requisition from the Governor of Iowa, which is the same thing, we will come to Jefferson City, or at any other place in Missouri, except GALLATIN, surrender ourselves, and take our trial for everything we have been charged with." He expressed the fear that they would be dealt with by a mob "if the militia of Daviess County could get their hands upon two of Quantrell's and Anderson's best men." They would not be taken alive, but would be glad to face a fair trial and to have "this long and sleepless vigilance on our part broken up." [22]

Missourians soon had reason to believe that Jesse had "returned" from Montana Territory, for, on January 31, 1874, the first train robbery in the state occurred. The spot selected was well suited to the crime — Gads Hill, a small village and flag station on the Iron Mountain Railroad, about one hundred miles south of St. Louis.

A few minutes before the train was due to pass at 5:40 P.M., five men walked into the depot and with pointed guns took control of the station agent and several visitors — practically the entire male population of the hamlet. A signal flag placed on the track brought the approaching train to a halt, and as the conductor stepped off the train he faced the muzzle of a six-shooter instead of a passenger. The highwaymen boarded the train, robbed the passengers of their money and jewelry, rifled the mail bags, and took the contents of the express safe, estimated at amounts varying from $2,000 to $22,000.

After ordering the trainmen to be on their way to Little Rock, the robbers made for the woods. Before departing, one of the bandits handed a crewman a written account of the incident, surprisingly accurate and even providing a blank space in which the amount of the loot could be recorded. Seven miles south, at Piedmont, the nearest telegraph station, the engineer reported the affair. Posses formed early the next morning but were too late to be effective.[23]

In the course of this robbery, a passenger suspected by the robbers of being a Pinkerton detective was taken to a private compartment and stripped of his clothing, apparently in the belief that search would reveal some mark that would establish his identity. The hands of each male passenger were examined to determine if he was a workingman, the robbers stating, according to reports, that they "did not want to rob workingmen or ladies, but the money and valuables of the plug-hat gentlemen were what they sought."[24] Their retreat evidently was westward across the state, and accounts were soon brought to the towns of their obtaining meals and lodging at farm homes along the way. Reportedly, they "conducted themselves as gentlemen, paying for everything they got."[25] In spite of the bandits' well-advertised solicitude for workingmen and of their gentlemanly habits, the governor of Missouri offered a reward of $2,000 for the "bodies of each one of the robbers."[26]

The Gads Hill bandits were generally believed to be the same men who had robbed passengers on a stagecoach between Hot Springs and Malvern, Arkansas, two weeks earlier. Reports of this robbery form the basis of another element in the James legend: the "We never rob Southerners" facet, which pleased many sympathizers of the Lost Cause and lent a patriotic motive to the gang's crimes. The truth is, the bandits did not differentiate between Northerners and Southerners except in this one instance. Here the leader, presumably Cole Younger, inquired if any of the victims had served in the Confederate army. One, G. R. Crump of Memphis, replied that he had. After further questioning, the bandit chief returned Crump's watch and money with the comment that the gang did not want to rob Confederate soldiers; Northerners had driven the members of the gang into banditry, and they intended to make Northerners pay. Among the passengers was John A. Burbank, former governor of Dakota Territory, and he lost heavily to the robbers.[27]

Few doubted that the crimes at Gads Hill and near Hot Springs had been committed by the James band, and even the St. Louis *Dispatch* carried an article connecting the band, of which the James and Younger brothers were now a part, with the series of robberies that began at Liberty. The article named Jesse and Frank James, Cole and Budd [sic] Younger, and Arthur McCoy as members of a gang that was originally much bigger, having included Dick Burns, Jim Devers, Andy McGuire, Payne Jones, and Al. [sic] Shepherd, who had all died by violence. The *Dispatch* reporter's informant, allegedly a St. Louis policeman, was in Richmond the day the bank was robbed and three citizens murdered, and he stated "positively and emphatically that he recognized Jesse and Frank James, and Budd and Cal. [sic] Younger among the robbers." The report ended with the prediction that these men would not be taken alive and that a posse would incur some losses in any attempt to bring in the bandits' dead bodies.[28] This prophecy, of course, did not encourage efforts to apprehend the robbers.

For the guilt of Jesse and Frank James to be proclaimed in a paper edited by Major Edwards was unthinkable. Edwards was in the state capital, Jefferson City, when the story appeared, and upon reading it he wired the city editor, Walter B. Stevens, "Put nothing more in about Gads Hill. The report of yesterday was remarkable for two things utter stupidity & total untruth."[29]

In the same issue that contained the article Edwards disapproved, he had written editorially about the crime at Gads Hill and in defense of Missouri, which he thought was about on a par with other states, "neither producing more reverence for the criminal and less respect for the law than the rest." However, he rated the Western highwayman as superior to the Eastern, for "he has more prowess, more qualities that attract admiration and win respect; but this comes from the locality . . . which breeds strong, hardy men — men who risk much, who have friends in high places, and who go riding over the land, taking all chances that come in the way, and spending lavishly tomorrow what is won today at the muzzle of a revolver." Edwards thus prefaced a long denunciation, bitter and unrestrained, of the practices of the Radical party during the war and reconstruction.[30]

A few months earlier Edwards had for the first time put together some of the most important ingredients of the James legend in a long article titled "A Terrible Quintette," which was published on November 22, 1873, as a special supplement of the St. Louis *Dispatch*.[31] It purported to be the fruit of interviews with Frank James, Jesse James, Arthur McCoy, and friends and acquaintances of Coleman and John Younger. These interviews were held when an Iowa sheriff and various Missouri law enforcement officers were making extensive, but poorly planned, efforts to capture the five men, following the train robbery in Iowa. Edwards ridiculed and belittled the officers' efforts.

Edwards' article provided an alibi for each of the five men for every robbery with which they were charged, starting with the bank in Russellville, Kentucky, and continuing through the train robbery in Iowa. If they had been implicated in earlier robberies, Edwards surely would have absolved them of guilt, for he declared them innocent of all charges. He vividly described incidents in the Civil War to show that all members of the "Terrible Quintette" had served the Confederacy with valor, either in the regular army or in guerrilla bands. The Jameses and Youngers had been driven from their homes to the guerrilla camps by Northerners' persecution of their families, but McCoy had, "at the first tap of the recruiting drum," left his work as a tinner in St. Louis and espoused the cause of the South by joining the First Missouri Confederate Infantry. After Shiloh, where the First Missouri was nearly annihilated, McCoy had joined Shelby's cavalry regiment.

Edwards set forth here, in what is surely the earliest written account, the story of the hanging of Dr. Samuel, the imprisonment of Mrs. Samuel, and the mistreatment of Jesse by militiamen. He told also of the raid by Kansas Jayhawkers on the Harrisonville properties of Colonel Henry W. Younger, the difficulties that sent Cole Younger to Quantrill, the murder of the Younger boys' father, and the persecution of their mother during and after the war. The five men, he wrote, "are eminently creatures of the war—three of whom lived upon the border and were tried in the savage crucible of border warfare."

A detailed account of Bill Anderson's raid on Centralia and of the subsequent routing of the forces of Major Johnson is an important part of Edwards' presentation. Frank and Jesse are given major roles in the happenings, and Jesse's killing of Major Johnson is described in every particular. Edwards' version of the Centralia massacre and the subsequent engagement between Anderson's and Johnson's men became the standard, to be repeated again and again. In Edwards' view, to be "credited" with killing Major Johnson undoubtedly added to the stature of Jesse James.

Edwards, knowing that few things aroused more hatred in Southern men in Missouri than mention of Jennison's name and of Ewing's Order Number Eleven, managed to include both in a story about Captain Emmet Goss. Captain Goss, Edwards said, at the beginning of the war owned a farm near Hickman's Mill (now a part of Greater Kansas City) that he worked soberly and industriously. He joined the Fifteenth Kansas Cavalry commanded by Jennison and, suddenly, became a terror to Southern sympathizers, seemingly possessed by a mania to kill. Goss had boasted that in helping to enforce Order Number Eleven he had "kindled the flames in fifty-two houses — of having made fifty-two families homeless and shelterless, and of having killed, he declared, until he was tired of killing." This Goss would "lavish his plunder and money on ill-featured mistresses, who were sometimes Indians, sometimes negresses, and but rarely pure white" — another goad to Southerners' rage.

Edwards' version of Goss's encounter with the guerrillas related that on November 22, 1864, Captain Goss, heading a force of thirty-two men, met by accident twenty-seven guerrillas, commanded by Fletcher Taylor and including Jesse and Frank James, at Cabin Creek in the Cherokee Nation. A fight ensued. "Nothing so weak as the Kansas detachment could possibly live before the deadly prowess and pistol practice of the Missourians." Twenty-nine of Goss's thirty-two men were killed; four guerrillas died. The manner in which Jesse James singled out Goss and shot him repeatedly Edwards described in gory detail. After dispensing with Goss, Jesse cornered the Reverend U. P. Gardner who, in his plea for mercy, said he was chaplain of the Thirteenth Kansas. Jesse, according to Edwards, merely turned his head slightly and put a bullet in Gardner's brain.

That Jesse James, but not Frank, could have been with the guerrillas that destroyed Goss's force is not impossible, for some bands had moved south along the Missouri-Kansas line into the Cherokee Nation and northwest Arkansas as Price retreated from Missouri, following the Battle of Westport. The time is after the death of Bill Anderson. According to the official report of Colonel Charles R. Jennison, two officers, Captain Orloff Norton, Company L, and First Lieutenant (not Captain) Emmett Goss, Company M, Fifteenth Kansas Cavalry, were "undoubtedly murdered while in charge of foraging parties in the vicinity of Cane Hill [Arkansas] on the 12th of November, as all search for them has proven fruitless, and when last heard from they were closely pursued by a large force of guerrillas said to be under the command of Lieutenant Tucks, C. S. Army." Jennison called Norton and Goss

N. H. Rose Collection, University of Oklahoma Library
Jesse James the Guerrilla

Union Pacific Museum, Omaha, Nebraska
Jesse James

The Kansas City Star
Jesse James: The One and Only

Library of Congress
Jesse James as Portrayed in *The National Police Gazette* Soon After His Death

Frank James the Guerrilla

This is said to be Frank James as he looked in 1871.

Frank James

Frank James at Age 55

Zerelda Samuel, Mother of the James Boys

The Children of Jesse James: Mary and Jesse Edwards

he James Home Near Kearney, Missouri, in the 1880's

Members of the James Band Killed or Captured at Northfield, Minnesota

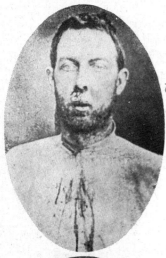

Jim Younger,
Captured

William Stiles, Alias
Bill Chadwell, Killed

Samuel Wells,
Alias Charles
Pitts, Killed

Clell Miller,
Killed

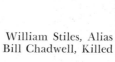

Cole Younger,
Captured

Bob Younger,
Captured

Colonel John F. Philips, Attorney for the Defense

William H. Wallace, Jackson County Prosecutor

Governor Thomas T. Crittenden

Major John Newman Edwards

A Widely Circulated Pitcure Which Purports to be Frank and Jesse James and Their Mother

Jurors Who Acquitted Frank James: standing, James J. Snyder, Benjamin F. Feurt, Charles R. Nance, James B. Smith, Abisha H. Shellman, William L. Merritt, Jason Winburn, Oscar Chamberlain; seated, William F. Richardson, Lonnzo W. Gilbrath, Richard E. Hale, James W. Boggs

Bill Anderson

William Clarke Quantrill

Fletcher Taylor, Frank James, and Jesse James (Original picture was probably made in 1864.)

Little Archie Clement, the Bloody Executioner at Centralia

St. Joseph (Missouri) Museum

Bob Ford

"two of the most efficient and faithfu. officers" of his command, and he characterized them as "always faithful in the discharge of their duties, never hesitating in the execution of any order, however hazardous." They had "endeared themselves to the entire command by their uniform kindness and affability toward all." [32]

Cole Younger was as cold-blooded as Jesse, according to the admiring Edwards. Once, after capturing fifteen Jayhawkers, he called for a new Enfield rifle he had seen the day before. He then ordered the prisoners tied in a row, belly to back, against a tree, in order, he said, to test the killing power of the gun at close range. He expected the first bullet to kill, or at least go through, ten men. When the first shot caused only three to fall writhing, he cried out, "Cut the dead men loose; the new Enfield shoots like a pop-gun!" Seven shots were required to complete the gruesome test, and "seven times had the avenging son feasted his eyes on the agonies of those who had been foremost in the murder of his father."

The basic theme of Edwards' essay was that these men, innocent of crime after the war, had been driven by war's aftermath into the status of fugitives from justice. McCoy was compelled to leave his farm home in Montgomery County, where he was living peaceably, by officers attempting to arrest him; wartime enemies of the Youngers had, in 1866 and 1867, made living at home impossible.

Edwards treated the James brothers' difficulties more fully than those of the other bandits, and the explanations he set forth as Jesse's statements in an interview became, in time and with slight variations, major elements of the James tradition. Edwards noted that Frank surrendered and was paroled in Kentucky and that Jesse was wounded on May 15, 1865, in a fight with Wisconsin cavalrymen while he was on his way to Lexington to surrender. Contrary to the generally accepted belief, Edwards reported, Jesse said that, though wounded, he surrendered on May 21. This report is followed with particulars of how he was cared for by friends, was moved first to the home of an uncle in Harlem, Missouri, thence to his mother's home in Rulo, Nebraska, and, after a long delay en route at Harlem, to the farm near Kearney. Jesse described his condition to Edwards: "Just able barely to mount a horse and ride about a little in the spring of 1866, my life was threatened daily, and I was forced to go heavily armed. The whole country was then full of militia, robbing, plundering and killing." Frank, after coming home "in defiance of the orders of the authorities and at his own peril," remained only a short time and then returned to Kentucky.

At Brandenburg in Nelson County, Kentucky, in June of 1866, Frank got into a fight with four Federal soldiers. He killed two, wounded a third, and was shot in the joint of the left hip by the fourth before he escaped.[33] Frank wrote for Jesse, who went to his brother even though he was weak, and he stayed until Frank had recovered. In October, 1866, Jesse returned to Missouri and during the winter nearly died of hemorrhages from his wound, which had not yet healed. Let Jesse's words, as Edwards reported them, tell what happened next:

On the night of February 18th, 1867, an effort was made to kill me. Five militia men, well armed and mounted, came to my mother's house and demanded admittance. The weather was dreadfully cold and I was in bed, scarcely able to get up. My pistols, however, I always kept by me. My stepfather heard them as they walked upon the front porch and asked them what they wanted. They told him to open the door. He came to my room upstairs and asked me what he should do. I requested him to help me to the window that I might look out. He did so. There was snow on the ground and the moon was shining. I saw that the horses hitched to the fence all had on cavalry saddles, and then I knew that the men were soldiers. I had but one thing to do — to drive them away or die. Surrender had played out for good for me. Incensed at my step-father's absence, they were hammering at the door with the butts of their muskets, and calling out for me to come down, swearing they knew I was in the house and would have me out dead or alive. I went down stairs softly, got close up to the front door and listened until from the talk of the men I thought I might be able to get a pretty good range. Then putting my pistol up to within about three inches of the upper panel, I fired. One hollowed and fell. Before the surprise was off, I threw the door wide open and with a pistol in each hand began a rapid fusillade. One I killed as he ran, two more were wounded besides the one on the porch, and the fifth man got clear without a scratch. So complete was the surprise that not a man among the whole five fired a shot.[34]

Jesse left home the next morning, shortly before a whole company of militia arrived to take him. The details of his flight are not part of Edwards' report, but in June of 1867 Jesse was in Nashville, Tennessee, under the care of a Dr. Paul Eve, who told him that his lung was too badly decayed for cure and that the best thing he could do was to go home and die among his own people. From Nashville Jesse went to Logan County, Kentucky, and after a brief stay there returned to Missouri in November. In December he returned to Kentucky; he and Frank were in a hotel in Chaplin, Kentucky, on the day the bank at Russellville was robbed. It will be recalled that this robbery was allegedly planned in order to provide funds for Jesse to go to a sunnier climate. In April of 1868 Jesse returned to Clay County, leaving Frank in Kentucky. "It was not safe for him to come to Clay County, and he did not always want to be killing."

On the recommendation of Dr. Joe Wood of Kansas City, Edwards'

54

article continued, Jesse went to New York and took passage on a ship for California. During the voyage, he made the acquaintance of a Major Gregg who, upon their arrival in San Francisco, took Jesse to the headquarters of General Henry W. Halleck, then commanding the Division of the Pacific. Together they reminisced about the fighting in Missouri during the Civil War. Halleck proffered assistance, but he advised Jesse to leave the Coast. Jesse thereupon went to the home of his uncle D. W. James, who owned the Paso Robles Hot Sulphur Springs, in San Luis Obispo County. The waters of the springs restored his health in the remarkable time of three weeks, and on October 28 he was again at home in Missouri. But there, Jesse said, he was threatened, and the militia swore that Frank should never be permitted to come home. In these circumstances, Jesse reported, he plowed day after day with three pistols strapped to him.

But Frank did come home, Edwards reported, and he and Jesse were working quietly on the farm when they were accused of the murder and robbery in Gallatin in December, 1869. Jesse, denying they were involved, offered an explanation of Captain Sheets's murder. Sheets was mistaken for Major S. P. Cox, who had boasted of killing Bill Anderson in Ray County in 1864, although Jesse was sure it was not Cox but some other member of his company who had killed Anderson. At least fifty of Anderson's followers had formed a league vowing vengeance against Cox. Any one of these might have killed Sheets, thinking he was Cox. Thus Jesse was willing for some other guerrilla to bear the guilt of Sheets's murder.

Through this piece and his other writings Edwards glorified outlaws, yet did not admit the guilt of his heroes. He had by this time presented, and would continue to present, to the public many of the elements of the James legend. To distinguish between fabrication and fact in his writings is not always easy, but his description of these now notorious brothers and the differences in their natures was no doubt correct, as far as it went:

Jesse James, the youngest, has a face as smooth and innocent as the face of a school girl. The blue eyes, very clear and penetrating, are never at rest. His form is tall, graceful and capable of great endurance and great effort. There is always a smile on his lips, and a graceful word or a compliment for all with whom he comes in contact. Looking at his small white hands, with their long, tapering fingers, one would not imagine that with a revolver they were among the quickest and deadliest hands in all the west. Frank is older and taller. Jesse's face is a perfect oval — Frank's is long, wide about the forehead, square and massive about the jaws and chin, and set always in a look of fixed repose. Jesse is light-hearted, reckless, devil-may-care — Frank sober, sedate, a dangerous man always in ambush in the midst of society. Jesse knows there is a price

VI

He said there is no man
With the law in his hand
Can take Jesse James when alive.

THE NOTORIETY of the James band now stimulated extraordinary efforts to capture them. The attempts to seize them had been limited mainly to those made by officers and residents in the localities of the crimes, who, if a local citizen like Captain Sheets was murdered, made every effort to find and punish the guilty. The general public was not seriously aroused over the plundering of banks and trains, however, since this was a period of protest against oppressive interest rates at the banks and questionable practices by the railroads.

D. G. Bligh's work after the robbery at Russellville, Kentucky, in 1868 is the first instance of a professional detective entering the hunt, and a detective named Westfall, from Chicago, arrested Clell Miller following the robbery at Corydon, Iowa. Unfortunately, detectives faced all the problems of local officials plus some of their own. They met with suspicion and even hostility in rural areas, where they were looked upon as enemies of workers and as tools of railroads and other corporations. In the absence of today's scientific aids, the detection of criminals was a hit-and-miss proposition at best, but lack of co-operation with, if not outright obstruction of, the investigators' efforts hampered them seriously. For instance, the very few persons who could describe Frank and Jesse James with enough accuracy to make them identifiable on sight refused to talk. Nor were photographs available. Friends shielded the ex-guerrillas willingly, and others protected them out of fear.

57

Rewards offered after the robberies undoubtedly attracted some detectives to the hunt, but not the employees of the Pinkerton National Detective Agency. This organization's services were obtainable only on a per-diem basis for each agent engaged, and its employees were not permitted to accept or to share in any reward.[1] Victims of the gang, in particular the railroads and express companies, employed them. Available records do not yield a complete picture of the Pinkertons' activities in Missouri, but it is possible to recount what they were believed at the time to have done. Portions of this account can be verified. William A. Pinkerton, son of Allan Pinkerton, the founder of the agency, on at least two occasions said that the agency was first retained in 1871, after the bank holdup at Corydon, Iowa.[2] Robert A. Pinkerton, also a son of Allan, was dispatched to the scene and with a posse followed the trail into Missouri.

In late August, 1873, following the train robbery in Iowa, the press reported that detectives hired by the railroad and express companies were again on the trail of the Jameses and Youngers. This time, in company with an Iowa sheriff, the investigators brought a party of men to Aullville in Lafayette County. There a group of "Lafayette County vigilants" joined them.

If an alleged newspaper interview with an anonymous member of the party can be believed, it provides an interesting commentary on the nature of a detective-directed search for desperadoes in 1873. According to this report, the party struck the trail of the robbers and captured "a magnificent mare belonging to one of the James" — losing horses evidently was becoming a habit with Jesse. The search party soon learned that the James boys had gone to join the Youngers at their home near Johnson City in St. Clair County. The vigilance committee, as it was called, made its way to Sedalia, eighty-five miles from the suspected rendezvous. The Missouri, Kansas and Texas Railroad supplied a special train that took the committee to a point about fifteen miles north of Johnson City. From there they rode in wagons to the vicinity of the town, arriving about midnight.

The committee made camp in the woods and sent out scouts. Within two hours the scouting party returned with information that the outlaws were in a house on the outskirts of the village. The entire group sped to the house and surrounded it, but because the men they hoped to capture were known to be desperate, they planned no move until sunrise. Despite their caution, however, they had just assumed their positions for the attack when an excited and impatient member of the group cried, "Close up on it!" No alternative remained, so the attackers moved in on the house and demanded surrender of the robbers. The inmates surrendered easily, for they were all women and children who, besides being frightened, resented having their sleep disturbed.[3]

Coincident with this episode another newspaper editor came to the defense of the Youngers. He was Augustus C. Appler, editor of the Osceola (St. Clair County) *Democrat*, who, in the course of the Civil War, had been so pro-Southern that his press at Hannibal, Missouri, had been destroyed by Union men. In discussing reports of this raid, some of which claimed that a battle had taken place, he labeled the charges against the Youngers as unfounded attempts by their father's murderers to have the boys imprisoned and thus to prevent their avenging the wrongs done their family. Appler stated positively that Cole Younger had attended church at Monegaw Springs on the day before the train robbery in Iowa.[4]

Seemingly, the inability of the officers to capture the fugitives pleased some of the public, including a writer on the staff of the Lexington *Caucasian*. This man boasted that the alleged bandits, including the James boys, had visited Lexington several times in the two preceding weeks: "These bold fellows only laugh at the authorities, and seemingly invite their sleepy enterprise, by bearding the legal lion in his lazy lair."[5]

The reputation of Missouri as the home and refuge of criminals troubled Governor Silas Woodson. At his suggestion Sheriff George E. Patton of Clay County called a meeting of citizens to plan means to correct the notion that "notorious law-breaking men" could harbor in the area.[6] Woodson took more direct action on October 13 by offering a reward of $2,000 for "the arrest and delivery of the bodies of said Frank and Jesse James, to the sheriff of Daviess County, Missouri."[7] The Governor's reward offer seems to have been the only one at the time that specifically named Frank and Jesse James, although thousands of dollars were offered in rewards for the perpetrators of the many crimes with which their names were associated.[8] None of these offers, however, resulted in the capture of the bandits.

After the robbery at Gads Hill the Pinkerton agency quickly sent men to Missouri to trace and arrest the culprits. These operatives were no match for the Jameses and Youngers, especially when they were eluding pursuit in their home environment; soon three Pinkerton men had died at their hands. Their first victim was John W. Whicher.[9] Although Whicher was only twenty-six years of age, the Pinkertons considered him an able and courageous detective, yet it would seem that his methods were amateurish and his courage overruled his discretion.

Whicher arrived in Liberty on March 10, 1874, and, seeming to know in advance whom he could trust, announced on the next day to D. J.

Adkins, president of the Commercial Bank, and to O. P. Moss, former sheriff, his plans for capturing the James boys. He would go to their mother's farm dressed as a farm hand and secure employment. After gaining the confidence of the family, he would capture the unsuspecting Jesse and Frank by suddenly confronting them with a cocked pistol. Adkins and Moss both tried to discourage him; they insisted the plan would not work. The James brothers were dangerous men and would kill him, Adkins argued; Moss is said to have added, "The old woman would kill you if the boys don't." When Whicher persisted, however, Adkins and Moss told him how to get to the Samuel farm.

It is difficult to think that an experienced detective would have believed that desperate men, constantly on the alert, would be duped by his simple disguise. Apparently unperturbed by any doubts of his success, Whicher left Liberty at 5:15 that afternoon on a slow freight train for Kearney. Arriving there about dusk, he left the train and started the four-mile walk to the Samuels' farm. What happened to him between then and about three o'clock the following morning is a matter of conjecture. He may or may not have reached the farm. Of record is the fact that the next morning an early traveler found his body with bullets through the head and heart along a roadside in Jackson County not far from Independence.

The only evidences of the manner of Whicher's death are his dead body and the story of the operator of the Blue Mills ferry, which plied across the Missouri River between Clay and Jackson counties. At three o'clock the ferryman was aroused by a party of four men who forced him to carry them across the river. When he noticed that one of the men was bound and gagged, the others said that they were officers who had captured one horse thief and were hot on the trail of another. From the ferryman's description, Deputy Sheriff Thomason believed the men were Jesse James, Arthur McCoy, and Jim Anderson, brother of the noted Bill, and their captive was Whicher.[10]

A few days after the murder of Whicher, the Pinkertons lost two other men in a fight with John and Jim Younger in St. Clair County near Monegaw Springs. Louis J. Lull, of Chicago, using the name of J. W. Allen, and John Boyle of St. Louis, under the name of James Wright, had gone to St. Clair County and had enlisted the aid of a former deputy sheriff, Edwin B. Daniel. The reports of how Daniel, Lull, and John Younger lost their lives are not in complete agreement as to details, but the general outline of what happened is fairly clear.

Lull and Daniel, while riding through the area, stopped at the home of Theodrick Snuffer, an old man whose sons were known to be friends of the Youngers, and inquired the way to the "Widow Sims'." By chance, John and Jim Younger were inside the house, eating their noon meal and aware of the strangers' interest in their family. After getting the information they asked for, Lull and Daniel rode away, but Snuffer and the two Youngers noted that they did not follow the old man's directions. Their suspicions were sharpened when Boyle, who had been riding some distance behind his companions, passed the house and joined Lull and Daniel.

John and Jim, heavily armed, decided to investigate. They rode after the detectives and upon overtaking them, ordered them to stop. Boyle, in fright, put the spurs to his horse and escaped. The Youngers ordered Lull and Daniel to unbuckle their cartridge belts, thus letting their guns drop to the ground. John then told his brother to ride after Boyle and bring him back, but Jim refused. One of the Youngers picked up the pistols and examined them, and the brothers then questioned the captives about their purposes, under the menace of cocked guns. Lull evidently concluded that he and Daniel were to be killed; he quickly drew a small pistol that he carried concealed in a hip pocket, cocked it, and shot John Younger through the neck. At that moment Lull's horse broke for the timber, but John emptied the load of a shotgun into the detective before falling unconscious to the ground. Daniel tried to escape, but Jim pursued him and killed him with a bullet that struck his neck.

John Younger was dead when his brother returned to him. Jim quickly removed his brother's pistols and the contents of his pockets, stopped long enough at Snuffer's house to report what had happened and to give instructions for the care of John's body, and rode to safety. After lingering between life and death for six weeks, Lull succumbed in a hotel at Roscoe, Missouri, in the presence of a brother and of his wife of less than a year.[11]

In addition to being known as a member of the James-Younger band, John Younger was wanted in Texas for the murder in January, 1871, of Acting Sheriff Charles H. Nichols of Dallas County. John killed Nichols while he was in the Sheriff's custody under the charge of attempted homicide; while on a drinking spree he had shot too close to the head of an old man — a charge that was not looked on, in that time and place, as serious. Nichols, who arrested John early the next morning, was a friend, and he allowed his prisoner to eat breakfast before taking him to jail. John, learning that Nichols had taken precautions to prevent his escape and considering this an unfriendly act, caught Nichols off guard, killed him, and escaped.[12] This was the brother about whom Cole Younger wrote, late in 1874, in the language of a preacher:

Poor John. He has been hunted down and shot like a wild beast, and never was a boy more innocent. But there is a day coming when the secrets of all

61

hearts will be laid open before that All-seeing Eye, and every act of our lives will be scrutinized, then will his skirts be white as the driven snow, while those of his accusers will be doubly dark.[13]

Billy Pinkerton did not consider the skirts of any of the desperadoes "white as the driven snow." He believed that the killings of Whicher, Lull, and Daniel were wanton crimes for which the criminals must be punished. A few weeks later he wrote confidentially that Boyle, the detective who had escaped the Youngers' attack, was "a dirty dog" and that if he had been "half a man, Captain Lull would now have been living."[14] Motivated by these beliefs, the Pinkertons continued their investigations and bided their outcome.

The murder of Whicher gave rise to the opinion, in other localities, that he had been betrayed by prominent persons in Liberty, specifically Sheriff George E. Patton, and the people of Clay County were accused of harboring and protecting the James boys. Both the *Globe* and the *Republican* of St. Louis attacked the reputation of Clay County in reporting an interview with L. E. Angell, the Pinkerton operative who went to Liberty to claim Whicher's body and investigate his death. Angell stated that the James boys had established terrorism over the county while maintaining that they robbed the rich and gave to the poor. They were secure in their county because their wartime depredations were recalled as the acts of friends.[15]

The *Republican,* although it usually avoided the sensational, became quite vituperative in its accusations of the officials, especially Sheriff Patton, and of the people of Clay County. It demanded action against the county's bandit gangs. If the governor and legislature were unable to devise effective ways to break up "the nests of thieves and cut-throats, then let them formally announce their inability to preserve the peace and dignity of the state and ask assistance from the federal government."[16]

Sheriff Patton, in an open letter, denounced the content of the *Globe* and *Republican* articles as a *"wilful lie,"* an *"intentional wrong,"* and *"maliciously false,"*[17] and he filed libel suits against both papers.[18] These actions were never pressed; a few months later the *Republican* commented that Patton was "a fearless and honest officer who has not flinched from performance of his duty as sheriff."[19]

While the officers and residents of Clay County were being charged with responsibility for the bandits' continuing crimes, Governor Silas Woodson, in a special message, placed the matter before the General Assembly of Missouri. Using stern language, he told the lawmakers that outlaws and murderers were bringing disgrace upon the state. Although he had done everything in his power to capture the bandits, he had failed. It was clear that in order to bring the desperadoes to justice a military organization as well as funds with which the governor could employ secret agents were needed. These he asked the legislature to provide. Should that body refuse his request, it would bear the blame for Missouri's bad reputation.[20]

Favorable response to the Governor's request was immediate. The Senate passed, by a vote of 28 to 1, and the House, 67 to 6, an appropriation of $10,000 for Woodson's use in hiring secret agents to capture the outlaws.[21] Over one-third of the members of the House, however, refrained from voting. Another effort, designed to compensate citizens for their losses through the outlaws' actions, fared less well. This was a proposal offered by a member of the House for "pensioning the widows and orphans of those killed at Monegaw Springs, or who shall hereafter be killed in attempting to arrest the Younger and James brothers, and tendering the thanks of the state to the Chicago detective force." This proposal was immediately tabled without a recorded vote.[22] To legislate against banditry in general was one matter; to legislate against outlaws by name was another. Nor was a militia bill passed.

Woodson's special message came at a time when newspapers in other states were criticizing Missouri for permitting banditry and Republican papers within the state were beginning to make lawlessness a political issue. This censure from within and without the state continued for a dozen years. Some that came from Republican states was primarily political in purpose. The ascendancy of the Republican party in national politics rested on tenuous ground, and every state counted. Missouri was again in the Democratic column, and there was little or no prospect of its reverting to the Republican, but the situation in Missouri might be used to deter other states from voting Democratic. In addition to politics, economic rivalries, sectional feelings, and the contemptuous attitude of the East toward the West made the press receptive toward news of lawlessness within Missouri. Then, too, the whims of newspaper editors obviously accounted for policies of some papers, without regard to other purposes.

In Chicago, where, according to one Missouri paper, nothing gave an editor more pleasure than to hear of bloodshed in Missouri, the press provided its full share of censure. The attitude of that city's press is indicated by the *Tribune*'s statement, "The murderous operations of the Missouri highwaymen . . . are a disgrace to that state, and argue a degree of inefficiency or cowardice upon the part of the state authorities." [23] The New York *Herald* charged that the Jameses and Youngers were alive "due to the unpardonable cowardice of the whole community." [24] And from the Pittsburgh, Pennsylvania, *Commercial* came the assertion that in the "bandit State of Missouri" the "whole machinery of law" was "set at defiance by a gang of notorious robbers and cut-throats, who plunder and terrorize the State with impunity, disturbed only by occasional visits from officers of other Commonwealths, who are promptly murdered on sight." [25]

The Democratic press in Missouri replied that misrule in Republican states surpassed in evil any situation in Missouri. The Kansas City *Times*, for instance, proclaimed that "robbers in Democratic Missouri are outlaws, with a price on their head . . . while robbers in Radical Kansas are elected to the highest offices in the State. . . . Democrats may not be good at catching fugitive thieves, but they can be counted on not to elevate such cattle to the highest offices in the State." [26]

In view of the blackening of Missouri's standing abroad and of the attacks on the Democratic administration by Republican papers in the state, Missouri's Democrats, in general, were not pleased with Woodson's message, which admitted inability to cope with lawlessness by routine methods. The James issue had been involved in politics earlier. In 1872 the charge that Governor B. Gratz Brown had failed to protect the state from lawlessness was used against him in his campaign for the Vice-Presidency of the United States as the nominee of the Liberal Republican party. The *Missouri Democrat* criticized him because the perpetrators of robberies committed in Missouri before he took office and in Iowa and Kentucky during his administration had not been caught. Even this early the paper had charged that Missouri's reputation was being injured by publicity in the Eastern press.[27] This was the beginning of a theme the *Missouri Democrat* harped on for a decade and a half. It soon was referring to the state with the expression, "Poor old Missouri."

The political situation in Missouri was favorable for the introduction of the issue of lawlessness into the campaign of 1874. Disfranchisement and other repressive measures taken against those who aided the Confederates had enabled the Republicans, or Radicals, to hold state office until 1870. In that year the combining of moderate Republicans and Democrats in the Liberal Republican movement rescued the government from the Radicals and elected B. Gratz Brown as governor, but Radical rule had left a legacy of hatred. By 1874 the Liberal Republican organization had disappeared, and the Democratic party was dominant. Its supremacy was challenged only slightly by a weak Republican party and a third party, the People's party, which represented discontented agrarians mainly and favored cheap money. Although numerically strong, the Democratic party in the state was weak in that its membership varied widely in political ancestry and differed greatly in opinion on the principal issues of the day. But on one issue there was complete agreement — opposition to the Republican party! The Radicals should never be returned to power in Missouri!

Realizing they had little or no chance to win, the Republicans cooperated with the People's party when it was to their advantage and at the same time looked for any issue that might divide the Democratic party. The Republicans never lost sight of the fact that their opposition was a coalition of ex-Confederate and ex-Union men. Any issue that could rouse old antagonisms was worth raising.

The controversy engendered by the Governor's special message on banditry played right into the strategies of both the Republican and the People's parties in 1874. Aware of the political implications of the message, the Democratic journals were quick to uphold the Governor and to defend the state against the charges that lawlessness prevailed. The impression that Missouri was in the possession of outlaws and that life and property were unsafe was due, they said, to accusations in the "Radical press" and not to activities of the outlaws. The public was also reminded that some of the crimes were committed when the Radicals were in power.[28]

This concern of the Democrats directed the attention of the other parties also to lawlessness in the state. The People's party met in convention in Jefferson City in early September and adopted a platform offering solutions for nearly every problem of the day. By implication it charged that lawlessness was preventing industry and capital from coming to the state; it demanded "the suppression of lawlessness and mob violence, and fearless execution of the laws, without regard to popular feeling in particular localities." R. T. Gentry echoed this demand in accepting his party's gubernatorial nomination.[29]

The Republicans had decided earlier to cast their lot with the People's party. The state central committee had resolved in July that since the People's party was charging the Democratic administration with recklessness and lawlessness and was opposing Democratic policies in general, the Republicans would support that party.[30] The Republican state convention in late September was little more than empty ceremony, for its delegates voted, after passing the usual resolutions upholding the national administration and the historic principles of the party, to adjourn without nominating candidates. A pungently worded resolution charged the state Democratic administration with misrule and incompetency that had led to "insecurity of person and property; prevention of immigration; the utter prostration of business, and the most ruinous depreciation of all values of property."[31]

The Republicans apparently believed that by bringing up the issues of lawlessness in general and the James boys in particular they might align Union Democrats against Confederate Democrats. There was little probability of success, but that a division of Democrats was not impossible is indicated by the threat made early in June by William F. Switzler to bolt the Democratic party if it failed to recognize Union members. Switzler, a former Whig and the editor of the Columbia *Missouri Statesman*, was an important figure in state politics. Among other things, he said that if the party nominated men of the "Gad's Hill type whose chief and only recommendation for office is that they were not Union men during the war, the *Statesman* will not support them." [32]

The Democratic state convention shrewdly evaded mention of lawlessness in its platform. It nominated a ticket that even a strong Union man like Switzler, albeit with some misgiving, could support [33] and thus dealt with the criticism of those who blamed the Democratic party for banditry in the state. Other issues soon became more important in the campaign, but none aroused the tempers of editors more effectively.

Perhaps the most important incident in connection with the issue of lawlessness was the attempt of no less a person than the reformer Carl Schurz to exploit it in his fight to retain his seat in the United States Senate. This widely known German immigrant, who had become a leader of the Liberal Republican movement in Missouri, was elected to the Senate as a Liberal Republican. His term of office was to end in 1875, and he was now a man without a party. A staunch Union man throughout the war, he had not seen fit to become a Democrat, nor had he yet returned to the ranks of the Republican party, as he later did. Instead, in 1874, he threw in his lot with the People's party and joined in the campaign for its candidates and principles.

In a speech in St. Louis, Schurz explained fully his views on the main issues of the election. He had been accused of referring to Missouri as "the Robber State." Near the conclusion of his speech he took up the charge, saying, "I pronounce that utterly false." He went on to state, however, that even European newspapers printed accounts of the Gads Hill robbery as a "racy anecdote to show what can be done in this commonwealth with impunity" and that he was embarrassed frequently when colleagues in the Senate brought him accounts of Missouri robberies. He denounced the Democratic platform for ignoring banditry while the other two parties condemned it. Those who committed robberies, those in power who permitted the crimes, the party that forgot the crimes when it defined its policy, and the newspapers that denounced those who brought the crimes to the public's attention all defamed the state and frightened away immigrants to the state. He believed lawlessness injured Missouri, prevented immigration, depreciated land values, hindered progress and prosperity within the state, and was a dishonor to the whole commonwealth. In concluding, Schurz suggested that if the Democratic party could not stomach the facts and provide a remedy, it was fortunate for the state that other people would.[34]

Schurz repeated these charges a few days later in Kansas City.[35] The Democrats were furious. Their newspapers, concerned that Democrats might be attracted to the People's party, excoriated him and reminded the voters that whatever lawlessness existed was as nothing compared to the general corruptness of the Radicals' rule in the years following the Civil War. The Radicals, the Democrats pointed out, during their years of control had not caught the James band, but Democrats had attempted to apprehend the outlaws. There was no truth to the charges that lawlessness had deterred immigrants from coming to the state and had depreciated property values.[36]

Schurz had not maintained a residence in Missouri during his term as Senator, and this circumstance now led to some humorous and cutting criticism. Henry J. Spaunhorst, editor of *Amerika*, commented that Schurz's speech explained why he had not lived in Missouri, had not invested money there, and was indifferent to the interests of the state. He continued: "We marvel only whence the German senator took the courage to put his feet on the soil of this terrible robber state and stay within its borders, though only for a few days." [37]

As was to be expected, the Democrats won the state election easily in spite of the charges growing out of lawlessness. Other issues had been more important, but none had aroused greater interest and feeling.

VII

His mother's right arm
It came to harm.
Detectives blew it off, sir.

T HE TRAIN ROBBERY in Iowa in July, 1873, and the one at Gads Hill, Missouri, in January of 1874, much more closely than the earlier bank holdups focused national interest on the James-Younger band. The killing of three Pinkerton detectives as well as the use of lawlessness as an issue in the 1874 political campaign in Missouri, which involved so eminent a figure as Schurz, added to the notoriety of both the outlaws and the State of Missouri. Also, the list of exploits attributed to the band grew, and the newspapers' interest in anything related to the outlaws rose.

The men who had committed the series of robberies from Liberty to Gads Hill had ruthlessly slain citizens, bank officers, and the engineer of a train under conditions that loaded the odds heavily against their victims. Whicher was a detective, acting in the line of duty, but his killing was a cold-blooded murder; John and Jim Younger had ridden out to their deadly affray with Lull and Daniel. One seeks in vain for gallantry in these acts. Yet, the Kansas City *Daily Journal of Commerce*, a paper never sympathetic to the outlaws or to their apologists, commented editorially in mid-April, 1874, that these were not "common or vulgar criminals" and that no case of common theft or individual robbery could be proved against them.[1] In spite of avowals of this sort, the suspicion was strong and openly expressed, especially in 1874 and 1875, that the Jameses and Youngers were involved in many robberies of stores, stagecoaches, and individuals that, although they are not usually included on the lists of their exploits, were certainly the acts of common and vulgar criminals. While the editor of the *Journal* reported that he had heard of "many generous deeds" by these men, he stated clearly that they were "outlaws by choice and against every inducement to be otherwise."

In the twelve months following the robbery at Gads Hill several events served to befuddle the public's thinking and thereby add to the sympathy for these criminals. The kind of admiration Major Edwards had expressed for them after the robbery of the fair at Kansas City in 1872 increased, and at the same time the belief became general that these were persecuted men — persecuted for unfounded charges. In April, 1874, following the Youngers' fight with the detectives at Monegaw Springs, a review of the family background and life of the Younger brothers made its rounds, assisted by the press in Missouri. This review stressed the prominence and excellent reputation of the Younger family and the injuries done the boys' parents by Federal soldiers during the war. All the boys — Cole, James, John, and Robert — had lived in Texas since the war, according to this account, but John had left there in 1871 after the killing of Sheriff Nichols. The other three, stated William F. Switzler's Columbia *Missouri Statesman*, "as late as the spring of 1873, were residing in Texas, and were looked upon as honorable and industrious gentlemen. . . . In appearance they are large and portly, with excellent address and more than average amount of intelligence, and connected with the best families of Missouri." [2] Apparently some readers would find it hard to believe that men so described could be common murderers and robbers.

Then there was the latest news of Jesse. "All the world loves a lover," and if he is dashing and daring, it loves him all the more. Hence, the announcement made in the St. Louis *Dispatch* in June that Jesse had married his cousin Zee was eagerly seized upon by other papers. Later it was established that the Reverend William James, Methodist minister and uncle of the parties to the contract, performed the ritual on April 24, 1874, at the home of the bride's sister near Kearney in the presence of a few relatives. The *Dispatch*'s report had been sent from Sherman, Texas, on June 5 by a correspondent who said he had seen Jesse and Frank in Galveston where Jesse awaited a vessel to take him and his bride to Vera Cruz; from there they planned to go inland and acquire a farm. Jesse had given this version of the marriage:

On the 23rd of April, 1874, I was married to Miss Zee Mimms, of Kansas City, and at the house of a friend there. About fifty of our mutual friends were present on the occasion, and quite a noted Methodist minister performed the ceremonies. We had been engaged for nine years, and through good and evil report, and not withstanding the lies that had been told upon me and the crimes laid at my door, her devotion to me has never wavered for a moment. You can say that both of us married for love, and that there cannot be any sort of doubt about our marriage being a happy one.

Jesse's confidant described Zee as a young lady "with an elegant form, beautiful eyes, and a face that would be attractive in any assembly." She was also a devout Methodist.[3]

This was not the only time that Jesse would claim to have been out of the country; fabulous tales were later told of his adventures in Mexico. Factually, it is doubtful that Jesse ever left this country, even for a honeymoon; probably he and Zee spent their first months of married life in Texas near Sherman, as she stated after his death, and Jesse and others of his coterie have been accused of holding up several stages in the area of San Antonio and Austin in the spring and summer of 1874. It was in one of these robberies that the leader is said to have told an Episcopal bishop, who protested the loss of his watch on the basis of his profession, that he did not need it, for Christ never owned one.[4]

Whether Jesse went to Texas or Mexico is of little consequence, for there was soon reason to believe that he had returned to Missouri. Late on the afternoon of Sunday, August 30, two omnibuses were stopped and the passengers robbed, one between Waverly and Carrollton and the other across the Missouri River from Lexington. The two robberies, about twenty-five miles apart, evidently were committed by members of the same band who had separated. Apparently, they were looking for, but did not find, someone carrying a large sum of money, who was expected to be on one of the stages. These holdups, it should be noted, were in the James boys' home territory.

The robbery nearer Lexington elicited greater publicity than the one between Waverly and Carrollton, for it seemed certain that one of the Youngers and the two Jameses committed it. Three armed and mounted men had been in the area all day, two of them spending some time in Lexington. These two had ridden on the ferry that transported the omnibus across the Missouri River on its late afternoon trip to the railroad depot at North Lexington, where it picked up passengers arriving by train.

The entire route the bus traveled was visible from the high bluff on the Lexington side of the river, and several Sunday afternoon strollers were along the road. They saw three men emerge from behind a house, stop the driver at gunpoint, and force the nine passengers, eight men and one woman, from the bus and to stand with their hands raised above their heads. The robber in command ordered one of his assistants to round up the strollers. One of them, Miss Mollie Newbold, defied him and ran to the ferry, under threats of death, to sound the alarm. The ferry crossed the river with the alarm of the robbery, which spread so quickly that soon a number of people stood on the bluff, witnessing the holdup.

While the helpless passengers were being robbed of money and valuables, one stroller watched with closer attention than the others — Miss Mattie Hamlet, who had known the James and Younger families for years. The newspapers reported that she recognized the robbers as Frank James, Jesse James, and Will [sic] Younger. The men whom she said were a Younger and Frank James exchanged greetings with her and, upon her entreaty, returned watches to two men and did not rob the woman passenger. When Miss Hamlet rebuked them for stooping so low as to rob travelers in an omnibus, they agreed that this was a bit small for them. Everyone — victims, witnesses, and highwaymen — seemed to enjoy the event; one of the passengers, a Professor J. L. Allen who had just arrived from Kentucky to establish a male academy in Lexington, is reported to have said that night that "he was exceedingly glad, as he had to be robbed, that it was done by first class artists, by men of national reputation." This happy man had been forced to trade his fine coat and vest for a worn and dirty linen duster.

In the peculiar climate of the time and place, this crime was judged by many as an exploit that merited just recognition. The publishers of the weekly Lexington *Caucasian* hurriedly brought out an extra edition in which they proclaimed that "in all the history of medieval knight errantry and modern brigandage, there is nothing that equals the wild romance of the past few years' career of Arthur McCoy, Frank and Jesse James, and the Younger boys. . . . Their desperate deeds during the war were sufficient to have stocked a score of ordinary novels, with facts that outstrip the strangest flights of fancy." But these extravagances served only to introduce the paper's admiring estimate of the gang's deeds:

Their fame has become national, aye, world-wide. Ever since the war closed, and left them outlawed, they have borne themselves like men who have only to die, and have determined to do it without flinching. For the last two or three years the whole country has rung with their daring and hardihood. These four or five men absolutely defied the whole power of Missouri. They have laughed at her Governor, and mocked him with epistles of burlesque penitence. They have captured and pillaged whole railroad trains. . . . They have dashed into towns and cleaned out banking houses in broad daylight. . . . Detectives, who have undertaken to ferret them out, have been slain. Sheriff's posses have been routed. The whole State authorities defied and spit upon by this half-dozen brilliant, bold, indefatigable roughriders.

Then came the details of the "Robin-Hood-like, rattling visit" with which they had honored Lexington.[5]

The Lexington *Register* did not share its rival's admiration for the bandits, but it, too, issued an extra; its account was limited to the details of the incident. Its editor, having no doubt as to the identity of the highwaymen, challenged the Governor of Missouri:

Governor Woodson said he did not have the James boys arrested because no one would make the proper affidavit charging them with any crime. The editor of this paper has this day forwarded to His Excellency an account of this robbery, and an offer to furnish, when and where demanded, the proper affidavit making the formal charge. The Governor can have a chance to show his zeal in the matter if he desires so to do.[6]

The editor of the *Caucasian* held fast for a time to his belief that the James band had committed the robbery; but Mattie Hamlet, who had conversed in easy familiarity with the bandits, upon receiving a letter from Mrs. Samuel announced, "After mature reflection on the subject, I am prepared to doubt the accuracy of my recognition." She refused to make a formal affidavit as to the identity of the men.[7] In the same vein, the Kansas City *Times* reported that it had reliable information that the Youngers were in St. Clair County on the day of the robbery and had been there all summer; Jesse James and his bride were in Mexico; Frank was confined to the bed with the recurrence of trouble from an old wound.[8]

By mid-October the editor of the *Caucasian* admitted his error in believing the Jameses had anything to do with the robbery. The occasion for this denial was the report of an interview with Mrs. Samuel while she was visiting in Lexington. Effusive comparisons of "Missouri's bold rovers" to medieval knights led to a startling boast: "If we must have banditti . . . Missouri, the Empire State of the West, should stand foremost — unequaled — unrivaled — in her freebooters. . . . And the James Boys have given her the proud preeminence that is her due." But in recent months some other band of desperadoes had been "plagiarizing on their reputation."[9]

It is not likely that Mrs. Samuel's trip to Lexington and the interview were accidental. All who knew her vouched for her shrewdness. Was she in Lexington to build sympathy for her family and confuse the public as to her sons' whereabouts? It would be characteristic for her to do just that. This was not to be the last of such appearances when accusations were being directed against her sons. Mrs. Samuel knew well the arts of showmanship, and she was at her best that day in Lexington, so that her interviewer was strongly impressed. He described her as a "tall, dignified lady, of about forty-eight years; graceful in carriage and gesture; calm and quiet in demeanor, with a ripple of fire now and then breaking through the placid surface; and of far more than ordinary intelligence and culture."

Her tale that day was essentially the same she continued to repeat until many years after the breakup of the James band. It included the family's respectable history, the death of the Reverend Robert James, the injustices suffered by the family during the war, including her own imprisonment, the guerrilla careers of her boys, all interlarded with the frequent repetition of, "No mother ever had better sons, more affectionate, obedient, and dutiful." She complained bitterly that others were committing crimes and then sheltering under the names of the James boys, who had been in Mexico for months. The editor of the *Caucasian* believed her story, he said, for Dave Pool, formerly a leader of guerrillas, and John N. Edwards verified it! [10]

There were, however, others — men secretly in the employ of the Governor — who did not believe Mrs. Samuel's story that the James brothers were in Mexico. Governor Woodson had employed J. W. Ragsdale and George W. Warren as investigators soon after the legislature appropriated money for this purpose. Ragsdale and Warren had been in the home area of the Jameses and reported to the Governor that a man in their employ had obtained work on a farm near the Samuel home. Curiously, all the parties of whom he made inquiries seemed to be friends of the Jameses and Youngers. [11]

After the holdup at Lexington, Acting Governor Charles P. Johnson, in the absence of Governor Woodson, called on the St. Louis Police Department, across the breadth of the state from the crime, for help; Flourney Yancey was assigned to this duty. Yancey's letters to the Governor reported that he spent several days trailing men he believed to be the Jameses and Youngers through Lafayette, Ray, Clay, Jackson, and Saline counties, and he was convinced that several minor robberies reported in that area had been committed by these men. He encountered difficulties in following the suspects because they were "mounted on the fleetest horses in the country and thoroughly versed in its geography." Nor did they stay in one place long enough for him to summon a posse to capture them. Besides, he found that nearly all the people were either in sympathy with or afraid of them; the only sheriff he had met whom he would trust was "Brown of Ray County."

Officer Yancey reported that on the morning of September 21 he flushed Jesse James and James Younger near the Clay-Ray county line and engaged them in a gun fight in which eleven shots were fired. He thought he had shot Jesse. The posse that pursued the fugitives failed to apprehend them, however. [12] Four Lexington citizens, including Mark L. De Motte, Republican editor of the Lexington *Register*, had volunteered their services to the Governor and worked with Officer Yancey. For this the *Caucasian,* when the fact became known, chided the four men with the suggestion that the James and Younger boys, upon hearing the names of the "Quartet of Blood Thirsty Warriors Leagued Against Them" had fled in "Wild Dismay to the Mountains of Hopsidam or the Bottoms of Wakenda." [13]

Excitement over the omnibus robbery had died down when, in late November, the Pleasant Hill *Review,* edited by Lycurgus Jones, brother-in-law of the Youngers, published a letter from Cole Younger that was reprinted widely. Cole expressed bitter antagonism toward Jesse James; the name of Younger would never have been associated with the Jameses had not Jesse published a letter stating that he, John Younger, and Cole were accused of the robbery of the Kansas City fair. The Youngers and the Jameses were not on speaking terms and had not been for several years; John had seen neither Frank nor Jesse for eighteen months before his death. Cole denied any involvement in the gang's crimes and offered to prove his presence in Jackson and St. Clair counties in Missouri and in Carroll Parish, Louisiana, at the times when the various robberies, beginning with that of the Kansas City fair, were committed. The fact that he did not concern himself with any of the holdups before 1872 may indicate that he did not consider serious the earlier charges against him. Younger appealed to the Governor to investigate his claims and challenged him to offer a reward for him if he did not believe him innocent.[14]

Shortly, an emotionally charged letter to the editor of the St. Louis *Dispatch,* signed JUSTITIA, accused the Radical press and particularly the Chicago *Inter-Ocean,* the St. Louis *Globe,* and the St. Louis *Democrat* in language very like John N. Edwards' of unjustly charging the James and Younger brothers with crimes. After passionately reviewing the wrongs suffered by the Younger family in wartime, the writer asked, "Is it right—is it just that they should still be deemed guilty of all the crimes perpetrated in Missouri since the war, and that they should be denied protection while engaged in clearing their names . . . ?" Professing to know that the Youngers had been making their living honestly since the war, he called upon the newly elected governor, Charles H. Hardin, to offer them amnesty.[15]

This letter, which was surely intended to influence its readers to accept its views, also represented a widely held belief in the Youngers' innocence that was discarded reluctantly, if at all, when the Youngers were caught, following the robbery of the First National Bank at Northfield, Minnesota, in September, 1876, and safely lodged behind prison walls. In the interval between publication of Cole's letter and JUSTITIA's appeal, two robberies occurred, and though the scenes were far apart the Jameses and Youngers were suspected, thus exposing their accusers to the ridicule of their defenders.

On December 7, four men robbed the Tishimingo Savings Bank of Corinth, Mississippi, of a sum reported at $5,000 and of jewelry valued at about the same amount. While two associates held the horses and stood guard, two bandits displaying "ugly looking knives" entered the bank, slashed the cashier across the forehead, and made away with the loot. News reports of the incident stated the James and Younger brothers were believed to be in the party.[16] The leader was said later to have been identified from a picture as Cole Younger.[17] This identification, of course, was uncertain.

On the afternoon of December 8, one day after the robbery at Corinth, a train on the Kansas Pacific Railroad was robbed in a spectacular manner at Muncie, Kansas, a few miles west of Kansas City. Five men on fine horses rode up to the depot, compelled section hands to pile ties across the tracks, and then locked the laborers in a small shed. As the train approached, the gang flagged it with a red scarf. After it had stopped, they forced crewmen to uncouple the passenger cars and then ordered the engineer to pull the express and baggage cars ahead some two hundred yards. From these cars the bandits removed an amount reported at $30,000. Then, seemingly in no hurry, they watched the crew recouple the cars before they rode away.[18]

Naturally, speculation as to the identity of the robbers led to the James-Younger band, and it was reported that Jesse James and one of the Youngers had been in Kansas City a few days before.[19] It became evident that serious efforts were to be made to catch the brigands, whoever they were. The press reported that the express company had offered $5,000 for recovery of the money or $1,000 each for the robbers, dead or alive; the Kansas Pacific Railroad Company offered a $5,000 reward and the governor of Kansas, $2,500.[20]

In a few days, Bud McDaniel, known to be a friend of the James boys, was arrested in Kansas City on a charge of drunkenness. A search of his person yielded over $1,000 in cash and several items of jewelry readily identified as part of the plunder from the express car at Muncie. Charges were filed against him, but he remained tight-lipped under questioning and would not expose his accomplices. Soon afterwards, he broke jail at Lawrence and was killed by a farmer in an attempt to capture him.[21]

Friends of the Jameses and Youngers often pointed to the incongruity of charging them with both the Corinth and Muncie robberies. Yet it is entirely possible that the leaders had separated and that some of the gang were in Mississippi and others in Kansas at the same time.

The depredations in 1874 of which they were accused had most assuredly made the James and Younger boys notorious the country over. Their notoriety produced varied reactions in the public, however, for many looked upon them as persecuted men and rationalized their acts. In Missouri the scars remaining from the Civil War and the postwar political injuries accounted for much of this feeling. Perhaps agrarian distrust of railroads and express companies was also a factor, for one writer suggested in his report of the robbery at Muncie that the funds seized by the bandits were "just as honestly earned as the riches of many a highly distinguished political leader and railroad job manipulator." [22]

Except for mention of the problem of banditry in the last message of the outgoing governor Silas Woodson to the legislature and in the inaugural address of Missouri's new governor Charles H. Hardin, interest in the bandits was at a low ebb through most of January, 1875. But on the night of January 26 a bungling raid upon the home of the James boys' mother created a greater sensation, generating more repercussions than anything yet credited to her sons. It also put the issue of amnesty for acts committed during the Civil War before the Missouri legislature, and the result showed that neither the war nor banditry was dead as a political issue.

At some time during this January night, Dr. and Mrs. Samuel were awakened by a noise outside and discovered a ball of cotton, saturated with some flammable substance, blazing in their kitchen. As they moved it into the fireplace, another flaming ball was thrown through a window. This, too, with poker and shovel the Samuels pushed onto the hearth, where it exploded with a powerful impact. A large fragment of the device struck nine-year-old Archie Peyton Samuel, half brother of Frank and Jesse James, and tore a hole in his side; he died within the hour. Mrs. Samuel's right hand was mangled so badly that amputation was necessary, and a Negro servant also was injured though less severely.

The press and local opinion immediately assumed that the assault had been made by Pinkerton detectives, probably assisted by local men, in an effort to capture Frank and Jesse. In support of this opinion was the fact that Jack Ladd, who had worked for some time as a hired man on Daniel Askew's farm, which adjoined the Samuels farm, disappeared from the community. The people, believing him a Pinkerton agent, thought he and Daniel Askew had aided the attacking party. It is possible that Ladd was the man whom Ragsdale and Warren had sent into the area and that he had alerted the agents that Frank and Jesse were at home. A special train on the Hannibal and St. Joseph and the St. Louis, Kansas City and Northern railroads then brought a force of detectives to a point near Kearney on the night of the attack. This train or another returned later to pick up the men. Many rumors circulated that some members of the attacking party were wounded or killed, and it was widely believed that Ladd was killed that night by either the James boys or the detectives, who were angered at the failure of their expedition.

The remains of the fireball that exploded indicated that the explosion was accidental. Apparently the iron ball held a flammable liquid that burned as it drained through a hole onto the rags with which it was wrapped and which served as a wick. Its purpose no doubt was incendiary, and it was expected to force the James brothers out of the house if they were there as was believed. The heat from the coals in the fireplace caused the explosion. That the detectives intended to endanger the lives of a whole family is doubtful; but the deaths of Whicher, Allen, and Wright had made them desperate, and they were careless.

A pistol bearing the letters "P.G.G." was found on the premises. This insignia of the Pinkerton Government Guard was attached to the guns of Pinkerton detectives, and to most people, finding such a gun provided evidence that the Pinkertons had attacked the Samuel home.[23]

Whether one or both the boys had been at home at the time of the attack became a question of first importance. The first person to reach the Samuel place after the explosion was a young man named James A. Hall, who lived with his parents on the farm that adjoined the Samuel farm on the south. His twelve-year-old brother E. P. had attended a neighborhood party that night with two of the Samuel children. James A., after viewing the gruesome scene at the Samuels' home, rode to Kearney for Dr. James V. Scruggs. Upon Dr. Scruggs's arrival, Mrs. Samuel asked everyone to leave the room for a brief interval — an interval in which, Hall believed, she bade someone farewell. Dr. Scruggs's horse disappeared from the Samuel barn, and two days later, it was found three miles away, completely jaded. It was suspected that Jesse or Frank had used the horse to escape.[24]

Regardless of whether the James brothers were guilty of the crimes charged against them, the murder of an innocent child and the maiming of their mother by law officers outraged people everywhere. Assuming that the Pinkertons were guilty, editorial writers expressed the general indignation and condemnation. In the state capital, Jefferson City, the news of the bombing was "the signal for a universal outbreak of indignation at the fiendish action of the Pinkerton detectives."[25] The Richmond *Conservator* commented that the "James boys never fired a dwelling at midnight."[26] The state's two leading Democratic newspapers, the Kansas City *Times* and the St. Louis *Dispatch*, were most condemnatory. The *Times* proclaimed: "There is no crime, however dastardly, which merits a retribution as savage and fiendish as the one which these men acting under the semblance of law have perpetrated." [27]

Major John N. Edwards, as could be anticipated, exceeded all others in his denunciation of "the dastardly dogs who were hunting human flesh for hire." In words calculated to revive Civil War hatreds, he cried out: "Men of Missouri, you who fought under Anderson, Quantrell, Todd, Poole, and the balance of the borderers and guerrillas . . . recall your woodscraft and give up these scoundrels to the Henry Rifle and Colt's revolver. It is because like you they were at Lawrence, and Centralia, . . . and wherever else the black flag floated." And he called for instant redress of this diabolical plot.[28] But Edwards' expression was too virulent, and the editorial did not receive general approval.

The state's General Assembly quickly took cognizance of the incident and passed a resolution asking Governor Charles Henry Hardin to investigate the bombing and report to the lawmakers. The resolution was introduced by one of the most powerful members of the Democratic party in the state, Stilson Hutchins, principal owner of the St. Louis *Dispatch*, who soon afterward bought the St. Louis *Times* and, in 1877, founded the Washington *Post*. In supporting the resolution, Hutchins offered no apology for the James boys, but he argued that a group of men under the guise of legally constituted authority had committed an outrage "upon the rights of the people of the State of Missouri which should be promptly investigated, denounced and punished." The other supporting speech in the House of Representatives was made by General James Shields, Union soldier who had been United States Senator from Illinois and Minnesota and who was to serve Missouri also in that office. He branded the incident as "the most cowardly and brutal outrage ever committed in the State." [29]

In the House the vote was 84 to 1 for the resolution,[30] but in the Senate it met more guarded approval. Republican members of the Senate spoke through half a day, condemning the measure and its supporters for not demanding the capture of the James and Younger brothers. The measure was then passed, 20 Democrats voting for it and 4 Republicans and 1 Democrat opposing it.[31]

It is evident that the Democratic press recalled the charges made against the party in the campaign a few months earlier and was willing now to exploit the unfortunate incident at the Samuel home to full advantage. On the other hand, the two leading opposition papers in the state, the Kansas City *Journal* and the St. Louis *Republican*, saw in the expressions of indignation evidence that the charges against the Democrats in 1874 were true. The *Journal* labeled the endangering of lives of children and servants as inexcusable, but, because the mother and stepfather had harbored the persons sought in the raid, the paper declared, "but few tears will be shed" for them. The editor of the *Journal* thought the attitudes expressed by the St. Louis *Dispatch* and Kansas City *Times*, representing "the controlling element" of the Democratic party, now fully warranted the charge that leaders of that party were in sympathy with the outlaws.[32] Hutchins' resolution asking an investigation occasioned a scorching editorial in the *Journal* that renewed the accusations against Democratic leaders:

It was hardly expected that the leader of the party, really the ring master of the dominant faction, would be so indecent as to take such decided ground in the legislature against those who attempt to capture them. The heat with which it was done is evidence of a greater regard for the outlaws than for the law and dignity of the state, and the object is evidently more to discourage future ventures of this kind than to protect the dignity of the state.[33]

As directed in the resolution, Governor Hardin ordered an investigation. He sent Adjutant General George Caleb Bingham to Clay County, and on February 4 he sent to the legislature as much of Bingham's report as he believed should be made public at the time. The full report was never divulged. In the absence of power to compel testimony, Bingham had obtained little information not already reported in the news stories. He did not think a fight had occurred at the Samuel home, for the bloodstains exhibited as evidence could have resulted from an accidental injury or nosebleed, and the bullet holes in the fence looked as if they had been there for a long time. Besides, there were seven holes, and he said the neighbors heard only four shots. He confirmed the information that special trains had conveyed the party to and from the area. Bingham could not learn from any reliable source that either of the James boys had been seen in the vicinity since the preceding April. He was convinced that the people of Clay County would be greatly relieved if the brothers could be captured and brought to justice.[34]

In presenting the report, Governor Hardin condemned "such outrages upon the peace and quiet of society" and pledged himself to use all his power to bring the offenders to trial. The same day Republicans in the House tried to get two resolutions considered, one asking the Governor to investigate the depredations of the James brothers and report to the legislature and the other calling on the Governor to explain how much of the $10,000 appropriated for the suppression of banditry had been expended and for what purposes. Skillful maneuvering by Stilson Hutchins and Democratic unity defeated the attempt.[35]

During March a grand jury in Clay County investigated the bombing and found indictments for the murder of Archie Samuel against Robert J. King, Allan K. Pinkerton, Jack Ladd, and five other persons whose names were unknown to the jurors. Witnesses included former Governor Woodson, who presumably was asked to explain how he had used funds appropriated for the suppression of banditry, members of the Samuel family, the doctors who had attended Mrs. Samuel, law enforcement officers of Clay County, officials of the Hannibal and St. Joseph Railroad, and Samuel Hardwicke.[36] There is no record of the testimony.

Samuel Hardwicke, Liberty attorney, reportedly admitted that he had been employed by Pinkerton, but only as an attorney. For several months he had been communicating by telegram in code with someone believed to be a Pinkerton agent. Rumors had already connected Hardwicke with the raid, but evidently he vindicated himself before the grand jury, for otherwise he would have been indicted. He moved into Liberty from his farm, a few miles away, soon after the raid, because, some said, he thought it safer in town. Several months later he moved to St. Paul, Minnesota.[37]

If any of the parties indicted were ever arrested, the records contain no evidence of such action. On September 13, 1877, the court ordered the case against the indictees continued generally, the state paying the costs.[38] This action was equivalent to dismissal of the charges. Pinkerton could very easily have been apprehended and extradited to Missouri. The fact that he was not arrested and brought to Missouri indicates either that there was little direct evidence against him, as some people believed, or that high officials knew the details of the raid, and their influence prevented Pinkerton's arrest.

In the weeks following the fireball explosion the build-up of a move to grant amnesty to the James and Younger brothers became evident. A long article in the Chicago *Times* of February 24, written by a special correspondent at Jefferson City, Missouri, presaged the introduction of a resolution offering amnesty. It presented a one-sided history of the Jameses and Youngers and argued that Radicals and Jayhawkers had prevented their settling down to peaceable lives after the war, that they had not committed the crimes charged to them, and that the mobbing and murdering of former bushwhackers made it unsafe for them to present themselves for trial.[39]

On March 8 the St. Louis *Dispatch* presented the case for amnesty in a long editorial. It charged that the failure of the Missouri Constitution of 1865 to provide a means of granting amnesty to ex-Confederates was responsible for the condition of the Jameses and Youngers, who had been "educated to desperation by cruelties perpetrated on them and their families during and since the war." They were now hunted only on suspicion; they should be given "the opportunity to come home and be honest and peaceful citizens, instead of being hunted like wolves by detectives, who are willing to sell their blood for the gold of a paltry reward." An offer of amnesty, the writer argued, would unquestionably be constitutional.

There followed shortly in Missouri papers, mainly in the form of letters, an array of argument, in the vein to which the people were by now accustomed, over the issues of the fugitives' guilt and innocence, the qualities of their characters, and the question of whether they were victims of persecution. It was evident that the bombing had created a climate of sympathy that favored an effort to obtain amnesty.

On March 17, Jefferson Jones of Callaway County introduced in the House a joint and concurrent resolution that instructed Governor Hardin to grant full and complete amnesty and pardon to Jesse W. James, Frank James, Coleman Younger, Robert Younger, James Younger, and others for all acts charged or committed by them during the Civil War and to offer them full protection and fair trials on charges of crime since the war. Such provisions would remove the discrimination that the resolution said was pronounced upon them by the Constitution of 1865. The wording of two sections in particular is even more important than the proposed amnesty in showing the feeling of those supporting it:

WHEREAS, Under the outlawry pronounced against Jesse W. James, Frank James, Coleman Younger, Robert Younger, James Younger and others, who gallantly periled their lives and their all in defense of their principles, they are of necessity made desperate, driven as they are from the fields of honest industry, from their friends, their families, their homes and their country, they can know no law but the law of self-preservation; can have no respect for and feel no allegiance to a government which forces them to the very acts it professes to deprecate and then offers a bounty for their apprehension, and arms foreign mercenaries with power to capture and kill; and

WHEREAS, Believing these men too brave to be mean; too generous to be revengeful, and too gallant and honorable to betray a friend or break a promise, and believing further, that most, if not all, the offences with which they are charged have been committed by others, and perhaps by those pretending to hunt them, or by their confederates, that their names are and have been used to divert suspicion from, and thereby relieve the actual perpetrators — that the return of these men to their home and friends would have the effect of greatly lessening crime in our State, by turning public attention to the real criminals, and that common justice, sound policy and true statesmanship alike demand that general amnesty should be extended to all alike, of both parties, for attacks done or charged to have been done during the war; *therefore be it resolved,* . . .[40]

There is some indication that the supporters of the measure had intended to offer amnesty for the crimes charged to the Jameses and Youngers since the war, but had refrained from doing so because of the doubtful constitutionality of such an act.[41] Jones made a fervent appeal for passage, and there can be no doubt that he honestly favored the measure, but the Kansas City *Journal* charged that he was not its real author. The resolutions, it declared, were drawn up in St. Louis, and Stilson Hutchins was to storm them through the legislature.[42] Clearly, the *Journal* suspected the hand of Hutchins' editor John N. Edwards in the project, but nowhere did it appear openly.

The time between introduction of the resolution on March 17 and the vote on March 20 did not permit a prolonged discussion of it in the press. Many papers ignored the measure, but the leading party organs took their stands. Defenders of the James boys were outspoken. Among them were people who believed that the Jameses were guilty, but that persecution had driven them into lives of crime. The eulogistic wording of the amnesty resolution did not admit this view, and obviously there were those who did not believe them guilty of any of the charges against them. As has been said, "The wish may have been father to the thought."

In support of amnesty, the Jefferson City *Daily Tribune*, important mouthpiece of the Democratic party, pointed out that it had always held that the Jameses and Youngers were not the perpetrators of any of the crimes charged to them because "there was never any better evidence against them than the cry of the populace, caught up and carried from mouth to mouth, without stopping to consider the facts." This clamor had made them outlaws. Unable to live peaceably at home, they were not willing to trust themselves for trial at the hands of people crying for blood. Recent occurrences had caused public sentiment to change in regard to them, and many papers that had formerly demanded their arrest and punishment now declared that they "have been more sinned against than sinning." The *Tribune* could see no harm in opening the way for the men to return to their homes.[43]

Certainly some Democratic papers opposed the resolution,[44] but the Republican Kansas City *Journal* stated the case against it most strongly. Its attack was bitter and laden with implications that the resolution served political considerations, but the paper recognized the realities of the situation. It first accused the framers of the proposal of basing it on the false premise that the state constitution had outlawed Confederates. In this the *Journal* was correct, for though the constitution did not extend amnesty to Confederates, it did not outlaw them. The *Journal* was right also when it pointed out that hundreds of Missourians who associated during the war with the men named in the proposal were granted full amnesty at the close of the war and had returned to their communities and the ways of peace. Bloodthirsty and lawless instincts had led these men to prefer a life of brigandage, with which the *Journal* accused the legislature of sympathizing while attempting "to save them from the consequences of their crimes." The protection that the measure required the governor to furnish the bandits if they surrendered would be such as to assure their acquittal. The *Journal* exclaimed over the legislature's apology that the offer of protection was all that it could do for the men under the constitution. The editorial concluded with the lament:

such is the barbarous depth to which this legislature has descended, that brigands, whose bloody deeds have shocked humanity and made them a terror to this and neighboring states, are to be made the special objects of its protection and the protection of the state. The law abiding citizens whom they have murdered are not to be avenged; society is not to be protected against them, and their crimes are not to be atoned for, but the brigands are to be given special protection, and secured alike against an outraged public sentiment and the decision of the courts.[45]

The *Daily Tribune* and the *Journal* had stated clearly two different views on the question of amnesty. On March 20, General Shields, reporting for the Committee on Federal Relations, to which the resolution had been referred, presented a substitute measure with a do-pass recommendation, which was accepted without a roll call. The eulogistic provisions were omitted, and no mention was made of guaranteeing a fair trial. Instead, the men named in the measure were to be "protected in their rights of person and property, as long as they remain peaceable and submit to legal proceedings." Arguments on the floor consumed half a day, and in the course of them one member sent to the clerk's desk and had read Governor Woodson's special message on outlawry of March 23, 1874. Then came the vote — 58 ayes and 39 nays. The measure had failed to pass because 58 was not the two-thirds vote required on concurrent resolutions. Subsequent efforts to get a reconsideration failed.[46]

Records show that 56 Democrats and 2 Republicans voted for amnesty, while 20 Democrats and 19 Republicans opposed it. For some reason Democratic sponsors of the measure had not been able to maintain party unity, and the number of Democrats who voted against it was more than the additional number needed to pass it. Analysis of the membership has revealed nothing that explains this vote except the fact that 10 Democratic representatives of a block of counties in southwest Missouri voted nay. In these counties Republicans had dom-

VIII

The people they did say,

For many miles away,

The bank was robbed by Frank and Jesse James.

D EFEAT of the amnesty bill did not end the flow of sympathetic and condemnatory reviews of the bandits' deeds. Nor did the acts of violence cease. On the night of April 12, 1875, Daniel Askew, the Samuels' neighbor who was suspected of assisting the detectives in the midnight attack on the Samuel home, was shot down at his doorstep. Naturally, the James brothers were suspected of either instigating or committing the killing to avenge his supposed part in the bombing.[1]

A tense situation was created by Askew's death. Others suspected of helping the detectives had been threatened, and the Liberty *Tribune* commented, "If this killing business is not put a stop to our county will be ruined." [2] Also, Sheriff John S. Groom, who in 1869 had vouched for the good standing of Jesse James, wrote Governor Charles H. Hardin that the county was "as greatly terror-stricken as at any time during the war" because the Jameses and their associates had threatened many men with Askew's fate. He pleaded with Hardin to assure the Jameses of a fair trial if they would surrender within a specified time. If they refused, the Governor should offer a reward to be paid for them "dead or alive." [3]

Since the killing of Archie Samuel and the crippling of Mrs. Samuel had engendered considerable hostility toward detectives in Clay County and throughout the state, the possibility that they had killed Askew to turn the tide of sympathy was not overlooked.[4] This theory was bolstered by a story from Chicago, where the Pinkertons' headquarters was located, that Askew had threatened to tell the details of the fatal raid and had been silenced.[5] Askew's death kept the political aspects of banditry before the people, for in reporting it the Kansas City *Times* mentioned that he was a Radical in politics. Republicans quickly charged the *Times* with attempting to mitigate the crime, for "to kill a Radical is no crime in the eyes of certain Democrats." [6]

It is interesting that the two leading anti-James newspapers in the state followed different lines at this time. The Kansas City *Daily Journal of Commerce* continued to blame the Democratic party and the eulogistic press for the gang's remaining at large; the St. Louis *Republican*, which had supported the People's party nominees in 1874, charged the citizens of Clay County, as it had after Whicher's murder, with the failure to apprehend the James brothers, and it berated the people of the county without mercy.[7] This paper undoubtedly stated merely what many in the state and elsewhere believed — that the James brothers made their home in Clay County, coming and going as they pleased under the protection of the people and that the law-enforcement officers looked the other way, for fear of vengeance. Those who denied these accusations probably came nearer to the truth. They said no one doubted that relatives and former bushwhackers befriended the Jameses and Youngers, but from beyond that circle they obtained little assistance. Most Clay Countians deplored the recent murders, but, realizing that Frank and Jesse were desperate men, they refused to risk their lives in an attempt to bring them to justice.[8]

That the reputation of Clay County was hurt by all the notoriety is certain, and probably many residents of the county were glad when the Samuels advertised their farm for sale and announced they would leave if they could sell it.[9] No purchaser appeared, however, and the Samuels continued to reside near their reluctant neighbors.

The outlaws and their crimes continued in the news. The Jameses and Youngers were suspected of robbing a store near Clinton in Henry County on May 13.[10] Rumors circulated that a long-standing feud between the two sets of brothers had been settled.[11] From Hopkinsville, Kentucky, came word of a band of twenty-three desperadoes, led by the James brothers, prowling in that vicinity. These reports from Kentucky continued through June and July.[12] Other news items about members of the band included a statement in mid-July that Cole Younger had passed through Jefferson City on his return to Texas after marketing livestock in the East [13] and an account of a conversation between Frank James and two citizens of Holt, Missouri, who met on a road near the Samuel farm.[14]

During this time, the usual letters to the newspapers, purporting to come from Jesse, were attempting to clear his name. The writer of these letters accused others of crimes attributed to him, reaffirmed his determination to vindicate himself, denied the rumor of his presence in Kentucky, denounced the Pinkerton detectives for the murder of Archie Samuel, and expressed appreciation to the St. Louis *Dispatch* and to the former Confederates in the Missouri legislature who had "stood up faithfully" for the James brothers.[15]

But the Jameses did not place all their reliance on their friends in the legislature. Jesse James believed in a personal God and, according to statements attributed to him, thought that, since he had done his best under the circumstances in which he had been placed, he was entitled to go to Heaven.[16] A portion of a letter first printed in the Nashville *Banner* in August, if actually written by him, expresses this view of divine justice:

Justice is slow but sure, and they [*sic*] is a just God that will bring all to justice. Pinkerton, I hope and pray that our Heavenly Father may deliver you into my hands, and I believe he will, for his merciful and protecting arm has ever been with me and shielded me, and during all my persecution he has watched over me and protected me from workers of blood money who are trying to seek my life, and I have hope and faith in him and believe he will ever protect me as long as I serve him.[17]

The letters that presented alibis and the expressions of faith in God did not serve to divert suspicion from the Jameses when another robbery occurred, even though it was far distant from Clay County. On September 5, 1875, four men robbed a bank at Huntington, West Virginia, of an amount reported at $10,000. The party was trailed into Kentucky, and near Pine Hill in that state two farmers fired upon the bandits and fatally wounded one of them. The dead bandit was identified after some delay as Thompson McDaniel, brother of Bud McDaniel, who had been arrested for the robbery at Muncie and had been killed after his escape from jail. Both brothers had been suspected of membership in the James band.

Several days later a man known in Missouri both as Jack Keene and Tom Webb was arrested in Fentress County, Tennessee. Unable to explain how he acquired the $4,500 found in his possession, he was returned to West Virginia, tried, and sentenced to twelve years in prison for participation in the robbery at Huntington.

Before the dead robber was identified as McDaniel, Missourians were informed that Jesse James had been killed, although the description of the dead man fitted Cole Younger more closely. When Webb (or Keene) was caught, reports circulated that Cole Younger had been arrested. No proof exists that any of the Jameses and Youngers were involved in the robbery at Huntington, but the presence of two Missourians nullified the argument that it had taken place too far from the gang's homes for them to be involved.[18]

The winter of 1875–1876 passed quietly so far as the gang's usual activities were concerned. In April the report that Frank James was a prisoner in the Missouri penitentiary was found to have no basis, but it attracted much attention.[19] Then in May, when a series of stagecoach robberies occurred in Texas, dispatches from Fort Worth said the robbers "are thought to be the notorious and desperate James boys, who have been at this work for several years in Arkansas, Missouri, the Nation and Texas." [20]

On the night of July 7, 1876, a Missouri Pacific Railroad train was robbed at Rocky Cut, near Otterville in Cooper County, Missouri, at a spot where a bridge was being constructed across the Lamine River. The band rode out of the woods and seized the watchman at the bridge, tied and gagged him, and used his red lantern to flag the slowly approaching train. Some of the bandits guarded the passengers and crewmen, while others rifled the safes of the Adams and United States express companies of over $15,000. To comfort the frightened passengers and crewmen, huddled under the guns of the guards, a minister who had been on board the train prayed loudly that the lives of all might be spared. In the thought that his prayers might go unanswered, he exhorted those about to be killed to repent of their sins while there was yet time. Following the prayer, the passengers mustered enough spirit to sing religious songs, an accompaniment to robbery odd enough to unnerve most bandits.

But these were practiced, nerveless thieves, and, as usual, the Jameses and Youngers were suspected of the holdup. It was, after all, committed on their home grounds. Besides, similarity between descriptions of the Jameses and Youngers and of some of the robbers gave firm basis to the suspicions. One reporter commented: "The robbery was well planned and well carried out. They were well versed in their business, evidently, as they are said to have been remarkably cool and courageous throughout the whole affair. No one was hurt, and no one loses anything save the express companies." After dividing the loot, the robbers apparently scattered, and the prompt pursuit by local citizens and officers was of no avail. That the prompt pursuit should be of no avail is not surprising, for in the climate expressed by the report — admiration of the cool and courageous bandits and lack of concern for the express companies' losses — efforts to capture the bandits could have been no more than halfhearted. As an official gesture, on July 8 Governor Hardin offered a reward of $300 for the capture of each participant.[21]

Information on the crime obtained by Chief of Police James Mc-

Donough of St. Louis caused him to send agents into southwest Missouri, where they arrested Hobbs Kerry and an uncle of the Younger brothers, Bruce Younger. Kerry had attracted attention to himself in the little town of Granby by flourishing a large sum of money. Correspondence between Kerry and Younger, intercepted by McDonough's men, led the Chief of Police to believe that Younger also was implicated in the robbery. Both men were brought to St. Louis, but Younger was subsequently released when he established an alibi.

Kerry was less fortunate. At Sedalia, less than twenty miles west of Otterville, he was identified by a farmer and his wife as one of a party of men who stopped at their house on Sunday before the robbery. Confronted by these witnesses, Kerry confessed that he had taken part in the robbery of the train, and he named as accomplices Jesse James, Frank James, Cole Younger, Bob Younger, Clem Miller, Charlie Pitts, and Bill Chadwell.[22] Larry Hazen, a noted Cincinnati detective, assisted McDonough and his men in the case; the railroad and express companies paid his expenses as well as those of the men from St. Louis.

Kerry had no criminal record. His association with the bandit gang had begun with a plan he and some friends had formed to rob a bank at Granby, in which they invited the Youngers and Jameses to take part. It was through this invitation that he met the more experienced bandits and became involved in the holdup of the train.[23] The very ease with which Kerry made contact with and joined the James and Younger brothers in a robbery demonstrates the easy familiarity with which they frequented western Missouri.

Hobbs Kerry's confession was followed by Mrs. Samuel's usual public denial of her sons' guilt and retelling of the wrongs her family had suffered [24] and by the customary letter purporting to come from Jesse James. The letter appeared this time in the Kansas City *Times*, preceded by the paper's indignant statement of disapproval of the manner in which detectives from St. Louis and other cities had invaded western Missouri. While the Jameses and Youngers were blamed by outsiders for every crime that occurred, the paper continued, the majority of the people in their home section were less sure of their guilt. Pretending to hunt the Jameses brought renown to the detectives; instead of trusting local officers, the higher authorities had employed "common 'thief catchers' who outrage farmhouses, carry off peaceable citizens, kill twelve-year-old boys, blow off the arms of old women," and so on.

The paper informed its readers that Frank and Jesse had been seen in Kansas City during the week before the robbery at Otterville and that Jesse was living in Kansas under an assumed name. One of Jesse's friends had ridden up to a *Times* reporter on the street and delivered the letter, which the newsman believed bore more evidence of truth than Kerry's confession. The letter was the usual dull denial of guilt and the usual offer to prove an alibi, this time by eight citizens of Jackson County. Jesse did not even know Kerry; more evidence of Jesse's innocence was to be produced later.[25]

Plainly, there was confusion among the staff members of the *Times*, for the very issue that carried Jesse's letter contained an editorial that condemned the robbers without naming them and urged strong measures to bring them to justice. The editorial deplored the romance that surrounded the gang's successful exploits and made them "the envy of thousands of green youths." Hundreds of their friends and contemporaries had "shared the wrongs and suffering that made them desperate" and were now living peaceably in their homes; this excuse for their lawlessness was not valid. They were outlaws by choice; only a determined attempt by the state to capture them could end their careers.[26]

When another letter, allegedly from Jesse, offered the additional evidence he had promised in the first, it also condemned the detectives and called Hobbs Kerry a "notorious liar and poltroon"; several men would swear that Jesse was not at Otterville. Then the writer of the letter charged that Bacon Montgomery, the leader of a posse from Sedalia that pursued the bandits, was the instigator of the crime. After getting his share of the loot he led the pursuers off the trail. The writer evidently knew that Montgomery was not popular with many former Confederates because he had commanded a unit of the state militia in Lafayette County during the administration of Governor Thomas Fletcher, first postwar governor of Missouri. The letter provided an opportunity to revile Montgomery for his postwar actions.[27]

The *Times* had been assured of the letter's authenticity by persons who knew the handwriting as Jesse's, but readers were warned to take Jesse's accusations with a "grain of allowance." The paper took Jesse to task for not surrendering for trial, arguing that mobs did not hang train or bank robbers:

The bold highwayman who does not molest the poor or the ordinary traveller, but levies tribute on banks and railroad corporations and express monopolies, is not generally such an object of popular detestation that he cannot secure a fair trial in our courts. It is the horse thief, the ravisher, the stealthy murderer of the innocent and helpless that fall victims to mob law. . . . The longer they come among us . . . the stronger the war of society against them. And eventually they must fall before it.

This warning by the *Times* indicated that the Kansas paper had altered its views considerably since John N. Edwards' editorial, "The

Chivalry of Crime," in 1872. There had been a change of ownership in 1875. Though still doubting the accused men's guilt, the *Times* recognized their folly in attempting to evade the law. The attitude of others was changing, too. Although some of the suspects had met violent deaths at the hands of mobs, the paper's statement that mobs did not form in vengeance when banks and trains were robbed was generally true. At this time western farmers were denouncing high freight rates and other exploitation by the railroads. As to the banks, credit was difficult to obtain, and interest charges were high. A natural reaction would be to ignore offenses against any financial institution or large corporation. In such a climate, even if the Jameses and Youngers were believed guilty, their crimes were viewed as indulgently as Robin Hood's. The writings of John N. Edwards and others who defended them undoubtedly helped to form this atmosphere.

Bacon Montgomery, the posse leader whom Jesse had accused of complicity in the robbery near Otterville, replied in an open letter that he was ready to be investigated on the charge of instigating the robbery if Jesse would come to Sedalia and submit to a similar investigation.[28] Jesse did not accept the challenge, nor did he reply. It is quite probable that he was on his way north to transact some bank business.

The Kansas City *Journal* complained that Jesse's letters of alibi were becoming "suspiciously — almost nauseatingly — monotonous."[29] Although it is doubtful that the writer of the letters was affected by this opinion, there were to be no more letters for nearly three years.

In the hunt for the James brothers that followed Kerry's confession, a raid was made on the farm home of Samuel Ralston in Jackson County. Twelve detectives who had arrived in Kansas City by train were taken in the night, again by train, to a point about two miles from the city, where they and their horses were unloaded. At daybreak on the morning of August 11, they surrounded and searched the Ralston home. A neighbor, Joseph Connelly, was found there, and he was put aboard the train, which had waited for the raiders and then moved westward. Connelly was released at Pomeroy, Kansas, where an unsuccessful attempt was made to find Frank and Jesse at the home of C. E. Wells.[30]

The reason for the raid on the Ralston home was apparent when it became known that Frank James had married the Ralstons' daughter Annie — according to the Kansas City *Times*, in July of 1875, but this is an error. The marriage took place in 1874 and probably in June, not long after Jesse had said his marriage vows.[31]

Frank James and Annie had eloped to be married, and her father did not learn the identity of his daughter's husband until several

91

months afterward. Under pretense of going to Kansas City to visit relatives, Annie Ralston had left home with a trunk and valise. On the train or in Kansas City she met Frank, and together they proceeded westward. In time Mrs. Ralston received this note:

Dear Mother:
I am married and going West.

ANNIE REYNOLDS

The Ralstons' first knowledge of the identity of Annie's husband was obtained when her brother met an uncle of the James boys in Kansas City. After learning he was a Ralston, the uncle said that his nephew Frank James had married Ralston's sister. The family concealed this information until the raid on their home.

Frank James, the *Times* stated, had visited Annie's parents three months before the raid. Ralston angrily asked James where his daughter was, and Frank merely said, "She is all right." Ralston said he wanted to see her, but Frank told him he could not for she was far away. In answer to another question he replied that they had been married in Omaha. The exchange became more heated, and Frank mounted his horse and rode away.[32]

In less than a month after the raid on the Ralston farm, the scene of the gang's activities shifted from their native state. The band's next crime removed all doubt about the Younger brothers' lawlessness and seriously weakened the belief that enemies had falsely accused the Jameses of banditry. On the seventh of September, exactly two months after the robbery at Otterville, eight men rode into Northfield, Minnesota. Three entered the First National Bank, two stood guard outside, and the other three waited on the outskirts of the town.

The acting cashier, Joseph L. Heywood, refused to open the safe to the intruders, even under threat, so the bandits killed him. The cashier's murder was singularly savage, even for this gang; the killer slashed Heywood's throat with a knife before shooting him. A. E. Bunker, a teller, escaped from the building, but was shot through the shoulder, though not fatally, as he ran. The usual smooth timing was now badly off schedule.

Citizens quickly became aware of the crime in progress and, led by Henry Wheeler and A. B. Manning, hurriedly obtained guns and began shooting at the guards in the street. The latter were attempting to clear the street of people, and in doing so they killed Nicholas Gustavson, a Swede who did not understand their orders shouted in English. As the firing intensified, the three men waiting at the edge of town rode to help their fellows. The shooting now was rapid and deadly;

two of the band and one of their horses were killed and another robber was severely wounded. The owner of the dead horse was carried out of town by one of the company who rode back under fire to pick him up.

In time the dead robbers were identified as William Stiles, alias Bill Chadwell, and Clell Miller. Belief that the Jameses and Youngers were among those who escaped stimulated the Minnesotans to organize the most widespread manhunt in Minnesota heretofore. The telegraph carried the warning that six desperadoes were somewhere in the area surrounding Northfield, and farmers and townspeople turned out by the hundreds to aid officers in the search for them. After several days of trailing, one of the hunted men was killed and three others captured. The man killed was Samuel Wells, alias Charlie Pitts, and the captives were Cole, Bob, and Jim Younger. Seriously wounded, hungry, cold, and nearly naked, the Youngers expected to be hanged at once. Instead, their captors fed them, dressed their wounds, and treated them with kindness.

But two members of the party escaped. They had separated from the rest of the band two or three days before the Youngers were taken. The wisdom of the fugitives' dividing into two groups was obvious, for in splitting up they confused their pursuers. It was generally believed that the two bandits who got away were Frank and Jesse James. According to some accounts, Jesse and Cole quarreled when Jesse proposed that they either abandon or kill the badly wounded Bob Younger, whose condition was retarding their flight. Cole reacted to this suggestion with such bitterness that Frank and Jesse left the Youngers immediately.[33]

The prisoners, after they had been fed and their wounds treated, were lodged in the jail at Faribault, Minnesota. Newsmen, photographers, detectives, and the curious came to see them. Determined efforts by officers and citizens restrained the demands for mob action, and the crowds were permitted to pass through the jail to view and talk with the captured men. Cole Younger shrewdly assessed the opportunity to win sympathy for himself and his brothers. He told of his family, spoke of his former interest in Sunday school and the Baptist church, quoted from the Scriptures, expressed regret for his crimes, and asked for the prayers of Christians. He was able to touch some of his audience, and when they wept, he allowed tears to roll down his cheeks. Then the visitor would usually reach a "wipe" through the bars for him to use in drying the tears. By this pose of piety, Cole moderated some of the feeling the murders of Heywood and Gustavson had engendered.[34]

The capture of the Youngers and the killing of Miller, Stiles, and Wells were a shock to many Missourians. None of the robbers wore or carried anything that would betray their identity, so that some time passed before all six could be identified conclusively. Five days after the robbery, Chief of Police McDonough of St. Louis wrote Governor Hardin that he doubted the Jameses and Youngers were involved in the robbery at Northfield, for at that very time his agents at Denison, Texas, were laying plans to round up the whole band there.[35]

Ten days later McDonough departed for Minnesota with an identification expert from his force; by that time he was convinced that the attempted robbery at Northfield was committed by the same band that had robbed the train at Otterville. He also believed that the gang had all left Texas by train for Minnesota on August 23, Hobbs Kerry's place in the band having been filled by a Texan named Cal Carter. McDonough had information, too, that Frank James's wife and child (they had no child at this time) were living at Carter's house in Texas.[36] Viewing the captured Youngers did not change McDonough's belief that Cal Carter was one of the Northfield robbers. He was sure that the man who claimed to be Jim Younger was Carter and that the two men who escaped were the Jameses.[37] He was, of course, wrong about Carter.

McDonough alerted the Minnesotans to the danger of letting so many people interview the captives and of confining them in a jail so poorly guarded. These were desperate criminals whose friends might undertake their rescue. The warning caused the stationing of a guard to surround the jail at all times. When the bandits' sister Henrietta Younger and their brother-in-law R. S. Hall arrived in Faribault to visit them, the guards' fears intensified, and tragedy resulted. That night an excited guard shot and killed another guard who approached the jail without making known his identity.[38]

In court Cole Younger was charged with the murder of Gustavson and with complicity in the murder of Heywood. Bob and Jim were charged with complicity in both murders. Under Minnesota law, the severest penalty for a defendant who entered a plea of guilty was life imprisonment. Rather than risk being hanged as the result of a trial they would surely lose, the Youngers pleaded guilty. They received the maximum sentence and were admitted to the Minnesota penitentiary at Stillwater.[39]

With Miller, Stiles, and Wells dead, the Youngers behind prison bars, and the James brothers generally believed to be the two who escaped, there was a great deal of speculation on two questions. Why did the band attempt to rob a bank so far from home? How was it that the people of Northfield were so successful in frustrating the attempt?

In no other town invaded by the outlaws had the populace dealt with them so effectively.

Some of the answers to the first question were amusingly absurd. For instance, it was said the band was in Minnesota to avenge the part Samuel Hardwicke, who had been living in St. Paul for six months, had played in the detectives' raid on the Samuel home. On the trip they ran short of money, and the robbery was merely an attempt to replenish their supply.[40] Judge Thomas Jefferson Younger of St. Clair County, uncle of the boys, said the group was on its way to Canada to settle, but on the way the James brothers lost all their money gambling. Unable to travel without funds, the Jameses persuaded the others, over the protest of Cole, to rob the bank. This, Judge Younger strongly implied, was the first robbery the Youngers had ever performed.[41]

In 1903 Cole Younger gave another answer to this question. Since he and his brothers could not live in peace at home they decided to make one big haul and with the money start life anew on some other continent. They selected the bank at Northfield because they had heard that General Benjamin Butler of Massachusetts and his son-in-law J. T. Ames had a large sum of money invested in it. Due to Butler's treatment of Southerners during the war, they "felt little compunction, under the circumstances, about raiding him or his." [42] This rationalization lent the attempted robbery and the murders at Northfield the stature of a raid by the South on the North and reinforced the legend of the outlaws as exiled Southern patriots.

A more feasible reason for the undertaking is that Stiles, being a Minnesotan, convinced the band that his state was a fruitful area for robbers. He evidently led them to believe that he knew enough about the people and territory to make an easy get-away with a large haul. Northfield was selected after their arrival in the state.[43]

The success of the people of Northfield in frustrating the gang was not due to any advance warning; it has been thought that the band simply erred in attacking a northern bank. The implication here is that in the South the people were not enough concerned over lawlessness to make the same effort at capture as the citizens of Minnesota. Cole Younger, however, blamed the gang's failure partly on the fact that shortly before the robbery, the three men who entered the bank had, without his knowledge, drunk a quart of whiskey.[44]

Certainly the robbery lacked the precision common to other raids of which the Youngers were accused, but to some degree both the bungling and the opposition they encountered in Northfield were accidental. The circumstances gave the citizenry an advantage over the bandits that was not enjoyed by the people in other towns whose

95

banks had been raided. To the acting cashier Heywood who, through his devotion to duty, upset the whole schedule of action in the bank, considerable credit is due.[45] Off to a bad start, the success of the robbery was further imperiled by the death of Stiles in the street, for upon him the desperadoes depended to guide them out of Minnesota. With a wounded man on their hands in a strange territory, they had little chance of escaping. Then, too, the inhabitants in the area turned out to hunt the robbers more enthusiastically and more generally than had the citizens of any community in Missouri.

It was time for self-examination by law officers in Missouri, and Republican newspapers did not overlook the opportunity to goad the authorities. The St. Louis *Globe-Democrat*, for example, thanked Minnesota for doing "what Missouri could have done — but, to her shame, did not do — ten years ago." [46] The Kansas City *Journal* held that there was no longer any doubt that the James-Younger band had perpetrated all the bank and train robberies with which it had been charged. The proof of their involvement at Northfield and the confession of Hobbs Kerry, among other things, settled any question about their guilt. Features common to all the robberies and the fact that all were executed with "a cool and desperate courage" of which few men are capable identified them as actions of the same band. The technique of each robbery, the inevitable alibi letters, the confusing statements of the women in the family, the legislative indignation over the bombing of the parental home, and the consideration of amnesty were all parts of "the ghastly comedy." And through all the acts of the comedy people knew the facts. Yet the gang's practice of killing anyone they suspected of giving information or of seeking it "spread abroad a sense of danger, of fear of assassination, that shut men's eyes and mouths in those localities where the friends, relatives or sympathizers resided." [47]

The *Journal* pointed out that it had never sympathized with either the band or those who attached colorful and romantic qualities to its members, but now it admitted that they possessed gallantry, cool courage, and genius that distinguished them from common thieves and robbers — characteristics that excited a kind of admiration from the crowd.

Following the fiasco at Northfield, the one plausible explanation of the beginning of Cole Younger's outlaw career was advanced. An anonymous friend of Cole who had, in 1868, operated a store in Lee's Summit, near the Younger farm in Jackson County, told the story. George Shepherd had come from Kentucky to get his brother Oliver and John Jarrette to help him rob the bank at Russellville. Jarrette induced Cole, who was industriously at work on his mother's farm, to go with them. Later, Cole returned home and admitted, after the mer-

96

chant questioned him, that he had helped in the robbery. R. S. Hall, Cole's brother-in-law, also blamed Jarrette for leading Cole into the career of banditry that he had pursued to the end at Northfield.[48]

One fragment of evidence supports this claim that Cole was living peaceably at home in early 1868, for in January of that year he and another man were credited publicly with capturing two members of a band of horse thieves near Lee's Summit and bringing them on a Sunday afternoon to the jail at Independence.[49]

The Youngers' imprisonment in Minnesota resolved for a time the questions of their guilt and their whereabouts, but the Jameses were still at large, still unconvicted of crime, and, in the opinion of some determined adherents to their cause, still innocent of wrongdoing.

IX

It was on Wednesday night,
The moon was shining bright,
They robbed the Glendale train.

THE TRAIL of the two fugitives led westward from Northfield, across Minnesota into Dakota Territory, and there it was lost. Chief of Police McDonough of St. Louis, believing as others did, that they were Frank and Jesse James, stationed men in Jackson County to watch for their return home. Both fugitives were known to have been hit by bullets during the fight in Northfield, and the bandit thought to be Frank suffered a severe knee wound.

In time McDonough's agents reported that the Jameses had arrived in their home territory, and on October 14 a squad of police officers from St. Louis, led by Sergeant Morgan Boland, raided the home of Dr. William W. Noland near Independence and arrested a man they thought was Frank James. He had a bullet wound in one knee, but he identified himself as John Goodin [1] of Cheneyville, Louisiana, and he explained that he had come to Dr. Noland for treatment of a wound received accidentally months before. This story did not convince the officers, and they removed Goodin to St. Louis.

Competent doctors in St. Louis held that Goodin's injury was about four months old, and acquaintances presented evidence to prove that the arrested man had told the truth about his identity. Belatedly convinced that a mistake had been made, McDonough released him. The police chief was sure that the Jameses had been in their home neighborhood at the time of Goodin's arrest because his raiders reported that, even though they met with no resistance, the roads in the area were picketed by guards to prevent the capture of the James brothers.[2] A few years later the rumor spread that the captured man had really been Frank James,[3] but this was never substantiated.

The confusion about the identity of Goodin points again to one of the factors that enabled the James brothers to evade arrest. Actually, the descriptions of participants in crimes who were believed to be Frank and Jesse had, through the years, been wildly inconsistent as to height, weight, shape of face, and color of hair and whiskers, except that usually at least one man had sandy whiskers. In most instances the descriptions had been formed after only a fleeting look and in highly excited circumstances. That law enforcement officers could not obtain descriptions that would make the bandits easily identifiable seems incredible, but the records indicate they could not. Until Jesse's death and Frank's surrender, both notorious gunmen moved about in complete freedom throughout Missouri and in other states.

Editors of Democratic papers in Missouri had been cautious, following the raid at Northfield, in their statements about the James-Younger band, but journalistic jibes in Republican papers upon the arrest and release of Goodin set off blasts and counterblasts in the press. The extraordinary proceeding of dispatching members of a metropolitan police force across the breadth of the state to raid a citizen's residence in the second most populous county of the commonwealth provoked acrid comment. Evidently, McDonough believed that local officers could not be trusted and that there was danger of opposition from local citizens if his purpose were known. Republican papers agreed with McDonough and attributed the Jameses' immunity to sympathy of Missouri Democrats for the brothers. The papers implied that friends, including law officers, would have protected the Jameses from arrest or would have rescued them after the arrest if possible. The failure of the raid in Minnesota was evidence that bandits could not elude justice in an area where the people were hostile.[4]

In assigning motives one can err, but surely politics accounts for much of the furor in the press. It is probable, too, that the papers' rivalry for readers and their desire to keep some issue boiling explain these mouthings. At this time, for instance, in St. Louis the Republican *Globe-Democrat* opposed the Democratic *Times*, and in Kansas City the Democratic *Times* contended with the Republican *Journal*. These latter two engaged in one of the roughest verbal slugfests engendered by the bandit issue.

The *Times* waited until Goodin had established his identity and then expressed indignation at the method used to remove him from Jackson County. The people had "ceased to regard the James and

Younger boys in any other light than as highwaymen and murderers" who had done "incalculable damage to Jackson and other counties in Western Missouri." [5] Local people could be trusted to assist in the arrest of the Jameses, but the St. Louis officers had shunned the help of Jackson County's law enforcement officers because they believed the contrary impression given by the *Journal* and other Radical newspapers.[6]

When the *Journal* rebuked the *Times* for this statement,[7] the latter attributed the attitude of the *Journal* and other Republican papers to their position when the Radicals controlled Missouri: "Their papers were forced to justify the high-handed usurpations and bloodshed of Radical rule by representing the people of Missouri as a set of robbers and bushwhackers who deserved no better treatment than savages and hyenas." And now, the *Times* charged, out of habit and because they could find no better grounds on which to attack the Democratic administration of the state, they presented a false and exaggerated picture of lawlessness and charged its continuance as the result of favor and protection by the community.[8]

In its next issue the *Journal* replied that the *Times* knew that these outlaws would long since have been in custody "if the officers of Jackson County had been like the officers of Minnesota." [9] To this, the *Times* retorted: "Fellow citizens of the Republican party in Jackson County, do you not every man of you know that this charge is as false as hell, a foul slander upon our whole people, and a malignant stab at the best interests of the county?" Then it pointed out that the marshal of Jackson County, who had made no attempt to catch the Jameses, was a Republican.[10] Three editorials on one page of the *Times* dealt with the *Journal's* charges.

While editors vented their feelings, Sheriff John S. Groom of Clay County, believing Frank and Jesse were at the home of their mother, led a posse there on the night of November 22 and quietly surrounded the house. Soon, a man approached the station of a posseman, who commanded him to halt. Instead, the man fired a pistol into the air and ran for the woods. Shots directed at him by the posse were ineffective, and he got away. Groom believed this was either Frank or Jesse, and the Liberty *Advance* commented that there was no doubt that the James brothers were at their mother's farm for several days during that week.[11]

The activities at the Samuel farm coincided with Mrs. Samuel's return from Texas, where she had gone a month earlier with the announced intent of making her home there permanently. Wide publicity accompanied her going, and her interviewers agreed that it was better for her to leave Missouri because of the injury her presence did her neighbors. She said she would have gone long before if she could have sold her farm, and then she repeated her familiar tale of woe.[12]

By early 1877 interest in the James brothers seemed to be lagging, for the whole state ignored a controversy in Clay County over the refusal of county officials to pay members of Sheriff Groom's posse who had hunted outlaws. But even though the Jameses had seemingly begun a three-year vacation from banditry, the public's interest in them, though less intense than a few years earlier, was not allowed to die. In August, 1877, Major Edwards returned to a newspaper desk as editor of the Sedalia *Daily Democrat*[13] and was on hand with comment as the occasion required. When the St. Louis *Republican* reported in the summer of 1878 that Jesse had spent three or four months in Callaway County under the name of James Franklin and had quickly left when detectives came looking for him,[14] Edwards branded the report a hoax. A strange man had been there and detectives had searched for him, but the man was not Jesse James, for Edwards knew positively that Jesse James had not "touched Missouri soil for one year." The James boys' career as train or any kind of robbers was over forever, and they were where the Pinkertons or any other detectives would never disturb them.[15]

In the "Kingdom of Callaway," in spite of Edwards' denial, the legend persists that Jesse spent some months there in the period after the robbery at Northfield, living first at the home of Washington R. Kidwell and later with Allen Womack. He taught a singing school in the Unity neighborhood, gave talks on religion in a local church, and, in the company of Dr. Martin Yates, who treated his wounds, ate at the Whaley Hotel in Fulton at the same table with the Pinkerton detectives who were searching for him. This bold gesture was followed by a disappearing act.[16]

The ten years that elapsed between the bank robbery at Liberty on February 13, 1866, and the holdup of the train at Otterville on July 7, 1876, must be regarded as a period for which much of the fact cannot be separated from the fiction; for the years from 1876 to 1882, the task of the fact-seeker is easier, although the Jameses' success in hiding themselves and their families was complete. Between 1876 and October of 1879 their reputations occasionally caused them to be suspected when a robbery occurred, and their names were then and later connected with some far-flung adventures, but no evidence points to them during this period. Stories of the men and their families between 1876 and 1879 abound. Writers of the early "histories" of the James band gave wild and romantic accounts of their living on the Mexican border. There they rescued beautiful maidens from abductors, fought cattle rustlers and horse thieves, engaged in a profitable cattle trade, or lived quietly with their families.[17] The origin of these tales is unknown, but they were repeated frequently without credit to any source. No evidence has been found to show that they were anything other than the products of prolific imaginations. One man wrote of recognizing two prominent Texas cattlemen, the Thompson brothers, as Frank and Jesse James in the summer of 1876. In 1878 he recognized the same men at Leadville, Colorado, where they were engaged in robbing stages.[18] Another report had them spending six months in 1879 in the region around Chaffee, Colorado, under the names of Tom Smith and Billy Green. There they worked, prospected, gambled, drank, and fought as other miners did.[19] In May of 1879 a telegraphed report to Eastern papers from Omaha told of Frank James encamped with a band of cowboys and deserters from the Army in the Wind River country of Wyoming, north of the Union Pacific Railroad. The Liberty *Tribune* branded this story, "Humbug big!"[20] And so the tales went.

No one shouted "Humbug big!" however, when the Jameses were charged with a daring train robbery on the Chicago and Alton Road at Glendale in Jackson County on the night of October 8, 1879. At dusk, several armed men rode up to the village store and took into custody its owner and a few farmers who were sitting around, discussing the issues of the day. The captives were marched to the depot, where the agent had been held at gunpoint while he witnessed the wrecking of the telegraph equipment. When ordered to lower the green signal and thus stop the next train, the agent at first refused, but he changed his mind when the muzzle of a cocked revolver was forced into his mouth and he was given a minute to decide whether he would obey the order. After the signal was changed, the outlaws piled rocks on the track to wreck the train if it failed to stop — proof of their callous disregard for the safety of passengers and crew.

At almost exactly eight o'clock captives and captors, waiting in the depot, heard the whistle of the train approaching from the west, and soon the cars and engine rolled to a stop. The outlaws took the members of the crew in command, and on both sides of the train the gunmen fired random shots into the air to intimidate the passengers and prevent their leaning out the windows and observing the holdup.

The express car was the robbers' objective. As two of them banged at the door on one side of the car to force it open, the express agent opened the safe and unloaded its contents into a valise in the hope that he could escape with it through the door on the far side. He was caught before he could jump from the car and the bag was wrenched from his grasp. One of the robbers knocked the agent senseless by a blow on the head with the butt of his revolver, the only injury in this holdup; the passengers were not molested.

The rifling of the express car completed, the bandits supervised the departure of the train. They then released their prisoners in the depot and disappeared into the darkness.

First reports placed the number of participants in the robbery at from fifteen to thirty men and the amount taken at $30,000 to $50,000. Both the railroad and the express company offered large rewards.[21] Later, the express company announced that the loot totaled about $6,000 and considerable non-negotiable paper; the number of bandits dwindled, too, in later accounts.

The manner in which the robbery was committed, rumors that Jesse James had been seen in Kansas City during the two weeks preceding it, reports that he was recognized as the leader of the bandits, and perhaps the habit of attributing Missouri train robberies to the James band fostered widespread belief that the robbery had been committed by them. Except for some skepticism about Frank being present at the scene, Missouri newspapers almost universally charged the two brothers with the crime.[22] Even John N. Edwards waited three weeks before accusing the press of associating the James brothers with the robbery "because the sensational aspect of the thing was all the greater . . . if these redoubtable men could be brought in somehow." For nearly three years, he continued, neither had been in Missouri, nor would either return. They were married, had children, and had "put all the past behind them."[23]

Edwards' belated alarm for the Jameses had sound basis, for in the three years between the robberies at Northfield and at Glendale attitudes toward bandits had changed, and there is evidence that the press now strove to arouse public sentiment to demand their capture. Mistreatment after the Civil War because of Confederate allegiance could have no relation to this robbery. If the James brothers were involved, they had chosen deliberately to renew their banditry for money and adventure. Nor was there evidence that new recruits to the gang were former bushwhackers or were even connected with the Confederate cause. Interest in the capture of the bandits rose.

But now, on November 4, Kansas City papers reported that Jesse James was dead; one-eyed George Shepherd had killed him. Shepherd was the guerrilla leader who had served a term in the Kentucky penitentiary for the robbery at Russellville in 1868. In 1879 he was living in Kansas City and working as a teamster. According to the story, Marshal James Ligget knew Shepherd's whereabouts, and he solicited his aid in the capture of Jesse. The plan was made for him to seek readmittance into the band, and after obtaining the confidence of the members, he was to betray them to Ligget and co-operate in their capture. This much Ligget confirmed.

When he reported Jesse's death, Shepherd related that, in accordance with Ligget's plot, he had gone to Mrs. Samuel's home, where he was blindfolded and led to the band's camp in the woods. Once the blindfold was removed, he faced Jesse James, Sam Kaufman, Ed Miller, Jim Cummings, and a man named Taylor. Miller was the brother of Clell Miller, killed at Northfield, and Jim Cummings, known also as Cummins, was a Civil War associate of the Jameses who had lived near Kearney, where he was known to be a horse thief. Kaufman and Taylor, who had bad reputations locally, were said to be sons of prominent families in western Missouri. In the course of the meeting Jesse said Frank James had died of consumption several months before.

Shepherd kept Ligget informed of the group's alleged movements, and from his information plans were made to capture or kill them as they robbed a bank in Short Creek, a small town near Joplin, Missouri. The plans collapsed, however, when the guard Ligget had stationed in the bank was discovered by Jesse on his final survey of the town. Shepherd said that he then determined to kill Jesse and to lead the others, who probably would pursue him, into an ambuscade of Ligget's men. He suddenly turned on Jesse as they rode along, accompanied by Jim Cummings and Ed Miller. Jesse drew, but Shepherd fired first, the ball hitting Jesse behind his ear. As the bandit chief fell dead, Shepherd fled, with Jim Cummings in pursuit, while Miller went to the aid of the fallen Jesse. The ambuscade was farther away than Shepherd had thought, and he and Cummings emptied their guns at each other in a two-mile chase. Shepherd was hit in the calf of a leg, and he believed he shot Cummings. Ligget and a party of men who went to the scene of the alleged killing near Galena, Kansas, searched for, but were unable to find, the body of the notorious Jesse James.[24]

Shepherd's tale was not accepted by everyone, but when Cole Younger heard it he said he believed it, for Jesse and George had been enemies since the latter's release from the Kentucky prison. Jesse feared that Shepherd might inform on him and cause his arrest, and there was also a difference between them over a woman.[25] Mrs. Samuel agreed with those who did not believe Shepherd; it would take a "two-eyed" man to get Jesse, she declared.[26]

The rumors that now circulated could be put together to finish the story. They went like this: The wounded Jim Cummings returned to Clay County and verified the details of Shepherd's accounts.[27] The Richmond *Conservator* reported that three well-mounted men escorted a wagon bearing a box across Ray County toward Clay, and the odor escaping the box indicated the presence of a decomposing corpse; the mortal remains of Jesse James rested therein.[28] A physician was said to have visited Ligget and to have told him that he attended Jesse and issued his death certificate before delivering his body to friends. Mrs. Jesse James was known to be at the Samuel home. The casket had actually arrived at Kearney by train, and a Clay County official had said that Jesse's body was "beneath Clay County turf." [29]

Shepherd was unhappy with the reaction to his "killing" of Jesse, and he complained that he had, as a result, received more abuse than the Jameses ever did. In answer to this complaint John N. Edwards reminded Shepherd that "from the days of Judas Iscariot down, all men despise those who follow his example." [30]

This incident has never been satisfactorily explained. That Shepherd was acting in good faith with Ligget and believed he had killed Jesse is hardly probable, and some suspected that he and Jesse were in collusion to divide the reward money and allow Jesse the advantage of being considered dead.[31] One doubter of Shepherd's story was Robert A. Pinkerton, if the press quoted him correctly:

No one should know more about Jesse James than I do, for our men have chased him from one end of the country to the other. His gang killed two of our detectives, who tracked them down, and I consider Jesse James the worst man, without exception, in America. He is utterly devoid of fear, and has no more compunction about cold-blooded murder than he has about eating his breakfast. I don't believe Shepherd would dare to shoot at him.[32]

Jesse evidently had made a believer out of this Pinkerton.

During November, 1879, when newspapers throughout Missouri were questioning Shepherd's claims and expressing an interest in the arrest of the robbers of the train at Glendale, the Kansas City *Journal* remained skeptical of the general sentiment. It still believed the bandits' friends were disguising their real sentiments, and it so charged in no uncertain terms:

At no time since these outlaws have been before the public has there been so much coldblooded lying and pretending done as is going on now. The friendly press in helping to secrete the robbers, by pretending that public sentiment is worked up and neighbors resolved on capturing, as it was when it had them embarking on the Galveston sands with tears in their eyes as they turned them for the last time on their native land. It is all stuff and twaddle. At no time has the work of hiding been more persistent, and at no time have spies been more numerous.[33]

Subsequent developments raise some doubt as to the accuracy of the *Journal's* analysis.

X

With the agent on his knees
He delivered up the keys
To the outlaws Frank and Jesse James.

By 1881 Frank and Jesse James had won a dubious renown that challenged even their abilities, but before the year was out the brothers had outdone fiction. It is apparent, however, that at the time they were plotting their new crime, political forces in the state were shaping to bring their outlaw career to an end.

The platform adopted by the Republican state convention in 1880 arraigned the Democratic party for "failure to prosecute notorious criminals of the state, and for permitting a Republican state [Minnesota] to perform that duty," and it charged that Democratic policy had "prevented immigration into the State and the introduction of capital and the growth and development of industries."[1] Connecting banditry and immigration both directly and by inference was not new; many responsible citizens of the state believed the depredations charged to the James band and the wide publicity given them deterred new residents from settling in Missouri.[2]

Thomas T. Crittenden, the Democratic nominee for governor, won the election. His record as a Union man, which was a factor in his selection by the party,[3] made it difficult for the Republicans to use the James boys as an issue in the campaign. Actually, Crittenden was the candidate of railroad companies and their political friends, who had bigger issues in mind.[4] Crittenden's firm determination to rid the state of outlaws was not evident until after his administration began, but it became an important factor in the state's efforts to break up the band.

Equally significant was the election of William H. Wallace as prosecuting attorney of Jackson County. He announced his candidacy with a pledge to make every effort to arrest and prosecute members of the James band. Defeated for the Democratic nomination, he ran as an independent and received the support of Republicans, who had no candidate. In the face of threats and warnings, he stumped the county, specifically naming the James brothers as perpetrators of train robberies, bank robberies, and murders in Missouri. In rural areas of Jackson County, Wallace faced strong opposition, but he was elected.[5] Analysis of the vote indicates that many Democrats supported him.

The first news of Jesse James in 1881 came from the Sedalia *Daily Democrat*, edited by John N. Edwards. Curiously, one of Edwards' associates on the paper's staff was Bacon Montgomery, accused of the train robbery at Otterville in one of Jesse's alibi letters. On January 7 the *Daily Democrat* reported that one of its staff, who could only have been Montgomery, had seen and talked with Jesse in Denver, Colorado. Jesse, according to the report, had found it possible to stay there for some time because "rebs" and "feds" were good friends there. He wanted to know what the possibilities were of being permitted to return to Missouri and live unmolested. Among other things, he claimed to have attended the Republican national convention of 1880 as a delegate from Mississippi and to have been one of the 306 delegates who voted for Grant's nomination for a third term.

Three days after the *Democrat*'s report, Governor Crittenden, in his inaugural address, expressed determination to bring the outlaw era to an end:

We should let all know that Missouri cannot be the home and abiding place of lawlessness of any character. No political affiliations shall ever be evoked as the means of concealment of any class of lawbreakers, but when crime is committed, pursuit and punishment will be inflicted under the forms of the law without fear, favor or affection.[6]

When, six months later, the next robbery in Missouri to be attributed to the James boys occurred, Crittenden's actions showed that he meant what he had said.

On July 11, 1881, four men robbed the Davis and Sexton Bank at Riverton, Iowa, of $4,000. The crime had all the characteristics of a James band operation, and they were suspected,[7] but it was soon determined that the robbery was the work of an outlaw band led by Poke Wells.[8] The Wells band's attack on the bank alerted public attention to lawlessness in the area.

Four days later Missouri was stunned with the news that a train on the

Chicago, Rock Island and Pacific Railroad had been robbed near Winston, in Daviess County, about sixty-five miles from the Kansas City depot, from which the train had departed at six o'clock that evening. Some of the bandits, variously reported to be from five to seven in number, had boarded the train at Cameron and others at Winston.

Darkness had fallen by the time the train was a few miles beyond Winston. At this point, the conductor, William Westfall, was collecting fares in the smoking car. He had progressed down the car to the fourth seat from the rear when a tall man with a heavy black beard and wearing a linen duster jumped up behind him, drew a revolver, and commanded him to raise his hands. As he gave the order the bandit shot Westfall in the back, then pumped a second bullet into him from behind as he tumbled out the door to fall from the rear platform, dead. In a fusillade fired now by the murderer and one or two of his companions, a passenger, Frank McMillan, was hit and killed.

As terror seized the passengers in the smoking car, two of the outlaws worked their way into the express car, beat down the messenger with their revolvers, took his key to the safe, opened it, and removed the money and valuables it contained. By this time other members of the gang had forced the engineer to stop the train on a siding. The robbers jumped off and disappeared in the dark.[9]

Even the earliest accounts of the robbery attributed it to the James brothers, and Mrs. Samuel made a hurried appearance in Kansas City to make her customary denial of their guilt and to explain that both Frank and Jesse were dead.[10] In spite of Mrs. Samuel's statements, rumors quickly strengthened the suspicions that one or both of the brothers led the band. Conductor Westfall, it was said, had been in charge of the train that carried the detectives to the Samuel farm on the night of the fatal bombing in January, 1875, and this fact introduced the motive of revenge into his murder.[11] J. W. Buel, who, in 1880, had published *The Border Outlaws* and *The Border Bandits* with the Jameses as subjects, announced that Frank James had offered him a proposition shortly before the robbery whereby a holdup and publication of a new Buel book would be timed together to promote sales. Buel stated that he had declined the offer, but he was positive that Frank and Jim Cummings planned the robbery. He had "unquestionable evidence," also, that Frank James had been recognized on the streets of Olathe, Kansas, a few days before the robbery.[12]

The usual grapevine reports placed Frank James, Ed Miller, Jim Cummings, Dick Liddil, and Jesse James in the neighborhood — Kansas City, Jackson County, and Daviess County — before and after the event, and Mrs. Frank James was said to be presently at the home of her parents in Jackson County. Men fitting the description of Jim

Cummings and Jesse James were said to have been in the vicinity of the robbery the week before it occurred, posing as father and son.[13]

Indignation and anger were now greater than at any time since the outlaws had begun their depredations, but John N. Edwards spoke in their defense. He said the press accused the Jameses of the crime only to make the story more sensational, for "the average newspaper would sell its soul for a sensation." This "journalistic mania" had permitted "many a Kansas horse-thief and highwayman" to go free.[14]

The outcry against the outlaws was in the main sincere, but political implications were not overlooked, especially by the Kansas City *Journal*, which stated its position beautifully:

We are not going to charge the Democracy of Missouri with being responsible for the late robbery and murder on the Rock Island road, until we learn exactly who committed the daring outrage. If it shall turn out that the James boys or any of their old gang had a hand in it, then the Democratic party of this state is responsible, for had it not been for sympathizing friends, all of whom are Democrats, the whole gang would long since have been caught and made to pay the penalty of their crimes. Such outrages as that at Winston are liable to take place in any state. They have occurred in Minnesota, Iowa and Kansas, but unfortunately for the good name of this commonwealth the perpetrators were all Missouri Democrats.[15]

The *Journal*, the St. Louis *Globe-Democrat*, and the St. Louis *Post-Dispatch* led the attack on Democratic officials for failing to apprehend the James boys. The *Post-Dispatch* was already exhibiting its independence of the party, though it was a Democratic paper. It had come into being in December of 1878 when Joseph Pulitzer combined the *Dispatch*, which he had bought at a sheriff's sale, with the *Post*. His differences with Crittenden no doubt colored the views expressed by the paper, but its many vehement statements on the James issue in the next four years cannot be explained so simply.

Democratic publishers in the state were much annoyed by the attack of these three critics of the state administration and also by the censure Missouri suffered in the press of other states. Chicago papers were the most scathing in their criticisms, but Missouri newspapers answered comments of papers in Massachusetts, Ohio, and Indiana also.[16] The Chicago *Times*, which had published an article favoring the amnesty proposal in 1875, now called Missouri "The Outlaw's Paradise," [17] and the Chicago *Inter-Ocean* declared that "in no State but Missouri would the James brothers be tolerated for twelve years." [18] Nearly every issue of the Kansas City *Times* in August, 1881, carried an editorial answering criticism of Missouri by Chicago papers.

The Kansas City *Evening Star*, which had first appeared in 1880, explained the critics' motivation:

The Chicago newspapers are making all the political capital they can out of the Winston robbery. Their chronic jealousy of St. Louis and Kansas City crops out on every occasion. They never neglect an opportunity to represent Missouri as a semi-civilized state, wholly abandoned to bandits and highwaymen, and in every way undesirable as a place of residence for quiet, law-abiding people. Their object is to keep immigration and capital away from this state and to retard, as much as possible, the development of the great section of country tributary to Kansas City and St. Louis.[19]

There was some truth in this explanation, even though it may have exaggerated the attitude of Chicago papers toward Missouri. Certainly the old rivalry between Chicago and St. Louis had left scars that the Chicago press exhibited regularly. Whatever the purpose, this criticism continued for several years. Missouri's Democratic journals answered with evidence that there was no more lawlessness in Missouri than in Republican states, satirized accounts of crime in other states, and presented figures to show that the value of land was as high in Missouri as elsewhere.[20]

At the same time that newspaper publishers in Missouri were exchanging insults with publishers in other states they were so stirred by the robbery and murders at Winston that they vied with one another in offering solutions to the problem of lawlessness. The *Globe-Democrat* urged the placing of armed guards on all trains; the *Missouri Republican* suggested time locks for express safes; the *Times* and *Evening Star* in Kansas City wanted the Governor to offer a reward up to $100,000; and the St. Louis *Chronicle* admitted that Missouri needed a little immigration of "those sharp-shooting, peace-compelling wheat growers of the north." [21]

In the absence of authority to offer a large reward on behalf of the state,[22] Governor Crittenden, with the help of Colonel Wells H. Blodgett, attorney for the Wabash Railroad, called a meeting of officials of railroad and express companies operating in Missouri. They met in St. Louis on July 26 and agreed to provide funds from which Crittenden would offer rewards for the capture of the robbers.[23] On July 28 Crittenden issued a proclamation offering a reward of $5,000 each for the delivery of Frank and Jesse James to the sheriff of Daviess County and $5,000 each for their conviction for participating in the train robberies at Glendale or at Winston or for the murder of John W. Sheets, William Westfall, or John McCulloch. A reward of $5,000 was offered also for the arrest and conviction of other participants in these crimes.[24]

For the governor of a sovereign state to seek the financial assistance of railroad and express companies to suppress lawlessness as Crittenden had done was, to say the least, unusual, and public reaction varied. The reward proclamation provoked many statements of commendation, and while no outright disapproval has been found, friends of the James brothers, foes of Crittenden, and perhaps some cranks could find in it grounds for criticism. Even John N. Edwards did not object to the offering of a reward for apprehension of the robbers, but he thought it unjust to point to the Jameses by name when there was "indubitable proof that for years they have been leading quiet lives."[25] The Kansas City *Times* complained because the money was contributed by the railroads and offered in the name of the Governor instead of in the name of the state; the Jefferson City *Peoples' Tribune* questioned the legality of Crittenden's action; the *Globe-Democrat* believed the reward would not accomplish its purpose as long as Missouri's population contained former bushwhackers and descendants of bushwhackers; the *Post-Dispatch* disliked the implied admission of weakness and of inability on the part of the state to cope with the problem and said the railroads were forced into the pool; and the St. Louis *Chronicle* suggested that competition between officials for the reward would prevent the robbers' ever being caught.[26]

In his autobiography Governor Crittenden later wrote that he was determined to rid the state of banditry and that he expected the reward offer to cause some member of the band to turn traitor. But, he confessed, a large element in his own party had more sympathy for such outlaws than with his undertaking to suppress them. "If not in full sympathy with them, giving the glad hand of welcome day and night, they acquiesced in their acts with suppressed joy, with eyes half closed on their crimes as those of a medieval saint upon the sins of his devotees."[27]

The excitement caused by the robbery at Winston and by the reward offer had barely subsided when, in bold defiance, the outlaws attacked again. On the night of September 7, they stopped a Chicago and Alton Railroad train by placing warning flags and a pile of rocks and logs on the track at Blue Cut (also called Rocky Cut) in Jackson County, a few miles east of Independence and near Glendale, the scene of the robbery in October, 1879. The engineer, Jack "Choppey" Foote, and other crewmen were held under guard and the passengers intimidated by the firing of Henry rifles into the air.

The outlaws forced Foote to provide a pick to break open the door of the express car, and the messenger, H. A. Fox, to open the safe. Its contents were quickly gathered into a sack carried by the bandits, who obviously were unhappy that the loot was not larger. The two who had entered the express car beat Fox senseless with their pistol butts and then directed the systematic search and robbery of nearly one hundred passengers. This rifling of the passengers' belongings was accompanied by angry threats and orders delivered in violent and boastful language. Perhaps a report that the next train to pass carried a shipment of $100,000 was true, and the outlaws' realization that they had, by miscalculation, stopped the wrong train shortened their tempers.

The leader of the band, again tall and black-bearded, was the only robber who wore no mask. He spoke loudly and boldly, declaring that he was Jesse James and that this attack was to avenge the Chicago and Alton's participation in the reward offer. When Engineer Foote was unco-operative at one point in the holdup, the leader held his revolver under Foote's nose and threatened to kill him, adding force to the threat by saying that this was the gun with which he killed Westfall.

Foote experienced another tense moment when he heard the whistle of the freight train that was following the passenger train. Frank Burton, the brakeman, also heard it and broke from the guarded group of trainmen to run along the track toward the approaching train to prevent a collision with the halted train. The bandits opened fire on Burton, and twenty-five to thirty shots were aimed in his direction before the cries of Foote made clear what he was doing. Burton was unhurt, but two bullets tore the tail of his coat. He succeeded in signalling the engineer of the oncoming train to stop.

When newsmen questioned Foote the next morning, he told them that after the robbery was completed, the leader escorted him back to his engine and then shook hands with him, saying, "You are a brave man and I am stuck on you, here is $2 for you to drink the health of Jesse James with tomorrow morning." As he spoke he placed two silver dollars in Foote's hand and then offered the services of his men to remove the stones from the track in front of the engine. Foote declined this proffered assistance; he later explained: "I was so tickled to get out of the scrape so smoothly that I told him not to mind the stones, we could take them off ourselves if he would only take himself and party off. He laughed and said, 'All right, Pard, good night,' and started up the bank with his men behind him." [28]

Governor Crittenden now called upon the people to "rise *en masse*" and pursue the bandits "by day or by night, until the entire band is either captured or exterminated." And, he warned, "If ordinary remedies are unavailing, heroic treatment must and will be resorted to. This foul stain shall be wiped from Missouri's fair escutcheon if the honest people of the state will but aid me in my endeavor." [29]

In a few days several young men from the area around Blue Cut were arrested and jailed at Independence, and it now seemed that "greenhands" had committed the robbery instead of the suspected veterans.

One of the prisoners confessed to the holdup and implicated three companions, who were held; the others were released.[30]

Yet, the belief prevailed that the real culprits had not been apprehended, and the seemingly serious suggestion was heard that the Governor call the state legislature into special session to appropriate funds for use in capturing the guilty parties.[31] Crittenden, believing he had already set the trap, probably gave this proposal little thought. The wheels of his machinery were turning.

In July, 1880, an unlettered countryman named Tucker Bassham, from a family of Quantrill men, had been arrested and charged with participation in the robbery at Glendale in 1879. He pleaded guilty and was sentenced to ten years in the Missouri penitentiary. In March, 1881, William Ryan, alias Tom Hill, was arrested in Tennessee and returned to Jackson County to answer charges for the same robbery. William H. Wallace, the new prosecuting attorney, persuaded Governor Crittenden to pardon Bassham to testify against Ryan.

The trial of Ryan, occurring in Jackson County near the greatest stronghold of sympathy for the James boys, in the latter part of September, 1881, was the first real test of efforts to break up the band of outlaws. In Jackson County, east of the city limits of Kansas City, was a heavily wooded area of several square miles, known as the Cracker Neck. Many of its male inhabitants were former guerrillas, and the area had long been considered a refuge of the James band. Glendale and Blue Cut were in its bounds, and it had been the home also of the Shepherd brothers, Bassham, and Ryan.

Residents of the Cracker Neck crowded into Independence for the Ryan trial, evidently to intimidate all who were to have a hand in convicting Ryan. Wallace and his associate in the prosecution, John Southern, were threatened; witnesses were warned against appearing; employees of the railroad company refused to give testimony; and an attempt at rescue was expected in case of conviction. When excitement was highest, Governor Crittenden rushed from Jefferson City to Independence and was reported to have dispatched large supplies of guns and ammunition to the scene.

Bassham testified that, in April, 1879, Ryan had come to his place and had suggested that he was a fool to work, for easier money could be made robbing trains. Bassham replied that he was not interested. Bassham's lack of interest did not deter Ryan from returning in October, two days before the robbery at Glendale, accompanied by Clell Miller's brother Ed. The two men told Bassham that Jesse James was to lead a group in the robbery of a train on the Chicago and Alton Railroad and that he had ordered Bassham to participate. At the appointed rendezvous on the night of the robbery, Bassham testified, he met Jesse James, Ed Miller, Dick Liddil, Bill Ryan, and "a man named Bob," identified by later confessions of members of the James band as Wood Hite, who rode with "Bloody Bill" Anderson in 1864.

Bassham, who was unarmed when he met the group, was given a shotgun and a revolver, both of which he recognized as belonging to acquaintances not in the group. Thus armed, he had helped rob the train; Jesse and Ed Miller, he testified, were the men who had entered the express car. When the loot was divided, Bassham's share was $900, and Jesse warned him not to attract attention in spending it. Bassham's testimony was sufficiently corroborated by circumstantial evidence to cause the jury to find Ryan guilty and to sentence him to twenty-five years in prison.[32]

During the trial Tucker Bassham's home in the Cracker Neck was burned, and afterward he received so many threats to his life and property that he moved from the area without leaving information as to where he was going.[33] While many considered his treatment and other incidents surrounding the trial disgraceful and indicative of the outlaws' large following in Jackson County,[34] the Kansas City *Times* boasted that the conviction of Ryan vindicated the county of charges that it sympathized with the outlaws.[35]

Prosecutor Wallace later claimed that the verdict convinced many people who had until this time been afraid to talk that it was safe to offer information about the bandits.[36] The tide was surely turning against the outlaws, for Missouri's former Confederate soldiers, in convention at Moberly, passed a resolution endorsing Governor Crittenden's efforts to end lawlessness in the state.[37]

XI

But that dirty little coward
That shot Mr. Howard
Has laid poor Jesse in the grave.

THE FREQUENCY and diversity of reports concerning the whereabouts and doings of the James brothers throughout 1881 provoked
the editor of the Liberty *Tribune* to comment that "the Irishman's
axiom, that nothing except a flea can occupy two places at the same
time, will have to be enlarged to include the James boys."[1] But tangible
evidence that the James band was rendezvousing in Kentucky caused officials to make extensive raids in Logan and Nelson counties of that
state in late October and early November. No members of the band
were captured, but there was little doubt that they frequently visited
relatives and old guerrilla friends there.[2]

One Kentuckian reportedly said he regretted that the raids had not
netted the outlaws. However, he expressed what was probably the typical viewpoint of people in that section when he added: "Personally, we
have no desire whatever to take in the reward offered for their capture,
unless we could purchase their bodies on credit and ship them C.O.D.
to Missouri."[3]

In February, 1882, another foray of officers into Kentucky was more
successful, and Clarence Hite, cousin of Jesse James, was arrested and
returned to Missouri. He entered a plea of guilty to participation in the
robbery at Winston on July 15, 1881, and was sentenced to twenty-five
years in prison. Reports varied as to whether he had implicated other
members of the band in a confession, and mystery surrounded the
handling of the case. The public, possessing little information, wondered why he had pleaded guilty instead of standing trial.[4]

In the last days of March, the farm boys arrested after the robbery at Blue Cut in September, 1881 — Creed Chapman, John Bugler, and John Mott — came to trial at Independence. John Land, the member of the gang who had confessed and on whose statements Prosecuting Attorney Wallace was depending for conviction, testified that the boys had joined older members of a band led by Jesse James and Dick Liddil. They had not shared in the loot, for Jesse had taken it all, with the promise, never fulfilled, to divide it later.[5] The case against these men was not completed, for Wallace decided that Land's confession was a fake. He entered a nolle prosequi in the case on April 6,[6] for other happenings had interrupted the trial.

On March 31 the press announced that Dick Liddil had surrendered,[7] and in time the details relating to his action came to general knowledge. Following the trial of Ryan in September, 1881, Liddil had become apprehensive that Jesse James suspected him of planning to give evidence for the state as Tucker Bassham had done. Ed Miller had disappeared, and there were indications that Jesse had killed him. Fearing Jesse, Liddil left him. Soon he was at the Ray County home of Mrs. Martha Bolton, sister to Charles and Robert Ford. Robert Woodson (Wood) Hite, brother of Clarence Hite and cousin of Jesse James, whom Bassham had testified was a member of Jesse's band, appeared at Mrs. Bolton's also. An argument started, and in the resulting fight Robert Ford and Dick Liddil killed Wood Hite. The real trouble between Hite and Liddil seemed to be rivalry for Martha Bolton's favors. Wood's body was moved upstairs, where it lay for a day, and then at night it was taken out and buried, wrapped in a horse blanket.

Liddil now knew that he might have to answer to both the law and Jesse James for the murder of Wood Hite, so he decided to turn state's witness. First, he sent Mattie Collins, his wife or mistress, to W. H. Wallace, who promised that there would be no prosecution against him in Jackson County if he gave himself up and assisted the officers by furnishing information that would result in the arrest of other members of the band. Since Wallace could guarantee nothing beyond immunity in Jackson County, a woman believed to be Martha Bolton visited Governor Crittenden, veiled so that he did not know her identity, and sought pardons for members of the James band.

As a result of this interview Liddil surrendered to Sheriff James H. Timberlake of Clay County on January 24. With information obtained from Liddil, officers were at work to complete the breakup of the band. Those most active were Sheriff Timberlake, Kansas City Police Commissioner Henry H. Craig, and Governor Crittenden.

When the news broke that Liddil had surrendered, Crittenden issued a public statement to the effect that before the surrender he had

had an interview with a lady, whom he did not know at the time, but with whom he had since become acquainted. He declined to promise pardons for the bandits in advance of their surrender, but did agree to use his influence to prevent punishment of any member of the band, except Frank and Jesse James, who would voluntarily surrender, make a full confession, and give information concerning the whereabouts of others.[8]

Clarence Hite's plea of guilt was no longer a mystery. Confronted by Liddil, he had chosen to accept a twenty-five-year sentence rather than stand trial. On April 3, 1882, with excitement still high over announcement of Liddil's surrender, dispatches from St. Joseph, Missouri, flashed the news that Jesse James was dead. His death had been reported falsely so often that many afternoon papers which received the brief message in time for their last edition warned readers to await confirmation. But the news was true this time! Almost as startling was the information that Jesse James, under the name of Thomas Howard, had lived in St. Joseph since November, 1881, with his wife and two children, and for the six months preceding the move to St. Joseph, the period in which the robberies at Winston and Blue Cut had occurred, the family had resided in Kansas City, where Jesse was known as J. T. Jackson.

Charles and Robert Ford, newly recruited, youthful members of the band, had been staying with Jesse and his family for several days. Charles had helped rob the Chicago and Alton train in September, 1881, but Bob had not yet participated in a robbery; plans were being made for the robbery of a bank in Platte City on April 4. Bob, however, had been in contact with Crittenden, Timberlake, and Craig for several weeks and through his older brother had gained Jesse's confidence. After breakfast on the morning of Monday, April 3, the three men went into the living room. Jesse removed his guns, laid them on a bed, and stepped up on a chair to straighten and dust a picture. Catching him thus off guard, Bob quickly drew his pistol and shot his host in the back of the head. Jesse fell lifeless to the floor.

Zee rushed into the room and, on seeing her husband lying dead, gave way to unrestrained grief and anger. As quickly as they could escape the house, the Ford brothers telegraphed Governor Crittenden, Timberlake, and Craig that they had killed their man and gave themselves up to the St. Joseph authorities. When townspeople appeared at the house, Zee first maintained that the dead man was Thomas Howard, but she soon broke down and revealed that he was indeed Jesse James. St. Joseph forgot the heated city election of the day, and the curious swarmed to the little house to view the murdered outlaw's body.

Doubt existed as to whether the dead man was really Jesse James, so identification of the body was the first important task to be performed. The grief of Jesse's wife Zee and of Mrs. Samuel, who arrived early the next morning, seemed so genuine and Mrs. Samuel's condemnation of the murderers so bitter and characteristic of her that those who observed the women were convinced that the body was Jesse James's.

Timberlake, Craig, and Wallace went to St. Joseph. Timberlake had known Jesse years before, having seen him last in 1870, and he recognized the body as that of his former acquaintance. Wallace took with him a Clay County farmer, William Clay, two former guerrilla associates of the James brothers, Harrison Trow and James Wilkerson, and Mattie Collins. They all identified the body as that of Jesse James, to Wallace's satisfaction. Photographs showed two scars from bad wounds on the right side of the chest, and the newspaper accounts pointed out that the tip of the middle finger of the left hand was missing and that there were scars from other wounds on the body. These wounds had long been part of the James legend.

Some were skeptical, however, and believed that a hoax was being perpetrated. This group was small. Countless others who claimed to know Jesse viewed the body, and no general opinion arose that the body was not his. The coroner's jury reached the verdict: "We the jury find that the deceased is Jesse James, and that he came to his death by a shot from a pistol in the hands of Robert Ford."

The gold watch worn by Jesse when he was killed was returned to its owner, John A. Burbank of Richmond, Indiana, who had lost it and a diamond stickpin in the stage robbery at Hot Springs in January, 1874. Other valuables that were identified as property of victims of robberies attributed to the James band were found in Jesse's possession. Horses and saddles in Jesse's stable had been stolen in northwest Missouri in recent weeks, but Jesse's friends charged the Ford boys with their theft. Many items found at the James house in St. Joseph were confiscated by officials and were then recovered by their rightful owners. Among the things unclaimed and later returned to Mrs. James was a copy of *Noted Guerrillas,* John N. Edwards' book-length defense of the Jameses and their fellows.

It was necessary for Governor Crittenden to ask that the body be turned over to Mrs. James before the St. Joseph officials would surrender it. Then a special train provided by the Hannibal and St. Joseph Railroad took the funeral party to Kearney, where hundreds of old acquaintances, friends of the family, and curiosity seekers viewed the corpse and attended the funeral. The Reverend R. H. Jones of Lathrop, Missouri, read from the Book of Job, beginning with "Man that is born of a woman is of few days, and full of trouble," and the fourth and fifth verses of the Thirty-ninth Psalm, which include the words,

"Lord make me to know mine end." Matthew 24:44, "Therefore be ye also ready; for in such an hour as ye think not, the Son of Man cometh," was the text the Reverend J. M. Martin of Kearney used for the funeral sermon. His discourse offered comfort to the family through faith in God and made the sudden, unexpected death of Jesse a warning to sinners. From the little church in Kearney the body was taken to the Samuel home and interred in a deep grave in the yard, beneath a huge coffee bean tree.[9]

The dramatic figure in these events was Mrs. Samuel, who gave vent to her grief and heaped curses upon the traitors who caused Jesse's death. When asked at the inquest if the dead man were her son, she replied that he was, but, "Would to God that it were not!" Upon meeting Dick Liddil as she left the inquest, she pointed an accusing finger at him and exclaimed, "Traitor! traitor! traitor! God will send vengeance on you for this; you are the cause of all this. Oh, you villain; I would rather be in my boy's place than in yours!" [10] When the funeral party reached Kearney she cried out to Sheriff Timberlake, "Oh, Mr. Timberlake, my son has gone to God, but his friends still live and will have revenge on those who murdered him for money." [11]

Crittenden, Timberlake, and Craig denied that they knew of Jesse's presence in St. Joseph and of Ford's intention to murder him, although they admitted that they knew Ford was with Jesse and intended to betray him.[12] Further, Bob Ford made a statement that exonerated them.[13] Whatever the arrangement with Ford, Governor Crittenden stood by the two brothers. A grand jury at St. Joseph indicted them for murder in the first degree. On April 17, they entered pleas of guilty, and were sentenced to be hanged. Crittenden received the news of the sentence by telegraph and that afternoon granted them a full and unconditional pardon.[14]

Was it the prospect of the reward that had motivated Bob Ford to kill Jesse James? Probably. How much reward did he get? Governor Crittenden boasted in his autobiography that "the proclamation of a reward accomplished its purpose in less than one year at a cost not exceeding $20,000, not one cent of which was drawn from the state." [15] However, he never revealed to whom the reward money was paid, other than the Fords, nor is it known how much they received. A part of the total undoubtedly went to those who apprehended Ryan and Hite. Some believed that Crittenden himself took part of the fund provided by the railroads, that others like Craig and Timberlake got a share, and that the Ford brothers' part was meager.[16] The search for the true story of the distribution of the reward is one of the elusive, but intriguing, pursuits of students of the James legend.

If the newspapers are to be believed, Crittenden, in his desire to get the credit for the killing of Jesse James, showed poor judgment. The *Post-Dispatch* quoted him as telling a reporter after the killing: "People have no idea how much trouble I have had in getting *my* men to work together and keep at it. *My* great point in the whole business has been secrecy. *My* success has been entirely brought about by keeping quiet and not revealing *my* information before I had effected *my* purpose." [17] He also boasted that he had no excuse or apology to render for his part in the affair, and he expressed the belief that the Fords deserved credit, not abuse, for the assassination.[18]

It was hardly to be expected that Crittenden would go unscathed for his role in Jesse's death, and quickly the wrath of his detractors struck him. Major Edwards, of course, came to Jesse's defense. In the first few days following the killing, the columns of Edwards' paper indicated that he doubted the reports of Jesse's death. Nevertheless, he denounced the killers and the officials leagued with them, and he printed comments of newspapers from throughout Missouri and the nation that disapproved the manner in which Jesse met his end. On April 13, no longer skeptical, Edwards came forward with a burning editorial that has become a classic bit of the James story. It began:

> Let not Caesar's servile minions,
> Mock the lion thus laid low:
> 'Twas no foeman's hand that slew him,
> 'Twas his own that struck the blow.

Once again appeared the explanation that the circumstances of war made Jesse James what he was, for after it ended he "refused to be banished from his birthright, and when he was hunted he turned savagely about and hunted his hunters." Edwards wished Jesse were still alive "to make a righteous butchery of a few more of them." The murder was "cowardly and unnecessary," and the state had leagued with "self confessed robbers, highwaymen and prostitutes" to have a citizen assassinated without knowing "that he had ever committed a single crime worthy of death. . . . Those with the blood of Jesse James on their guilty souls" were saying everything that might be said about him to justify the manner of his killing, but "such a cry of horror and indignation . . . is . . . thundering over the land that if a single one of the miserable assassins had either manhood, conscience or courage, he would go, as another Judas, and hang himself."

The violence of Edwards' denunciation grew as he discussed claims that capture by legally constituted authorities of Missouri was impossible. He called upon Jesse's comrades for vengeance and concluded:

Why the whole State reeks today with a double orgy, that of lust and that of murder. What the men failed to do the women accomplished. Tear the two bears from the flag of Missouri. Put thereon in place of them as more appropriate, a thief blowing out the brains of an unarmed victim, and a brazen harlot, naked to the waist and splashed to the brows in blood.[19]

Earlier remarks on the death of Jesse by this apologist for the James band had already incited comment. On the same day his now famous editorial appeared, his paper quoted the Independence *Sentinel* as follows:

We are not surprised that the Sedalia *Democrat* should raise a fearful and doleful howl over the execution of its friend Jesse James, as the incident of the presentation of the magnificent gold watch must still be fresh in the memory of its gift (ed) editor.

This remark referred to a story long current that, at the time of the robbery at the Kansas City fair, Jesse James had presented Edwards with a fine gold watch, evidently loot from a holdup, in appreciation for his editorial on the robbery. Edwards now admitted that a watch was once offered to him, but said he refused it because it was not his habit to take gifts from anyone. Jesse James was "infinitely ahead" of James E. Payne, editor of the *Sentinel*, whom Edwards branded as a liar and a slanderer, and he suggested that Payne, being a Missourian, knew his remedy for being so branded.[20] Payne ignored this broad provocation for a duel.

Edwards did more for his heroes than write editorials. He was active in raising a subscription of several hundred dollars in Sedalia for the benefit of Mrs. Jesse James; the *Democrat's* local competitor, the *Bazoo*, started a fund for the widow of Westfall, the conductor murdered at Winston.[21]

Edwards was one of a very small number of newsmen who actually defended Jesse James, but many disapproved the manner of the killing and the suspected bargain between the assassin and Governor Crittenden. A traitor is never admired, and in this case the picture in the mind of the typical American of Jesse James as a dashing Robin Hood, even if untrue, was so in contrast to his end — shot in the back while unarmed — that expressions of condemnation were spontaneous. Newspapers in Missouri were crowded for days after the shooting of Jesse with recounting of the deeds charged to him and his band. In them Jesse was pictured as the boldest of men. News of his assassination created a sensation throughout the entire country. The James brothers had enjoyed a record unequaled in America for evasion of the law, and the telling of their exploits rang with descriptions of courage and recklessness seldom rivaled.

Personal friendship, sympathy growing from their activities during the Civil War, and an element of hero worship, then, account for part of the admiration of Jesse James and criticism of those who brought him to his end. Add to this the political and personal dislike of Governor Crittenden and a sincere belief that the method employed in ending the bandit's career was wrong, and one has the sources of most of the critical reactions in Missouri that followed the killing.

Republican papers in Missouri were not united in their censure of the Governor. For instance, the St. Joseph *Herald* and the St. Louis *Globe-Democrat* disapproved of his hiring "assassins" to accomplish what the authorities had failed to do, but the Kansas City *Journal* remained consistent to its earlier demands for suppression of lawlessness and praised Crittenden's action. The *Journal* saw, as did Republican members of the state legislature that was meeting in special session, an opportunity to make political capital of the killing. It editorialized that the legislature must pass a resolution approving the removal of Jesse James in order to vindicate the good name of the state and urged Republicans to introduce it if the Democrats failed to assume responsibility.[22] Democratic papers warned Democratic representatives to be on guard against the move, for if such a resolution was killed by Democratic votes it would be termed a rebuke of Crittenden by Missouri Democracy; if passed, Republicans could charge that Democrats approved assassination.[23]

Twice Republican members of the House of Representatives proposed resolutions commending the Governor and approving the death of Jesse. The second of these ended with this statement: "But the fact that the assassination was, or had to be, resorted to, to accomplish the desired end, is a humiliating confession of the inability of the party in power to execute the laws, and a dark stain upon the escutcheon of the State."[24] The presiding officer declared both resolutions out of order, in that they were not embodied in the call for the special session, and he was sustained by an almost straight party vote on an appeal from his decision — 84 Democrats supporting his ruling and 35 Republicans, 3 Greenbackers, and 1 Democrat opposing.[25]

The Republicans next offered two more resolutions, one demanding that the Governor report to the legislature on the manner in which he had disposed of public funds in his charge and the other asking for an account of any funds paid or promised to be paid by the Hannibal and St. Joseph Railroad Company as rewards for the capture of members of the James band. The first was tabled by a partisan vote almost identical to the one that quashed the earlier resolutions, and the second was declared out of order by the chair.[26]

Two resolutions introduced by Democrats approving the removal of Jesse James were declared out of order by the Speaker, and in one of these instances his decision was sustained by another party division.[27] As a final effort, Republican William H. Wade offered a resolution granting the use of the legislative hall after adjournment to those who approved Governor Crittenden's actions in the death of Jesse James. This, too, was ruled out of order.[28]

The Confederate wing of the Democratic party in Missouri recalled the manner in which a faction made up mainly of Union men and controlled by a group opposed to state regulation of railroads had forced Crittenden's nomination through the state convention of 1880, and they were never friendly to his administration.[29] Among the Union men who spoke out to uphold Crittenden's action in breaking up the James band was James S. Rollins, a former Whig and president of the Board of Curators of the University of Missouri. He wrote Crittenden a long letter of commendation, in which he bitterly criticized those who upheld the James band.[30] On the other hand, the *Post-Dispatch*, which certainly was not Confederate in sympathy, was one of the loudest denouncers of Crittenden and his method of ridding Missouri of Jesse. Pulitzer, the paper's owner, may have been sincere in this denunciation, but it is also true that he was disgruntled because of Crittenden's appointments in St. Louis and other administrative policies.

That Crittenden's policies as governor were a hot issue within his party is evidenced by the fact that the Democratic state convention, meeting at Jefferson City on July 26, 1882, did not endorse the state administration, nor did it consider a resolution on the Governor's actions in connection with the death of Jesse James.[31] Criticism that was politically motivated and criticism that was sincere combined to give the impression abroad that the majority of Missouri's people resented the killing of Jesse. Assassination at the hand of a traitor did much to raise him to heroic standing. The intensification of the heroic image was foreseen by an editorial writer in the St. Louis *Chronicle* who commented, on the day after Bob Ford shot Jesse, that it would have been better if he had been "delicately choked between the head and shoulders. There would have been no pathos about that, and it would have been a better end for a man than the half-heroic death he died."[32] The manner of his death gave every admirer of the James band and every critic of the Governor an opportunity to praise their hero and condemn Crittenden. Soon, the cruel and unreasoning slaughter of innocent citizens and the pillaging of property were forgotten in a general admiration for the dashing highwayman.

An editorial in the *Howell County* (Missouri) *Journal* illustrates well the beginnings of this metamorphosis:

We have no milk and water sentiment for Jesse James. No matter if he was brave and fearless as a lion; no matter if he was generous and liberal; no matter if he rewarded a kindness; no matter if he loved his wife and children with a tender and passionate love; no matter if the hand of all mankind was turned against him and ostracised him from society, we have no sentimental sympathy for a man who delighted in the blood of his fellow men; who struck terror to every peaceful, law abiding community; who made traveling on our great highways, the railroads, unsafe; who deterred capital from investing in, and the people from immigrating to the grand old state of Missouri. Law, order, peace, justice and the preservation of good society all demanded his LEGAL extermination.

But it is the cowardly manner in which the deed was committed; it is the fact of a beneficiary turning upon his benefactor; a serpent sending his poisonous venom into the bosom that warmed it to life, that excites the indignation of all honest men. It is the prostitution of the fair name of our State; it is the picture of a vain, egotistical, incapable Governor disgracing the state of Missouri in the eyes of the civilized world by associating himself with hired criminals, plotting and making blood bargains. It is this and placing the State of Missouri on the same level with the Jameses, by murdering, in a cold and more cowardly manner than ever they murdered; in placing the Executive Department of the State in the same category with red-handed bandits, that we protest against.

The great parallel that will go down in history will be Crittenden and James, and the very ashes of Jesse James will cry out in disgust and righteous indignation at the comparison.

The Ford boys should be tried as other criminals and Governor Crittenden with them as an accessory before the fact.[33]

Charges of this kind against Crittenden, Timberlake, and Craig made by the Sedalia *Daily Democrat*, St. Louis *Globe-Democrat*, St. Joseph *Herald*, and a few rural newspapers were ably answered and bitterly condemned by the Kansas City *Journal*, St. Louis *Missouri Republican*, Jefferson City *Peoples' Tribune*, Kansas City *Times*, Richmond *Conservator*, and other papers. The *Conservator* touched some of the real causes of the criticism of Crittenden when it charged that the Republicans opposed Crittenden's action chiefly because he was a Democrat and "a liberal one." Likewise, it said, "The Quantrell wing of the Democracy are dissatisfied because an ex-Union soldier has brought their chief and pride to bay." The *Conservator* concluded that the "crank" was "displeased because it is his nature to be a crank."[34]

The death of Jesse James gave Eastern papers that were so inclined an opportunity to castigate Missouri. It made no difference whether Missourians upheld Crittenden or sympathized with Jesse James. Both attitudes were indications of the uncivilized and barbarous state of society in Missouri. Missouri newspapers reported and answered comments of the New York *Herald*, New York *Mail*, New York *World*, Boston *Globe*, Boston *Advertiser*, and other Eastern papers.[35] The more sensational illustrated papers capitalized on the event. On April 11, 1882, the New York *Daily Graphic* devoted its entire front page to a picture of a monument to Jesse James. On it was this inscription:

HIC JACET

JESSE JAMES

The most renowned murderer and robber of his age. He quickly rose to eminence in his gallant and dangerous profession and his exploits were the wonder and admiration and excited the emulation of the small boys of the period. He was cut off in the prime of his strength and beauty, not by the hands of the hangman but by the shot of a base assassin of whom the Governor of the State of Missouri was the accomplice. He was followed to his grave by mourning relatives, hosts of friends, officers of the law, and the *reverend clergy*, who united in paying extraordinary honors to his memory. Go thou and do likewise.

Under the inscription appeared the familiar quotation with lines drawn through the words "Kingdom of Heaven" so that it read, "Of Such is the State of Missouri." Around the base of the statue a throng of children carrying revolvers, rifles, daggers, and other implements of crime gazed at it in admiration of their hero.

The assassination of the bandit chief provided for those in the East who held the West in contempt an opportunity to cultivate this contemptuous view toward the West. The New York *Illustrated Times* did it well in a long article comparing the East and West:

. . . Missouri is under the bloody sway of a band of cut-throats, outlaws and assassins and has been so for the last fifteen years and more.

The outlaws were well known; yet they robbed, wrecked, plundered and assassinated with impunity. The injury which the Jesse James gang inflicted upon Missouri is beyond calculation. The emigrant hastened through it and on to Kansas; no man ventured within its borders unless the stern necessities of business compelled him; when a traveler got into a Missouri train he did so with the same feeling that a man has when going into battle — with little expectation of getting through alive.

The names of these soul-ensanguined and savage outlaws were well known to the authorities; so were many of their haunts; yet they lived and depredated; robbed and rioted in a manner for which the European freebooters of the dark ages furnish no parallel. Claude Duval, Robin Hood and Brennan-on-the-moor, were effeminate sunflowered aesthetes compared with the Jameses and their sworn confederates.

When Jesse James met the fate which all such men inevitably do meet — when society is ridded of this monster — does he get the burial of a dog, which his crimes would deserve? Not at all. The railroad company, which he and his men had doubtless often plundered, furnish a special car to carry the body to Kearney, for burial. At Kearney the casket was opened and the immense crowd invited to view the remains. The scene is said to have been terrible. Shrieks, moans and curses mingled in wild diapason; and then Sheriff Timberlake and Deputy Sheriff Read helped to carry the body to the grave, and at the grave two reverend gentlemen, Jones and Martin prayed and sang his soul to a place in the mansion of the blest.[36]

The *Illustrated Times* was consistent in its position. It upheld Governor Crittenden, saying, "The safety of society is of more consequence than the life of a blood-thirsty outlaw." The *Inter-Ocean, Tribune,* and *News* of Chicago used Jesse's demise to continue their criticisms of Missouri, and the St. Louis *Missouri Republican* took the lead in answering them and hurling countercharges about crime in Chicago.[37] The Cincinnati *Enquirer* predicted that "the soil upon which Jesse James flourished will produce another perhaps as gifted as he. . . . The business will be carried on at the old stand, and travelers will do well to bear that fact in mind." [38] Obviously, Chicago and Cincinnati, towns that still remembered their competition with Missouri for immigration and western business, were not averse to reinforcing an unfavorable impression of the western commonwealth.

Perhaps some of these comments on Missouri and its outlaws were made with tongue in cheek; attempts at humor can be found, too. *Texas Siftings*, published at Austin, headed a column with a drawing of Jesse portrayed as an angel. Borne aloft by wings, he carried a huge revolver in one hand and a rifle in the other. A long satire followed on the question of whether he had gone to Heaven as his wife, mother, and others claimed. The writer was skeptical, for somehow he could not fit Jesse into his picture of Heaven.[39] The minister who had baptized Jesse lived in Austin, and *Texas Siftings* charged that he was morally an accomplice in the bandit's crimes because he had not drowned him when he had a chance.[40]

The Judge, still in its first year, satirized the death of Jesse with drawings on the back cover of its April 22, 1882, issue. Included was a proposed monument to Jesse and scenes depicting train and stage robberies. The central feature was a portrayal of the home life of "the gentleman of the road." In the midst of guns, daggers, and revolvers that decorated the walls were three plaques bearing these inscriptions: "God Bless Our Home," "What is a Home Without A Revolver," and "What A Friend I Have in Jesus and My Revolver." Three men in the room were drinking liquor, apparently supplied from the jug on the table; two well-armed women, their hair pinned up with daggers, and two children, a boy with pistols bulging from his pockets and a baby in a cradle holding a pistol in one hand and a dagger in the other, completed the domestic scene.

The assassination and the outlaw's career motivated the production of many pieces of doggerel. *The Judge* published one, entitled "A Missouri Roundelay," that satirized Jesse's life. The last stanza follows:

> At home with the boys all my household joys are aesthetic
> and chastely gay;
> We have prayers with meat, and there's always a seat
> when the parson comes our way;
> For pa wore the cloth, and though I may be off, ma
> hasn't forgot her place,
> And there's never a dollar that I may collar to which
> she don't say grace.
> > In fact, in Missouree
> > It's just such gents as me
> > As rule the roost,
> > And well may boast
> They're the pride of our great countree, tree —
> They're the pride of our great countree.

To this was added the postscript:

> By treachery's bolt, from an army Colt, I was kicked
> into Paradise,
> And now I frolic, on wings angelic, in the mansions of
> the skies.
> I've a job on hand, and it looms up grand — just whisper
> to them at home:
> Jack Sheppard and me has it fixed, you see, to capture
> the golden throne.[41]

With Jesse receiving all this publicity, it was natural that the public should be avid for every available item about his family. There was interest also in places connected with the events of his life, and on April 10, only seven days after his slaying, the St. Louis *Missouri Republican* told of thousands of curious people visiting the house he had occupied in St. Joseph. The owner, seeing an opportunity for gain, charged an admission fee of ten cents, a modest amount, in view of the fact that the fence and stables were almost demolished by relic hunters who carried away splinters of wood from the structures as souvenirs.

Thus the death through treachery of Jesse James, already famous, and public reaction to it did much toward clothing him with immortality. One of the persons who comprehended the workings of these factors was the staunch and loyal Democrat Jacob T. Child, who published the Richmond *Conservator* and who was, within three years, to accept appointment by President Grover Cleveland as Minister of the United States to Siam. In an editorial entitled "The Prince of Bandits," Child pleaded for an end to the sensational treatment of the outlaw's death and aptly summarized the events and correctly appraised their significance:

It would seem that the shooting of Jesse James continues to be the leading sensation of the day and the insane gush of the papers and their eager desire for sensation has caused them to convert a dead train robber into the Prince of Bandits and exalt him into a grand historical character, whose deeds will be embalmed by the poets and crystalized by the historian. Articles eulogistic and condemnatory have been written, bitterness has been engendered. . . . Major Edwards . . . has caused the hair of many a one to raise by calling on "the red slayer to slay." . . . In the meantime praise and censure are lavished on Crittenden, the Fords are locked up in jail and then convicted and pardoned and Jesse sleeps the sleep that knows no waking beneath the grass of his mother's yard and a host of silly people preserve bloody splinters and pieces of his home at St. Joe as relics of a man that has bid the law defiance for twenty years. . . . Let the senseless gush stop, and let his deeds and memory be forgotten.[42]

The gush did not stop, and Jesse's memory and deeds have not been forgotten.

XII

It was his brother Frank
Who robbed the Gallatin bank
And carried the money from the town.

THE JAMES LEGEND did not end with Bob Ford's killing of Jesse James on April 3, 1882, for Jesse's death opened the book on the chapters of his life that had been the subject of speculation and imaginative tales since the time of the first announcement of his marriage. Too, Frank James remained to be reckoned with.

At the inquest, Zee stated that she and Jesse were married at Kearney on April 24, 1874, and that they had gone immediately to Texas for about five months. They then returned to Kansas City. She could not recall definite dates, but after some months in Kansas City, perhaps as much as a year, they had gone to the Nashville area in Tennessee. Jesse had used the name J. D. Howard during their residence in Tennessee; their two children, Jesse Edwards and Mary, were born there. The family returned to Kansas City in 1881.[1]

The accepted date of Jesse Edwards' birth, December 31, 1875, indicates that his mother arrived, at the very latest, in Tennessee early in December. Their neighbors and acquaintances in Tennessee, upon learning the true identity of the man who had lived among them as J. D. Howard, began to supply details of his life, and Nashville newsmen pieced together the story of his residence in the area. He had worked at farming and hauling, but was also known as a trader and wheat speculator. Also, he showed a penchant for gambling and horse racing. At times, his neighbors said, he was absent from home for three or four weeks, and Mrs. Howard and the children — Mary was born on July 17, 1879 — also were absent for similar periods of time.[2]

The public, soon after Jesse's death, learned of his stay in Tennessee, but it did not know immediately that Frank, also, had lived there. Dick Liddil told the officials to whom he confessed that Frank had resided in the same area as Jesse under the name B. J. Woodson, but they held their tongues. Rumors about Frank were numerous at the time of Jesse's death. These included reports of his presence in St. Joseph immediately after the murder, of his attendance at the funeral, and of his being recognized in St. Louis, New York, and Kansas City and in places in Texas and Kansas. The belief that he would avenge Jesse's death was widespread.[3]

As the months passed, this possibility seemed to grow more remote, but behind-the-scenes arrangements for his surrender were being made.[4] On August 1 John N. Edwards wrote to Frank James from Sedalia as follows: "I have just returned home from the Indian Territory [one of Edwards' ways of saying he was now sober after a drunk] to find your letters. Do not make a move until you hear from me again. I have been to the Governor myself, and things are working. Lie quiet and make no stir."[5]

The full story of the negotiation of the surrender has never been revealed, but Edwards probably made the arrangements with Crittenden; he evidently composed the long letter Frank sent to the Governor. Mailed in St. Louis on September 30, it reviewed the agonies of his life as a fugitive, expressed the desire for an opportunity to prove that he was not as bad as pictured, and asked the Governor for some hope of amnesty.

To this plea Crittenden replied that the constitution of the state did not permit him to grant a pardon before conviction for a crime, but he assured James of a fair trial and protection of his rights under the law. The courts would determine his guilt or innocence, and "after the voice of the court is heard, then if it becomes necessary, I will decide what my action shall be."

One senses that these two letters were intended for public consumption and had little to do with the real negotiations for the surrender. Crittenden released them to the press at the party that celebrated Frank's surrender.[6]

On the night of October 4 Edwards and James arrived in Jefferson City on an eastbound train. They registered at the McCarty House as "Jno. Edwards, Sedalia," and "B. F. Winfrey, Marshall, Mo." The next morning they strolled about the city and then spent the afternoon at the hotel. The arrangements with Crittenden had evidently been completed, for shortly before five o'clock the Governor invited several state officials into his office, where a number of newspapermen had already assembled. The Governor was in a jovial mood, and, according to one account, he talked as if he had a "Christmas box" to open. Then he showed the gathering his letter from Frank James. As the group discussed the letter, Edwards and James entered the room and walked toward the Governor. Attention turned to Edwards as he said, "Governor Crittenden, I want to introduce you to my friend Frank James." The men exchanged greetings, then Frank removed his pistol and cartridge belt, and, offering them to Crittenden, said, "Governor Crittenden, I want to hand over to you that which no living man except myself has been permitted to touch since 1861, and to say that I am your prisoner."[7] The newsmen and officials then accorded Frank a friendly reception.

The Governor instructed his secretary Finis C. Farr to deliver Frank into the custody of the sheriff of Jackson County at Independence, but the prisoner was permitted to return to the hotel with Edwards to await Farr's arrangements for the trip. The word quickly spread over the city that Frank James had surrendered, and in the next few hours several hundred people came to the McCarty House to view the noted outlaw. Even the Governor came, bringing Mrs. Crittenden for a brief visit. Early the next morning a party made up of Farr, James, Edwards, and Frank O'Neill, a reporter for the St. Louis *Missouri Republican*, left for Independence.[8]

News of the surrender had covered the state, and as the train progressed toward Independence, people along the way thronged to the stations for a glance at Frank James, and hundreds were on hand to witness his arrival at Independence where his wife, mother, and small son greeted him. The family and the officials spent the day at a hotel, and crowds milled in and out for hours. Because one of Jackson County's charges against Frank was the murder of Whicher, the Pinkerton detective, he was not admitted to bail, and late in the afternoon he was committed to the jail.[9]

Frank O'Neill had known of the pending surrender for several days, and he had prepared a long feature article based on interviews with Frank. This was published in the *Missouri Republican* with the account of the surrender. It characterized Frank as a refined gentleman rather than a bandit, reviewed his life, and told of his desire to start anew and make good.[10] With this, the story of Frank's residence in Tennessee at the same time as Jesse began to unfold as Tennesseeans who had known B. J. Woodson and J. D. Howard now came forward with additional information.

In 1878, J. D. Howard brought suit against one Johnson for appropriating to his own use proceeds from the sale of corn to which Howard claimed he was entitled. After Frank's surrender, Howard's attorney John P. Helms made available for publication in the Nashville *American* the letters he received from Howard during the litigation. The first letter, written from Johnsonville, Tennessee, on January 17, 1878, was that of a man indignant that this Johnson had obtained money "under false pretenses" and had made false statements. Howard charged that besides causing him $56 expense, Johnson "has acted to injure my credit." A week later Howard wrote from Johnsonville that he was badly needed at home and was willing to drop the suit if Johnson would pay him the money due. The third letter, as all except the first two, came from Box's Station (then on the outskirts of Nashville). Dated April 20, 1878, it asked that Helms make every effort to bring the case to trial. But more important in the James story than his dealings with Johnson is his mention that he was having bad luck, two of his children, twins, dying, and his wife being in bad health. On May 12 Howard wrote Helms again to tell him that the witness whose name the attorney had failed to make out was "B. J. Woodson, whose post-office address is Eaton Creek, Davidson County, Tennessee. Let him know, and he will be present."

Howard indicated throughout the series of letters an understanding that the case would come to trial in June, but it came up on May 30, and he was not on hand. He then offered to provide a new bond and asked Attorney Helms if "Mr. Woodson" would be allowed to give the bond for him.[11]

The publication of these letters documents well some of the story of the Jameses' residence in Tennessee. In Dick Liddil's revelation to Missouri officers that Frank James had lived in Tennessee as B. J. Woodson he had also said that Frank's wife Annie was known there as Fannie Woodson and Zee had gone by the name of Josie Howard. Liddil made no mention, and may not have known, of the twins born to Jesse and Zee. They were named Gould and Montgomery for the two doctors who attended Zee. Robert Franklin James, the only child of Frank and Annie, was also born in Tennessee, on February 6, 1878. Annie, in her later years, talked very little about the years in hiding, but one of the stories she told her son in grateful remembrance was that Zee had nursed him as a baby after the twins had died, when she herself could not produce the milk to sustain him.[12]

The date at which Frank and Annie took up residence in Tennessee as B. J. and Fannie Woodson has not been determined. For that matter, the date of their marriage is in question. The first public announcement of it reported her father as giving the date as 1875.[13] In a later interview he stated that she left home in 1874 and he did not know the date of her marriage.[14] Robert James believed, on the basis of information from his mother, that 1874 is the correct date and that his parents went to Tennessee soon afterward,[15] but no one seems to have identified them there before the winter of 1876–1877.

The question of whether Frank and Jesse made forays from their Tennessee homes for plunder and whether they visited the locations where the folklore of several western states has placed them in the time that elapsed between the robberies at Northfield and Glendale probably will never be answered. The evidence indicates that Jesse worked less and was away from home more than Frank, and it was Jesse, not Frank, who was responsible for the resumption of train robbery at Glendale in 1879. He had grown restless and edgy and perhaps needed funds he did not want to work to get. Probably Frank counseled against the robbery, and certainly he did not go to Missouri with Jesse.

Dick Liddil claimed that his first association in crime with Jesse James was in the robbery at Glendale, but he had seen Jesse, Frank, the Younger brothers, and others of their band at the home of Robert Hudspeth in Jackson County several times in the years from 1870 to 1875. In his confession Liddil was careful not to implicate himself in crimes committed where the jurisdiction of Missouri could not protect him, but he did say that Jesse and Bill Ryan were the guilty parties in the robbery of a sightseers' stage near Mammoth Cave, Kentucky, in September of 1880. There was little doubt that Jesse was there, for the watch stolen that day from Judge R. H. Rountree of Lebanon, Kentucky, was found among his possessions at St. Joseph, and Zee was wearing the diamond ring, resized to fit her, that had been taken from Judge Rountree's daughter Lizzie. Liddil also stated that Jesse, Frank, and Ryan had robbed a government paymaster, Alexander Smith, at Muscle Shoals in Alabama on March 11, 1881.[16]

It was later in March of 1881 that Bill Ryan, using the alias of Tom Hill, got drunk in a small Tennessee town, and his threatening talk and flourishing of guns brought his arrest. He was held until identification could be established and then returned to Missouri. Ryan's arrest motivated Frank and Jesse and their families to give up their habitat in Tennessee, fearing that if they stayed, their identity would be detected.

It is astounding that when Jesse fled Tennessee with his family he went to Kansas City to live. Could he have thought his chances for safety and protection greater there than anywhere else? Or was this an act of courage, daring defiance, and boldness? With his death, details of his residence in Kansas City and St. Joseph became known. The confessions of Bassham and Liddil and, later, of another member of the band, left little doubt that he had been at Glendale, Winston, and Blue Cut. Frank James, now that he had surrendered, would not admit that his activities from March, 1881, coincided with those of his brother Jesse. The attempt to prove that they did would create a sensation in Missouri and would stir up a political storm.

During the weeks in jail at Independence Frank James welcomed old friends and a procession of others. Countless gifts were bestowed upon him. The anti-James press (or was it anti-Crittenden?) bellowed with rage at this easy-going reception of the outlaw. The Kansas City *Journal* commented: "The triumphal ride of Frank James from the state capital to Independence was ample evidence that the red-handed murderer and train and bank robber is not without friends among the Missouri moss-backs. Had the train stopped long enough he would have been given an ovation at nearly every station." [17] The St. Louis *Globe-Democrat* remarked that it was not entirely clear whether Frank James surrendered to the State of Missouri or the State of Missouri to Frank James.[18] It was hard to believe that Frank would have come in without some promise of pardon, and rumors circulated that he had an understanding with Crittenden about a pardon in case of conviction.[19] The *Post-Dispatch* commented that in the Democratic sentiment in Missouri and the character of Governor Crittenden as a politician, "the last surviving hero of Quantrill's band has ample assurance of amnesty, safety, and an honored place in civil life." [20]

By throwing himself on the mercy of the law, Frank James weakened the chances of convicting him. This act indicated his faith in acquittal, and his pathetic plea for amnesty brought sympathetic response. A Boonville paper commented, "He has undoubtedly touched a responsive chord of sympathy in the breast of all of us." [21] The Kansas City *Times* said, "Frank James' appeal preceding his surrender is a manly one." [22] Judge John Ward Henry of the Supreme Court of Missouri openly urged that Frank be pardoned: "He has won my sympathy already. If I were the Governor, I would pardon him right away." [23] The editor of the Neosho *Times* favored pardoning Frank if he were convicted, but he believed that "the idea of convicting him, in Missouri courts, may as well be dismissed"; an indictment should be maintained in Missouri, however, as grounds for refusing to grant requisitions from other states. By thus preventing his trial and possible conviction in neighboring states, the editor thought, Frank would be assured of an opportunity to become a good citizen and thus to vindicate himself.[24]

Frank James knew that the statute of limitations on crimes for which there was no indictment against him, together with the difficulty of obtaining witnesses, would probably prevent his trial for any robberies in Missouri preceding the Glendale affair of 1879. Hence, he denied that he had participated in any of the crimes charged to the band during the four years preceding his surrender. Observing this strategy, the Kansas City *Times* warned of the obstacles to convicting him and told the people not to be disappointed if the state failed.[25]

In addition to the effect of Frank's voluntary surrender and the legal difficulties in the way of convicting him, another factor entered the situation. This was the attitude of the large segment of Missouri's population that had sympathized with the South in the Civil War. No expression described this attitude and its sources more accurately than an editorial in the Sedalia *Weekly Democrat*, following the surrender, that reviewed the war in Missouri and the guerrillas' role in it. This, the writer said, explained the attitude of ex-Confederates toward the James boys:

Was it wrong for the Confederates of this State — when the war had closed — to look with some degree of gratitude upon the men whose vigilance saved hundreds of rebel homes and thousands of rebel lives from unmilitary desecration? The East had no Jennison, or it would have appreciated a Quantrell. It is an unsettled question whether, when the white-winged messenger of peace had supposably settled down upon the country, the Jameses could not have returned to peaceful pursuits. They have always claimed that the barbarity of remembered wrongs forced them back into the saddle, and they became hunted animals. With their history as defenders of the faith, how natural it was for a generous people to extenuate the crimes that for seventeen perilous years have been charged to these men. If the Confederate women crowned the Jameses with unfading laurels, there were also plain, practical, unsentimental men who could not forget the hands which sometimes stood fearful guard over their household treasures. But there should be no mistake about this feeling toward the outlaws. The gratitude and remembrance were for Frank James, the Confederate defender — not for Frank James the bandit. Therefore we repeat, that his surrender necessarily destroys the last vestige of the disturbing recollections of the war, and will tend to remove at once the unhallowed divisions that would otherwise have perished with the return of peace.[26]

It remained to be seen if the surrender would remove "the last vestige of the disturbing recollections of the war." Frank's friends would hardly consider the war ended until their hero was freed, and those old comrades and others who rallied to his cause directed their strategy toward making his trial a war issue.

The son of Governor Crittenden once wrote of John N. Edwards that he, too, came in when Frank James surrendered. This is more than figuratively true. Edwards was no longer the composer of the bitter condemnatory editorial printed after the killing of Jesse James, but instead a man intent on saving a friend from the noose. If this meant that Edwards was Crittenden's friend and defender also, he was that unwaveringly. His part in the developments must be pieced together from fragments of information. In the week that Frank surrendered, Edwards joined Bacon Montgomery and Harvey Plattenburg in a new journalistic venture, the Sedalia *Dispatch*, a daily. The paper lasted less than six months, and no files are extant. After its demise Edwards was out of the newspaper business for a time, but in June, 1883, he joined the editorial staff of the St. Joseph *Gazette*. Thus, his editorial comment is lacking for nine months.

Before Frank's surrender, Edwards had started arranging for legal assistance for him by asking Charles P. Johnson, prominent lawyer and former lieutenant governor of Missouri, to defend his friend. He pointed out that James had no money, but he promised Johnson that James's friends would remember him if he assisted. Johnson replied that he would co-operate to the best of his ability. The *Globe-Democrat* interpreted this arrangement to mean that after Johnson had cleared James, "he will stand forth as the candidate of the Edwards-James wing of the Democratic party for Governor of Missouri." [27] In this comment there was foreboding of the effect the trial of Frank James was to have on Missouri politics.

When Frank arrived at Independence, two indictments of long standing were pending against him in Jackson County. He was charged with the murder of J. W. Whicher, the detective, and with robbery of a bank in Independence in 1867. This latter indictment is difficult to explain, for at no time had Frank been connected publicly with this crime, nor had Jesse. In late January, 1883, Prosecutor Wallace dismissed these Jackson County charges when he found it impossible to establish proof of guilt, but in the meantime another indictment had been found, charging James with participation in the robbery at Blue Cut on September 7, 1881. [28]

Rumors were abroad that the governor of Minnesota would attempt to remove Frank to that state for trial on charges growing out of the robbery at Northfield. Governor Crittenden stated emphatically that he would not honor a requisition from another state until all Missouri charges had been disposed of. The governor of Minnesota did, in January, 1883, send a requisition to Crittenden for the removal of James to Minnesota. It was based on a complaint filed with a city justice of Northfield and not upon an indictment. Crittenden refused to grant the requisition, on the ground that charges against James were pending in Missouri. [29]

The indictments against Frank James in Daviess County charged him with the murder of John W. Sheets in the bank robbery at Gallatin in 1869, participation in the train robbery at Winston on July 15, 1881, and, in that robbery, the murder of Conductor William Westfall and of Frank McMillan, a passenger on the train. Through agreement between Wallace and Prosecutor William D. Hamilton of Daviess County, Frank was removed from Independence to the jail at Gallatin to await trial on these charges. He had declined to give bond on the remaining Jackson County indictment.[30]

It became evident that to present convincing evidence against James on any of the pending charges would be exceedingly difficult. Bill Ryan and Clarence Hite, both in the Missouri penitentiary, and Dick Liddil were the only persons who could give the information needed. In view of the difficulty of convicting Ryan, Wallace could hardly offer him a pardon in return for testimony against Frank, nor did Ryan give any indication that he would co-operate. According to rumor, Hite had given information to Wallace, and he would be pardoned in return for evidence against James; before the trial occurred, however, Hite died of tuberculosis.[31]

Of the witnesses who might be called to testify against James, only Liddil remained, and there were difficulties in the way of using his testimony. In August, 1882, Liddil was arrested by federal officials and removed to Huntsville, Alabama. On October 20 he was indicted for complicity in the robbery of Alexander Smith, the government paymaster at the river improvement project at Muscle Shoals. Others indicted for this robbery of $5,000 were Frank James, Jesse James, and Bill Ryan. At his trial, Liddil admitted that he had been a member of the James band, but he said the paymaster had been robbed by Frank, Jesse, and Ryan while Liddil was in Kentucky. He knew nothing of the crime until after it was done. The judge, in instructing the jury, made it mandatory to find Liddil guilty of complicity if the evidence showed that he was a member of the band that committed the deed. The jury pronounced Liddil guilty, but recommended executive clemency. The judge suspended sentence until the next term of court.[32]

It was now doubtful that Liddil's testimony would be admissible against Frank James, hence a move was started to obtain Liddil's pardon from President Chester A. Arthur. Timberlake, Craig, Wallace, United States Senator Francis M. Cockrell, and R. T. Van Horn, publisher of the Kansas City Journal and representative in Congress from his district, wrote letters asking Arthur to pardon Liddil because of his indispensability as a witness against James and as a reward for carrying out his part of the bargain to aid in breaking up the James band.

Governor Crittenden also wrote to Arthur in Liddil's behalf, claiming that Liddil's conduct in helping to break up the James band warranted this recognition. Members of the jury that convicted him, two clerks of the court, one United States marshal, and four deputy marshals signed a petition urging the President to grant the pardon, and the trial judge in the case, John Bruce, telegraphed approval of the pardon. The federal district attorney, William A. Smith, objected, however, on the ground that one robber and murderer should not be pardoned to convict another.

United States Attorney General Benjamin Brewster, to whom Arthur referred the matter, agreed with District Attorney Smith and refused to recommend the pardon. Because of the insistence of Senator Cockrell the matter was referred to Brewster's department three times, but his decision remained unchanged, and the President refused to grant the pardon.[33] Judge Bruce, however, on April 10, 1883, released Liddil on his own recognizance without sentence. This action was considered a final settlement of the case, and Liddil was free to testify against James.[34]

Because of Crittenden's later actions, his attitude toward the pardon of Liddil at this time is of special interest. In an interview with representatives of the press he emphasized that he made the application for Liddil's pardon "on the sole ground of the important service he had heretofore rendered the state, and in the firm belief that Liddil's reformation was sincere and permanent, that he was entitled from the state of Missouri to such recognition for his services in bringing the old gang to justice." [35]

While the prosecution was busy assembling witnesses and evidence, the partisans of Frank James were not idle. All former guerrillas apparently were on his side, but it cannot be said that all former Confederates were. William H. Wallace made much of the fact that he and his family were victims of Ewing's famed Order Number Eleven, and he long insisted that the driving force behind the overthrow of the James band and the attempt to convict Frank James came from ex-Confederates.[36] The strategy of Frank's defense, however, was to exploit every shred of sympathy that could be gained by recalling the Civil War in Missouri; the fact that there were no Republicans in his camp added political flavor.

The pro-James press, instead of arguing that Frank should be acquitted because of his Civil War activities, declared that he should not be convicted because of them. For instance, on May 22, 1883, the Sedalia *Daily Democrat* appealed to the people to give Frank James a fair trial:

Everybody has been forgiven and forgotten except Frank James, who has come at last to seek rest and refuge within the confines of a magnanimous commonwealth, trusting all to the honor and honesty of a people for whom he has imperilled his life. . . . It is time to draw the veil of charity over the terrible past, and to deal honorably and fairly with Frank James.

One suspects that the intent of this argument was to create, subtly, the feeling that Frank's career as a guerrilla should excuse his later banditry.

After several delays and continuances the defendant came to trial at Gallatin, Missouri, on August 21, 1883, for the murder of Frank McMillan.[37] Nearly fourteen years had passed since the killing of Captain Sheets in the Gallatin bank, but the hostility toward the Jameses it had engendered was not all gone. One bit of evidence suggests that John N. Edwards tried to minimize this bitterness, for the St. Joseph *Gazette*, of which he was editor, published on the opening day of the trial a "Special to the Gazette," which pinned the robbery and the killing of Sheets on Jesse James and Jim Anderson in no uncertain terms. Even this admission of a James's guilt bore Edwards' notion of extenuating circumstance: They had mistaken Sheets for Major Cox, the killer of Bill Anderson, against whom the two had sworn vengeance. The language of the "Special" was less literate than that of Edwards, and it contained many errors of fact. There had been a time when Edwards would have condemned publication of a charge like this against Jesse James.

On both sides the array of counsel was formidable. William H. Wallace and the prosecuting attorney of Daviess County, William D. Hamilton, were assisted by four prominent Gallatin lawyers — John Shanklin, Marcus A. Low, Henry C. McDougall, and Joshua F. Hicklin. Edwards had done well in gathering legal talent to defend the accused. Defense counsel consisted of former Lieutenant Governor Charles P. Johnson, former Congressman John F. Philips, James H. Slover, C. T. Garner, John M. Glover, Joshua W. Alexander, and William M. Rush. All were aspiring Democratic politicians, and Philips was at the time a commissioner of the Supreme Court of Missouri. Philips and Johnson had served in the Union army during the Civil War,[38] and they made the most of this fact during the trial.

In order to accommodate a larger portion of the crowd that poured into Gallatin, Judge Charles H. S. Goodman heard the case in the local opera house. He warned that anyone found armed in the courtroom would be fined. Tickets of admission were issued by the sheriff, George Crozier.

Selection of the jury was watched with close interest, for the opinion was widely held that the outcome of the trial would depend more upon the membership of the jury than upon the evidence. Out of a panel of one hundred men, almost equally divided as to party membership, the twelve finally selected were all Democrats. All were comparatively young men and substantial farmers. Only two had served in the Civil War, both on the Confederate side. Frank James's defenders were pleased with the membership of the jury, and Edwards' St. Joseph *Gazette* admitted openly: "All are Democrats and well-to-do, thrifty farmers. There is much speculation on the jury. The prosecution tried to appear hopeful, but evidently apprehended that the jury will acquit. The friends of the prosecution who wanted a conviction are dissatisfied with the jury." [39]

Before the trial ended, a rumor circulated that Sheriff Crozier had impaneled the jury from a list provided him by William M. Rush, an attorney for James.[40] Wallace and his fellow prosecutor Hamilton planned to sign affidavits to the effect that Crozier was not following the law in impaneling the jury and to demand of Judge Goodman that he depose the sheriff and direct the coroner to summon the jury. Judge Goodman heard of their plan and warned Wallace and Hamilton that he would refuse their demand "in order to prevent bloodshed." Wallace said that he then packed his grip to leave, but his colleagues convinced him that he was the only one with sufficient knowledge of the case to lead the prosecution, and thus they persuaded him to stay. Thirty years later Wallace wrote that he knew, at the time of the trial, that Crozier obtained the panel from men about the courthouse yard in Gallatin and that he saw Crozier using a list in making selections.[41]

Dick Liddil, the prosecution's main witness, had served a term in the Missouri penitentiary for stealing horses in Vernon County, but had been released under the three-fourths time rule — that is, for good behavior upon completion of three-fourths of the sentence. Missouri laws forbade the admission in court of the testimony of a convicted felon unless he had been pardoned. The defense attorneys objected to Liddil's competence to testify, on the ground that the circumstances of his release from prison did not constitute a pardon. But Judge Goodman's interpretation of the law was that release on the three-fourths time rule was accompanied by a pardon, and he permitted Liddil to take the witness stand.

The state attempted to show that the robbery at Winston was committed by Frank James, Jesse James, Dick Liddil, Clarence Hite, and Wood Hite and that Frank James killed Frank McMillan. Liddil swore that in 1881 he, Wood Hite, and Bill Ryan were living in Nashville, Tennessee, with Frank and Jesse James. In March, 1881, after Ryan was captured and returned to Missouri, the others became apprehensive lest they, too, should be trailed to Nashville, and they decided to leave. From Nashville they went to Kentucky, and there they were joined by Clarence Hite. In Kentucky the men made plans for the robbery of a train and then departed for Missouri. Liddil told of their visits in the homes of Mrs. Samuel, J. T. Ford, and Mrs. Martha Bolton in the weeks preceding the robbery at Winston. As to the execution of the robbery, Liddil said that Wood Hite, Jesse James, and Frank James entered the passenger and express cars while he and Clarence Hite commandeered the engine. After the robbery, Frank told Liddil that he had killed one man and Jesse the other.

Several witnesses corroborated parts of Liddil's story. Passengers on the train described the man who killed McMillan, indicating that he resembled Frank James, but none of them positively identified him as the murderer. Witnesses on both sides told of Frank's residence in Kentucky from 1876 to 1881 and vouched for his good behavior while there. Sarah E. Hite and her father Silas Norris corroborated the statement made by Liddil about the party's visit in Kentucky on the way to Missouri; both said that Frank was in the group.

Martha Bolton, her children, and her father J. T. Ford told of Frank's being at their homes in Ray County, Missouri, with the other members of the band several times before and after the robbery. Several residents of Daviess County identified Frank James as a man they had seen in that area in the days preceding the robbery and murder. Members of the band, while scouting the area, had stopped for meals and lodging and had visited places of business in the vicinity of the crime.

An interesting bit of evidence to this effect was given by the Reverend Jamin Machette. On the day before the robbery a man who said his name was Willard and another named Scott stopped at Machette's home for a meal. Machette identified the defendant as Willard, and he told of their argument over Bob Ingersoll, a contemporary agnostic, in which Willard obviously bested the parson. Machette recalled that they discussed Shakespeare also, and Willard quoted long passages from his works. Frank James's propensity for reciting Shakespeare was well known.

Jonas Potts, a blacksmith of near Winston, said that a few days before the robbery he had shod the horse of a man whom he now identified as Frank James.

In refutation, the defense presented witnesses who had also seen the man identified by the state's witnesses as Frank James. These denied that the defendant was the man seen in Daviess County.

In the cross-examination of witnesses the defense brought out the fact that Dick Liddil and Bob Ford had killed Wood Hite at the home of the Ford brothers' sister Martha Bolton. The implication, clearly made, was that Liddil's surrender and his testimony against Frank James were due to his desire to escape the consequences of this crime.

At first the defense did not question Liddil's statement that five men participated in the robbery, and the strategy pointed to a plan to identify the fifth man as Jim Cummings. However, this was soon abandoned for the claim that only four bandits committed the crime and that Wood Hite was mistaken for Frank James.

The alibi to explain his absence was presented in Frank's testimony. He told that he had lived peaceably in Tennessee without engaging in any crime from 1876 to 1881, but his tranquillity was disturbed by the capture of Ryan, and, fearing arrest, he decided to move. He sent his wife and small son to Missouri, with instructions to ask General Jo Shelby to appeal to the governor of Missouri for a guarantee of a fair trial if he would surrender. He had, he admitted, gone to Kentucky with the other members of the group, but he had not accompanied them to Missouri. From the home of his uncle George Hite, in Nelson County, Kentucky, he had gone to Louisville and from there to the home of his sister Susan Parmer, near Denison, Texas. He arrived in Texas in the first part of June and remained until the early part of July, when he went into the Indian Nation. While in the Nation he heard of the robbery at Winston. He returned to his sister's home after having been absent for three or four weeks and remained there through August and a part of September. From Texas he returned to Nelson County, Kentucky, where he awaited news of his wife's efforts to negotiate his surrender. Mrs. James, convinced by General Shelby that an appeal to the governor would be useless, joined her husband in Kentucky late in October. After a few months of wandering, they established a home at Lynchburg, Virginia, where they were living when they heard of Jesse's death.

In support of this alibi, Allen and Susan Parmer repeated the story of Frank's visit at their home, but their statements were indefinite as to dates, and they were very poor witnesses. Mrs. Samuel swore that Frank was not with the other members of the band when they were at her home before and after the robbery. No one, not even Mrs. Samuel, offered any cover-up for Jesse on this job.

General Jo Shelby told of Mrs. James's visit to his home at Page City, Missouri, and of his persuading her that it was hopeless to appeal to the governor in Frank's behalf. Shelby also stated that while other members of the band had visited him in 1880 and 1881, he had not seen Frank James since 1872.

Shelby's appearance as a witness was a highlight of the trial. He entered the courtroom inebriated; unable to find the witness chair, he was helped to it, and then he demanded to see the Court. Judge Goodman was pointed out to him, and the General greeted the Judge and expressed a feeling of good will toward him. It was clear that if Shelby could have found some way to get to Goodman he would have shaken hands, but the expression on the Judge's face intimated that it was well for the witness to defer the formality. Shelby then inquired, after surveying the room, where the jury was. When he located it, he bowed in a friendly manner and settled himself to answer questions.

The cavalry commander did not remain settled, however, for soon he identified Frank James. Rising, he asked the Court's permission to "shake hands with an old soldier," but was refused. He argued with Wallace on the cross-examination and applied uncomplimentary epithets to Liddil. The Judge threatened him several times, and John F. Philips insisted that because of Shelby's condition the questioning should be stopped. But Shelby did not want to stop. Upon the completion of his testimony, he asked again for permission to shake hands with James and was again refused. So, as he left the room, the General nodded at the accused and said, "God bless you, old fellow."

On the next day, Shelby again appeared in court and apologized to Judge Goodman for his conduct on his previous appearance, but he made it clear that anything he had said about Wallace stood. Goodman reprimanded Shelby and fined him ten dollars for contempt of court. Despite the General's behavior in court, the appearance of one of the best-loved heroes of Missouri's ex-Confederates as a witness did the cause of Frank James no harm.

Governor Crittenden was, perhaps reluctantly, a witness for the defense. He testified that Liddil had told him that after the robbery Frank asked Jesse why he had killed a man, in spite of their agreement that there would be no killing. Jesse replied that he had killed to make the gang a band of common murderers and thus retain their loyalty. Liddil now accused Frank James with the murder.

Three days were required for all the lawyers on both sides to make their pleas to the jury. Each competed with the others for the appropriate simile, metaphor, or other figure of speech with which the public expected speeches to be embellished. The speeches of Wallace and Philips have been preserved in entirety, and from them it is apparent that almost as many words were devoted to the Civil War as to the evidence in the case. Philips made the James band "the last remnant of unreconciled and unaccepted parties of the local predatory struggle, suing for reconciliation," and the prosecution worked hard to offset this attempt to link the gang and their crimes with the Southern cause.

If one ignores the florid oratory and considers only the evidence, it appears that the only direct statement of Frank James's participation in the robbery and murder was that of Dick Liddil, a convicted horse thief, accused murderer, and traitor to the band, who was trying to evade the punishment his crimes deserved. No one else testified that Frank James was the man who killed McMillan. The statements about his being the man who visited Daviess County in the days before the robbery were conflicting. On the other hand, James's alibi was extremely weak and was substantiated only by members of his family.

Faced with this evidence and instructed to acquit if any reasonable doubt existed as to the guilt of the defendant, the jury could easily justify an acquittal. After three and one-half hours of deliberation it found the defendant not guilty. "At the sound of the words 'Not Guilty' the defendant embraced his devoted wife, and then one loud prolonged sound of applause marked the closing scene of the great drama. . . . There were many in the audience, however, who were sorely disappointed with the verdict. . . ." [42]

In a few days Frank James received this letter:

St. Joseph, Mo., Sept 11th, 1883

My Dear Frank:

I need not tell you how great a joy was the verdict. The employment of Philips was an inspiration. What a true, brave, splendid man he is. And what a speech he made.

I left Gallatin in accordance with his orders — and those of Rush and Johnson. . . . I am quietly now watching the expressions of public opinion, and building up some breastworks. Never mind what the newspapers say, the masses are for you. The backbone of the prosecution has been broken. I have been through hell myself since I saw you, but I have driven out the pirates, and got the vessel again.

Write to me.

Your friend, as ever,

J. N. Edwards

Remember me to Sheriff Crozier. He is a *man* that is everything.

XIII

And Governor C.
He laughed with glee
And fixed a price to suit him.

Two FACTORS — the sincere and widespread belief that Frank James was guilty and the papers' ever-present alacrity to utilize the James issue for political purposes — account for the uproar that followed his acquittal at Gallatin. Some critics, but not nearly all, were calmed with the explanation, which many Democratic papers offered, that the verdict was the logical outcome of a prosecution based on the uncorroborated testimony of a convicted felon and confessed traitor.[1] The protests centered around two circumstances: the connection of prominent Democrats with the defense and the Democratic make-up of the jury. Republican papers and the independent Democratic St. Louis *Post-Dispatch*, still raging against the Crittenden administration, seized upon John F. Philips' participation in the trial. He was a prominent Democrat, Union man, former representative in Congress, law partner of United States Senator George Graham Vest, and, at the time of the trial, a commissioner of the Supreme Court of Missouri. His appointment to the latter position occurred after he had promised to defend Frank James, and Philips kept his pledge in spite of public expressions of disapproval.

The bitterest attacks upon Philips appeared in the *Post-Dispatch*. On September 5 it commented: "If Frank James is not convicted Mr. Philips' [the *Post-Dispatch* consistently misspelled his name] connection with the case will make all the world ascribe the defeat of justice to political influence, and the crowning shame of this outlaw business will be fixed as an indelible stain upon the escutcheon of Missouri." What the paper termed "the reigning powers" had selected Philips to be the next governor. If they failed, they could at least ensure him a seat in Congress from the Kansas City district. "Either of these promotions would shed a crimson light on the political features of this James trial." In condemning Philips for taking part in the trial while a commissioner of the supreme court, the *Post-Dispatch* suggested that, "If there is any manhood in the Legislature, any respect for the purity and dignity of the judiciary, there will be an investigation of this thing and somebody will be impeached." [2]

The Democratic press generally approved Philips' action, and the St. Joseph *Gazette*, whose editor surely knew the facts, stated, "He was appealed to in James' behalf by men whom Philips had known for years, men who stood as high as the highest in the land, and as a lawyer he accepted." [3] Certainly a question of professional ethics was involved. Normally, commissioners of the supreme court do not engage in private practice, and they disqualify themselves in any case before the court in which they have had an earlier interest. But Philips considered it right to keep his commitment to defend Frank James, a prisoner entitled to a fair trial with competent counsel, regardless of his guilt or innocence. If Philips' political standing influenced the jury's verdict, such influence was not unusual in a trial in a rural community.

The Kansas City *Journal* and the St. Joseph *Herald* led Republican papers in attributing the verdict to the exclusion of Republicans from the jury,[4] but no Republican paper was so vitriolic as the *Post-Dispatch*, in an editorial titled, "Yesterday's Verdict."

For fifteen years it had been the burning disgrace of Missouri that the bandit chief and his gang had so many sympathizers and so much political influence that they could rob and kill and terrorize where they would, without fear of arrest in the most populous counties of the state. Yet never was this political influence displayed with such successful bravado as at this trial in the Court House which had echoed the pistol shots that killed Captain Sheets.

The editorial stated that "loud-mouthed and bullying partisans of the prisoner" had thronged to Gallatin, where two Union soldiers and aspiring politicians, Johnson and Philips, had paid "homage to the political influence of James' friends by appearing as the ardent defenders without fee." With this "bold parade of political influence on his side" and with "a rustic jury already inclined to pardon him the vengeance he had taken for the wrongs they believed he had suffered," the prisoner had little to fear even though "the evidence was strong enough to have hung . . . any other man undefended by the influence that protected

Frank James." Thus, the editorial proclaimed, "the James Boy brand" had been "burned deeper into the politics of Missouri." [5]

The *Post-Dispatch* and the St. Joseph *Herald* also directed an attack on the St. Joseph *Gazette* and on Major Edwards as well as the other Democratic friends of Frank James. When George E. King withdrew from the *Gazette*'s employ a few days after the trial because of disagreement with the policies of the paper, the *Post-Dispatch* attributed the following statement to him:

I was not in sympathy with the work in which the Gazette was engaged. I have charity and friendship for the people of the lost cause, but at this late date don't choose to discuss or be their champion. I have always been for the supremacy of the law, but the final and chief cause of my withdrawal was in the fact that the Gazette, in spite of all my efforts, espoused the cause of the Gallatin outlaw, and is the apologist, if not the organ of the James boys, and I just simply chaffed and fretted until liberty and freedom from the establishment was my greatest desire, and I have retired from it because I was distressed at its work.[6]

The *Post-Dispatch* maintained that King expressed the feeling of a majority of the Democrats in every county in Missouri, and it warned of trouble within the party if its leaders and papers did not recognize and respect this sentiment. The *Herald* followed the same line; it blamed Missouri's bad reputation on the "anti-James" Democratic newspapers because they had not exposed the Frank James-Bourbon element within the party and the "James press." [7] The self-righteous *Post-Dispatch*, in an editorial titled "Who Slanders the State?" claimed that every Democratic paper in the state with a candidate on hand had to uphold the Gallatin verdict as being in accordance with the law and evidence. It also said:

If the Democratic party is to be saddled with a defense of that partisan trial and verdict, or if the impression goes abroad that no candidate for Governor can get the Democratic nomination unless he or his newspaper supporters stand forth as conspicuous upholders of that verdict, such a consummation will be the crowning shame of the James Boy business.

Nowhere in this Union are the people more unanimous than in Missouri in their absolute conviction that Frank James was guilty as charged in the indictment and that the evidence proved his guilt clear of all reasonable doubt. If the honest sentiment of the party and of the State continues to be misunderstood and misrepresented abroad, it will be due solely to the truckling homage which candidates and politicians pay to the James Boy influence in the Democratic party.[8]

Thus, Republican criticisms and dissension within the Democratic party over the Frank James trial opened the way for an issue that was to arouse intense feelings in Missouri politics for the next year and a half.

Crittenden and Wallace timed the public release of confessions by Dick Liddil and Clarence Hite to coincide with the outburst of criticism following the trial, Liddil's appearing on September 9 and Hite's on September 12.[9] Apparently, the confessions were released in order to substantiate the testimony given by Liddil at the trial.

Liddil's confession, made shortly after his surrender and before the death of Jesse James, named Wood Hite, Ed Miller, Tucker Bassham, Jesse James, Bill Ryan, and Liddil as members of the band that robbed the train at Glendale on October 9, 1879. The participants in the robbery at Winston were the same he had named in the trial at Gallatin; the robbery at Blue Cut, he said, was committed by Frank James, Jesse James, Wood Hite, Clarence Hite, Charlie Ford, and himself.

Hite's confession, made at the Missouri penitentiary in the presence of Governor Crittenden, H. H. Craig, and Sheriff Timberlake shortly before Hite's death, agreed with Liddil's statement in the essential details of the robberies at Winston and at Blue Cut. Hite had joined the band in the spring of 1881. Most astounding in both accounts was the evidence of the utter freedom with which all members of the band visited by day or night towns like Kansas City, Richmond, Liberty, Gallatin, and Independence in Missouri, and Nashville, Louisville, and others in neighboring states. They traveled on public conveyances or across country on horses as they pleased. So few people knew them that there was practically no danger of being recognized, and friendship or fear of reprisal silenced those who knew them.

The confessions admitted that the relatives of all the members of the band harbored and protected them, but beyond that group, very few acquaintances gave them shelter and aid in the years Liddil and Hite were in the band. Among those mentioned as sheltering them were Robert and Lamartine Hudspeth, Ben Morrow, and Jo Shelby. The home of J. T. Ford and that of his daughter Martha Bolton were refuges, and in Nelson County, Kentucky, the sheriff, Donny Pence, looked out for their interests. If half the stories told by Hite and Liddil of their "borrowing" horses for an indefinite length of time are true, the James boys' reputation as train and bank robbers is greatly overrated, and their achievements as horse thieves are vastly underestimated.

Despite criticism of the trial and publication of the two confessions, Frank James retained two staunch friends. One, of course, was Edwards, and the other was Shelby, whom the Chicago *News* characterized as "the leader of an organized band of horse thieves, a gang of night-prowling bandits, who never knew what legitimate warfare was,

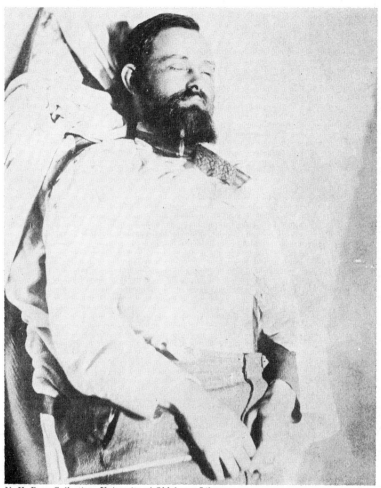

N. H. Rose Collection, University of Oklahoma Library

Jesse in Death

PROCLAMATION
$5,000⁰⁰
REWARD

FOR EACH of SEVEN ROBBERS of THE TRAIN at
WINSTON, MO., JULY 15, 1881, and THE MURDER of
CONDUCTER WESTFALL

$ 5,000.00

ADDITIONAL for ARREST or CAPTURE

DEAD OR ALIVE
OF JESSE OR FRANK JAMES

THIS NOTICE TAKES the PLACE of ALL PREVIOUS
REWARD NOTICES.

CONTACT SHERIFF, DAVIESS COUNTY, MISSOURI
IMMEDIATELY

T. T. CRITTENDEN, GOVERNOR
STATE OF MISSOURI
JULY 26, 1881

State Historical Society of Missouri

Spurious Reward Proclamation Which Perpetuates Belief that Reward Offer
Was for the Outlaws "Dead or Alive"

PROCLAMATION

OF THE

GOVERNOR OF MISSOURI!

REWARDS

FOR THE ARREST OF

Express and Train Robbers.

STATE OF MISSOURI,
EXECUTIVE DEPARTMENT.

WHEREAS, It has been made known to me, as the Governor of the State of Missouri, that certain parties, whose names are to me unknown, have confederated and banded themselves together for the purpose of committing robberies and other depredations within this State; and

WHEREAS, Said parties did, on or about the Eighth day of October, 1879, stop a train near Glendale, in the county of Jackson, in said State, and, with force and violence, take, steal and carry away the money and other express matter being carried thereon; and

WHEREAS, On the fifteenth day of July 1881, said parties and their confederates did stop a train upon the line of the Chicago, Rock Island and Pacific Railroad, near Winston, in the County of Daviess, in said State, and, with force and violence, take, steal, and carry away the money and other express matter being carried thereon; and, in perpetration of the robbery last aforesaid, the parties engaged therein did kill and murder one WILLIAM WESTFALL, the conductor of the train, together with one JOHN MCCULLOCH, who was at the time in the employ of said company, then on said train; and

WHEREAS, FRANK JAMES and JESSE W. JAMES stand indicted in the Circuit Court of said Daviess County, for the murder of JOHN W. SHEETS, and the parties engaged in the robberies and murders aforesaid have fled from justice and have absconded and secreted themselves:

NOW, THEREFORE, in consideration of the premises, and in lieu of all other rewards heretofore offered for the arrest or conviction of the parties aforesaid, or either of them, by any person or corporation, I, THOMAS T. CRITTENDEN, Governor of the State of Missouri, do hereby offer a reward of five thousand dollars ($5,000.00) for the arrest and conviction of each person participating in either of the robberies or murders aforesaid, excepting the said FRANK JAMES and JESSE W. JAMES; and for the arrest and delivery of said

FRANK JAMES and JESSE W. JAMES,

and each or either of them, to the sheriff of said Daviess County, I hereby offer a reward of five thousand dollars, ($5,000.00,) and for the conviction of either of the parties last aforesaid of participation in either of the murders or robberies above mentioned, I hereby offer a further reward of five thousand dollars, ($5,000.00.)

IN TESTIMONY WHEREOF, I have hereunto set my hand and caused to be affixed the Great Seal of the State of Missouri. Done at the City of Jefferson on this 28th day of July, A. D. 1881.

[SEAL.]

THOS. T. CRITTENDEN.

By the Governor:

MICH'L K. McGRATH, Sec'y of State.

BURCH & FERGUSON, STATE PRINTERS, JEFFERSON CITY, MO.

State Historical Society of Missouri

Reward Proclamation Issued by Governor Crittenden

THE DAILY GRAPHIC

AN ILLUSTRATED EVENING NEWSPAPER

39 & 41 PARK PLACE

VOL. XXVIII. All the News. Four Editions Daily.	NEW YORK, TUESDAY, APRIL 11, 1882.	$12 Per Year in Advance. Single Copies, Five Cents. NO. 2814.

THE APOTHEOSIS OF JESSE JAMES.

THE NEW YORK
Detective Library.
PRICE TEN CENTS.

No. 373. {COMPLETE.} FRANK TOUSEY, PUBLISHER, 34 & 36 North Moore Street, N. Y. {PRICE} Vol. 1,
New York, January 18, 1890. {Issued Every Saturday.} {10 CENTS}

The Subscription Price of The New York Detective Library by the year is $5.00; $2.50 per six months, post-paid. Address
FRANK TOUSEY, PUBLISHER, 34 and 36 North Moore Street, New York. Box 2730.

OLD SADDLE-BAGS, THE PREACHER DETECTIVE;

OR,

THE JAMES BOYS IN A FIX.

By D. W. STEVENS.

LOG CABIN

NEW STORIES OF STARTLING LIBRARY ADVENTURE BY THE BEST AUTHORS

Entered According to Act of Congress, in the Year 1889, by Street & Smith, in the Office of the Librarian of Congress, Washington, D. C.
Entered as Second-class Matter at the New York, N. Y., Post Office, Thursday, April 11, 1889.   Issued Weekly.   Subscription Price, $5.00 Per Year.

Vol. I.   STREET & SMITH, Publishers,   New York, April 11, 1889.   Price 10 Cents.   No. 4.
            31 Rose St., N. Y., P. O. Box 2734.

JESSE, THE OUTLAW
A·NARRATIVE·OF·THE·JAMES·BOYS·
BY CAPT. JAKE SHACKELFORD, THE WESTERN DETECTIVE.

"THROW UP YOUR HANDS, CURSE YOU!" THUNDERED JESSE JAMES, COVERING US WITH HIS REVOLVER,
AS WE ALL CAME TO A STARTLED HALT.

The Judge Satirizes Treatment of Frank James After His Surrender

THE NEW YORK DETECTIVE LIBRARY.

PRICE TEN CENTS.

Entered according to Act of Congress, in the Year 1890, by FRANK TOUSEY, in the Office of the Librarian of Congress, Washington, D. C.

Entered at the Post Office at New York, N. Y., as Second Class Matter.

| No. 416. | COMPLETE. | FRANK TOUSEY, PUBLISHER, 34 & 36 NORTH MOORE STREET, N. Y. NEW YORK, November 15, 1890. ISSUED EVERY SATURDAY. | PRICE 10 CENTS. | Vol. 1. |

The Subscription Price of The New York Detective Library by the year is $5.00; $2.50 per six months, post-paid. Address
FRANK TOUSEY, Publisher, 34 and 36 North Moore Street, New York. Box 2730.

Frank Reade, THE INVENTOR, Chasing the James Boys
WITH HIS STEAM TEAM.

A THRILLING STORY FROM A LOST DIARY.

THE NEW YORK
DETECTIVE LIBRARY.

PRICE TEN CENTS.

Entered according to Act of Congress, in the Year 1891, by FRANK TOUSEY, in the Office of the Librarian of Congress, Washington D. C.

Entered at the Post Office, at New York, N. Y., as Second Class Matter.

No. 470. {COMPLETE.} FRANK TOUSEY, PUBLISHER, 34 & 36 NORTH MOORE STREET, N. Y. | PRICE | **Vol. 1**
NEW YORK, November 28, 1891. ISSUED EVERY SATURDAY. | 10 CENTS. |

The Subscription Price of THE NEW YORK DETECTIVE LIBRARY by the year is $5.00; $2.50 per six months, postpaid. Address
FRANK TOUSEY, PUBLISHER, 34 and 36 North Moore Street, New York. Box 2730.

THE MAN ON THE BLACK HORSE:
OR,
The James Boys' First Ride in Missouri.

By D. W. STEVENS.

NOV 24 1891

Telegram from Governor J. W. McClurg to Sheriff of Jackson County

THE FIVE CENT
WIDE AWAKE
LIBRARY

Entered according to Act of Congress, in the year 1892, by FRANK TOUSEY, in the office of the Librarian of Congress, at Washington, D. C.

Entered at the Post Office at New York, N. Y., as Second Class Matter.

No. 538 | { COMPLETE. } | FRANK TOUSEY, PUBLISHER, 34 & 36 NORTH MOORE STREET, N. Y.
NEW YORK, December 27, 1892. | ISSUED EVERY WEDNESDAY. | { PRICE }
{ 5 CENTS. } | Vol. I

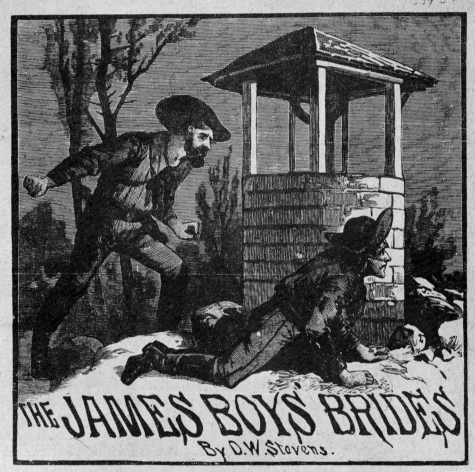

THE JAMES BOYS' BRIDES
By D. W. Stevens.

JESSE JAMES AS AN ANGEL.

Texas Siftings, published in Austin, depicted Jesse as an angel in ridiculing his funeral service.

and whose most gallant charges were made upon unguarded stables and chicken coops." Reaction to this denigration of the veteran Shelby was, in general, outrage; even the *Post-Dispatch* termed the *News's* characterization "wanton slander." Shelby framed an open reply to this and other charges: "I am aware how the press of the country is yelping. Let them yelp. It only nerves me to stand the closer by an ex-Confederate who is in trouble. We clamor not for mercy; we despise sympathy. All we require in the James case is evidence of reliable men." [10]

John N. Edwards sensed that the reaction to the trial might influence Crittenden's thinking on matters pertaining to James, and he took no chances. On October 5 he sent a letter for publication to the editor of the *Missouri Republican* in which he refuted most emphatically the charges that Crittenden had promised, as part of the surrender agreement, to pardon Frank James if he were convicted. Edwards wrote that no pledge was ever asked, and none was given. The men representing James had too much respect for Crittenden personally and for the high office he held to ask for a pledge or promise of any sort. What Crittenden had said about the surrender was the complete truth.[11] On October 17 Edwards explained in a letter to Frank James why he had made the statement:

Every wolf on your track was lying against Gov. Crittenden, in order to poison him against you, and to put him in a false attitude if he ever had your case to come before him. . . . Whatever I do at any time or upon any occasion is done with an eye simple to your interests. As for myself, I do not care one tinkers damn what is said, I shall stay till the end.

Frank James, then, was well aware, as he sat in the Gallatin jail following the trial, that the efforts on his behalf continued. On the motion of Prosecuting Attorney Hamilton, the court on November 5 entered a nolle prosequi in the indictment for the murder of Westfall, granted a continuance of the case for the murder of Captain Sheets, and remanded Frank to the authorities in Jackson County.[12] On December 13 he was released on bond in Jackson County and was immediately rearrested and returned to Gallatin. A few days later the court at Gallatin permitted his release on bond.[13]

The news now spread that James would be arrested and removed to Alabama by federal officials for trial for complicity in the robbery of the paymaster at Muscle Shoals in March, 1881, and Crittenden became much concerned. He sought the help of Senator Vest, and he wrote to Judge Arnold Krekel of the federal court in Kansas City, arguing that the federal courts had no jurisdiction until all Missouri cases were disposed of. James's bondsmen brought him to Judge Krekel and approved an arrangement by which James was released on his own recognizance, to appear to answer federal charges after final disposal of Missouri cases. Thus the question of priority was amicably settled, and it was assured that James would stand trial on federal charges before he faced Minnesota justice.[14]

Interest was high in James's approaching trial in Jackson County for the robbery at Blue Cut. On January 30 his attorneys applied for a change of venue on grounds of unreasonable prejudice against Frank James in Jackson County, and the court set February 11 as the date for a hearing on the application.[15]

On December 17, 1883, the state supreme court ruled, in another case, that the testimony of a felon was not admissible in court unless he had been pardoned, and the court indicated that it did not consider as a pardon release from the penitentiary on the three-fourths time rule.[16] The law in question was one passed by the legislature in 1879, so that there was doubt that the decision of the court was applicable to the release of Dick Liddil in 1877.[17] However, William H. Wallace concluded that the court's ruling did make inadmissible the testimony of Liddil unless he had a full pardon from the governor. Wallace appealed to Governor Crittenden to pardon Liddil in order that he could be used as a witness in the case pending against Frank James in Jackson County. Crittenden refused, with the weak explanation that a pardon would reflect on Lieutenant Governor Henry C. Brockmeyer, who, as acting governor, had released Liddil from the prison. Brockmeyer had held that, at the time, Liddil's release from the penitentiary was accompanied by a complete restoration of citizenship.[18]

Wallace could have made the courts decide the issue of Liddil's legal competency to testify, but, instead, on February 11, the day set for hearing on the application for change of venue, he dismissed the case against Frank James. On the same day, W. P. Hamilton dismissed the charges remaining against James in Daviess County. Wallace ascribed his action to the refusal of Crittenden to pardon Liddil.[19] One can understand Wallace's dismay at Crittenden's refusal, but he now had a means of ridding the state of a problem and passing the responsibility for its solution to someone else. James was removed to Huntsville, Alabama, to await trial for robbery of the paymaster.[20]

Crittenden's critics now descended upon him. The dismissal of the cases, the St. Louis *Missouri Republican* said, "caused a large amount of talk, and a great deal of indignation is expressed at Governor Crittenden's refusal to pardon Liddil, and the charge is openly made that he did so for the express purpose of acquitting James." [21] The *Post-Dispatch* charged Crittenden with trying to avoid the problem of pardoning Frank James after conviction.[22] It upheld Wallace's action, explaining, "It appears that he did it to save Missouri from further disgrace in trying James with the whole influence of the present Governor and Supreme Court unmistakably arrayed against his conviction." [23]

In the following June, when Wallace was a candidate for representative in Congress, he published a long and bitter statement that Crittenden's refusal to pardon Liddil caused the dismissal of the James cases. The *Post-Dispatch's* editorial comment on the article called it "a severe arraignment of our Governor" that added unneeded proof of his "utter unfitness for the high public trust he held." The newspaper labeled Crittenden's administration "a disgrace to the state second only to that inflicted on it by the James boys." [24]

Republican papers also lambasted Crittenden. The St. Joseph *Herald* termed the matter as clearly political: Crittenden had refused to pardon Liddil because of political pressure on him; such influence could be expected as long as Democrats controlled the state.[25] The Kansas City *Journal* considered the refusal as proof that Frank James had surrendered under a compact with the Governor to protect him from harm.[26]

Crittenden's actions in connection with the breaking up of the James band had not, certainly, been above question. The manner in which he hastened to claim the credit for Jesse's shooting, his failure to reveal all the negotiations with the friends of Frank James in connection with the surrender, and his appearance at Frank's trial as a witness for the defense all aroused comment. Crittenden had also boasted that in breaking up the James band he had spent $20,000, not one dollar of which was furnished by the state, yet he never revealed who received the money. In addition, his refusal to pardon Liddil at this time is difficult to reconcile with his earlier appeal to President Arthur to pardon Liddil in recognition of his service to the state in breaking up the band.

A study of Crittenden suggests a man who lacked the astuteness to measure up to his own estimate of himself. He never admitted any misgiving over the manner in which Jesse James was killed, and to point it out is not to argue the propriety of his role in the killing. After Frank James had stood trial once without conviction, Crittenden came to believe that further prosecution in Missouri would be a hounding of the man that would serve only to prevent his becoming a law-abiding citizen. Crittenden was willing to take the criticism that refusal to pardon Liddil would bring, for he was accustomed to it; most of his official acts as governor had brought attack from one quarter or another.

It is possible that John N. Edwards had made Crittenden a "believer." At least Edwards was the Governor's most outspoken defender and the bitterest denouncer of "Wallace and Company," who, he said, were trying to save themselves from ridicule and condemnation by making Crittenden their scapegoat. After all, he noted, Liddil was not a witness in the case against James for J. W. Sheets's murder in Daviess County, which had also been dismissed. "Overmastered there [Gallatin] in every way — in skill, in management, and in legal knowledge and ability — they whined out something about a packed jury, and hurried ignominiously back into Jackson County." Upon the bare suggestion that Liddil was not a competent witness, Edwards continued, they now dismissed all the indictments against James in their control and took "refuge for their sham, deceit and imbecility behind the so-called sympathy of Governor Crittenden for the prisoner. . . . Praying for a way out from the muck where vociferous assertion and vain glorious boasting had landed them, the Federal indictment came as a God send and liberated the whole conglomerated outfit of tools, fools and shallow schemers." But for Crittenden, "not one of the lot today would be higher in the scale of legal notoriety than a pig pen reared up against a cathedral." [27]

Crittenden would not be a factor in the Alabama trial of James, however, and that hurdle was the next for the outlaw's partisans. On April 17, 1884, he was arraigned in federal court at Huntsville on charges of participating in the robbery of Paymaster Alexander Smith at Muscle Shoals on March 11, 1881. Edwards had helped secure counsel headed by General Leroy Pope Walker. James W. Newman, an Alabama lawyer whose brother was the commissioner of labor statistics for Missouri, was also helpful.[28] Mrs. James and "Little Robbie" were on hand to sit with the defendant. General Shelby would have been there, but the death of his stepfather in Lexington, Kentucky, prevented his attendance.[29]

The prosecution's principal problem was that of identifying James as one of three men who had waited at a saloon near the river works until Smith passed and had then followed and robbed him. Smith and others who had seen the bandits testified that they believed Frank was one of the men, but none would identify him positively. The description of a horse also entered into the testimony, and the Alabamans described the horse ridden by the man they thought was James almost exactly as Dick Liddil described the horse Frank rode away from Nashville. Liddil told of Frank's return to Nashville after the incident and of Frank, Jesse, and Ryan admitting the robbery. Because of his effrontery during cross-examination, Liddil was not an effective witness.

The defense offered the alibi that Frank was in Nashville at the time of the robbery and presented several citizens of Nashville who said they had seen him there on March 11, 1881. Among them was Jonas Taylor, a blacksmith, who swore he had shod Frank's horse on March 11 and had seen him again on March 12. He had brought his record book to the trial to substantiate his statements. The witnesses from Nashville had known Frank as B. J. Woodson.

In the absence of positive identification and in the face of a fairly well established alibi, the jury found the defendant not guilty.[30] The verdict excited little comment in Missouri, the Kansas City *Journal* remarking that it caused no surprise, since the trial was in the sympathetic South.[31]

Upon announcement of the jury's verdict, "Not guilty," Sheriff John F. Rogers of Cooper County, Missouri, stepped forward and placed the defendant under arrest. Governor Crittenden's requisition had already been honored by the governor of Alabama, and arrangements were complete for the return of Frank James to Missouri to answer charges of participation in the train robbery at Otterville in 1876. Rogers had registered at a Huntsville hotel under the name of Jones and had given his address as Versailles, Kentucky. Thus, no chances were taken of letting James fall into the hands of Minnesota officers if any were in Huntsville as rumored.[32] The arrest was quickly recognized as a hoax, and the St. Joseph *Herald* branded it the work of ruling Bourbons in Missouri.[33]

The issues that had developed around the James band still complicated Missouri politics. William H. Wallace resigned as prosecuting attorney in May to seek the Democratic nomination for representative in Congress from the Fifth District of Missouri. One Democrat analyzed his action: "During the recent trials of Frank James he sprang into some notoriety the upshot of which causes him to resign his position to run for Congress." [34] Wallace's candidacy ran into rough weather, for the district nominating convention refused to seat the delegates from Jackson County who supported him. These delegates bolted the convention and nominated Wallace; the convention nominated Alexander Graves. The Democratic state committee suggested a primary, to be held on September 16, to settle the dispute, and the Fifth District Democratic committee met on September 6, with all members present, to arrange for the primary. The meeting was held behind closed doors, but it became known that the committee did not allow representatives of Wallace to suggest names for judges and clerks. The one Wallace supporter on the committee objected to the procedure and refused to take part. After the election officials had been selected in this way, Wallace declined to submit his name to the voters; Graves's men said that Wallace withdrew from the race because he knew he would lose.[35]

Whatever the cause for Wallace's withdrawal, the Republican press had its own explanations. The election judges appointed were Wallace's political and personal enemies, and many were good friends of Frank James; to beat Wallace, the Democratic machine had called to its aid the friends of train robbers and of the Lost Cause who were thirsting for revenge. Fourteen years later, an anonymous biographer attributed Wallace's defeat to the fact that "he had displayed unnecessary vigor and pertinacity in the prosecution of train robbers." Undoubtedly, his earlier role as the prosecutor of bandits had defeated his ambitions for a seat in Congress, and John N. Edwards was pleased. He wrote to Frank James, "Well, Wallace has been beaten. It was thoroughly done and showed much skillful management." [36]

Crittenden did not fare well, either, at the hands of Democrats in 1884. He wished strongly to attend the Democratic national convention as a delegate-at-large from Missouri. Edwards supported his candidacy, but the pro-James Sedalia Daily Democrat remarked, "He has done enough to divide and mortify the Democracy of the State, without sending him to pose as the ideal Democratic dude of the great commonwealth of the West." [37] The state Democratic convention denied Crittenden this honor in a close vote.[38]

Crittenden's defeat was due, in large measure, to the growth in strength of the faction in the party that had opposed his nomination in 1880. This group wanted laws regulating the state's railroads that would supplement provisions of the state constitution of 1875. Also, his method of handling problems concerning the St. Louis Police Board had cost him the support of a majority of the St. Louis delegates.[39]

The James issue may have turned a few votes, but actually it had little share in causing Crittenden's defeat. Nevertheless, some Democrats feared that Republicans in other states would attempt to discredit Democrats in general by asserting that Missouri Democrats did not approve the extermination of the James band. Recognizing this possibility, the Richmond Conservator commented:

However, here in Missouri, our majority is so large that we can afford to blunder. But what shall we say to the struggling Democracy of the doubtful States? Missouri has been thrown up to them as the "robber State" much to their injury. At last a Democratic Governor arose, in the person of Gov. Crittenden, who has so wisely administered our affairs that our credit is equal to that of the Federal Government. . . . He has suppressed outlawry and made train and bank robbing among the lost arts. Our Democratic brethren of other States have been referring our calumniators to his heroic work. Now, they are to be told that Missouri's Democracy do not endorse this. What shall we say to them? Let those who did the deed frame the reply.[40]

The Democratic state convention, meeting in August at Jefferson City, nominated John S. Marmaduke for governor. He had been Crittenden's leading opponent for the nomination in 1880 and represented the antirailroad faction in the party. His record in the Missouri militia and the Confederate army made him acceptable to former Confederates, who were thinking strongly that it was time for a Southerner to head the state ticket. Concessions were made to Union men in the selection of other candidates. Crittenden's administration was endorsed in the platform, but no mention was made of the James band or of banditry.[41]

Later in August, the Greenback-Labor party held its convention, adopted a platform that invited the co-operation of all to oust the Democrats, and authorized the state central committee to nominate a ticket. The committee endorsed Nicholas Ford's candidacy for the governorship.[42] The expectation that an agreement could be made with the Republicans and that the two parties would unite in opposition to the Democrats was obvious. The St. Joseph *Herald*, which supported Nicholas Ford for governor, set forth the line the campaign would take, soon after the Democratic convention, when it charged that the nomination of Marmaduke was "a crystallization of the old rebel spirit — the spirit which created and made possible the existence of the James and Younger boys." All non-Bourbons were urged to unite to support Ford for governor.[43]

The Republican state convention was scheduled to meet at Moberly early in September. By a coincidence that might have been accidental, the Moberly Fair Association had invited Frank James, free on bond, to appear at the fair to function as a race starter. The fair was scheduled at the same time the convention was to be in session. James had been earning money in this way, and fairs profited financially from the crowds of the curious who were attracted by his presence. Nevertheless, the Republicans became indignant, and, seeing the opportunity to exploit the situation politically, the Republican state committee voted, 10 to 7, to hold the convention in Jefferson City instead of at Moberly.[44]

The Republicans were now the object of many barbed comments. According to one report, the committee considered moving from Moberly to Kansas City, but gave up the idea when it learned that a pair of Frank's old boots were on exhibition at a pawnbroker's shop. The Kansas City *Times*'s offer to move the boots out of town for two days was not accepted.[45] Another source announced that Frank was to be in Jefferson City on the first day of the convention and added, "Delegates . . . can be comforted by the fact that woods commence close to town."[46] The comment of John N. Edwards must have irritated

Republicans: "Of all the weak, silly illogical things done in the name of the Bloody Shirt, the substitution of Jefferson City for Moberly, as the place of holding the Republican state convention, was the most hopelessly and helplessly idiotic." [47]

When the Republicans met, the Democrats received no mercy. The convention endorsed the candidacy of Nicholas Ford for governor and divided the other nominations for state offices between Republicans and Greenbackers. One part of the strategy of this combination, known as Fusionists in the campaign, was obvious: Divide the Democratic party between Union and Confederate factions. Resolutions and platform were designed for that purpose:

We indict the Bourbon Democracy of Missouri with persistently ignoring the Union element of the State. While the Republican party has obliterated every disability growing out of the rebellion, the Democratic Party still insists in prosecuting men for their loyalty, and in making service in war against the government a condition for the important offices of the State and for Senators and Representatives in Congress. Against this policy we protest as an insult to a Union State and an example fraught with demoralization to the patriotism of the youth of the country in all future times. Also, for its alliance with and protection of notorious and confessed banditti, whose presence in Missouri has driven out immigration from its borders and capital from its industries. All these have been most offensively repeated in the nomination of the present Bourbon State ticket, at the head of which has been placed a man whose only claim to notoriety was his conspicuous position in the army recently waging war on the government by which he was educated; . . . we believe the time has come in the history of the State of Missouri when all should lay aside party prejudices and unite in wresting the government of the state from the hands of that party.[48]

The Republicans, who no doubt expected to gain the votes of some Union Democrats with these charges, aroused Democrats to anger, and they retorted that the Republicans damaged the reputation of Missouri and insulted all Missourians.[49] The Republicans, said the Sedalia *Daily Democrat*, were "more anxious to vilify their state than to confine themselves to the truth," and it termed the inference about Frank James "the dirtiest, vilest mass of lies that any party, in any country, ever gave their endorsement to." [50]

In the campaign the Democrats presented enough comparisons of population and economic development in Missouri with those of neighboring states to force the Republicans to drop the charge that Missouri was losing immigrants and capital because of Democratic policies.[51] The campaign against Marmaduke became personal, and the opposition attacked him for supporting the Confederacy during the war and for expressing sympathy for former Confederates in the campaign. Repeatedly the Republicans charged that it was the Confederate element in the Democratic party, already standing accused of friendship for Frank James, that supported Marmaduke's candidacy. William H. Wallace, loyal to the Democratic party in spite of its rejection of him, took to the stump to deny these charges against Marmaduke.[52]

The combined opposition to Marmaduke proved to be much stronger than the opposition to Crittenden had been in 1880, but it was not sufficient to defeat him. His plurality over Ford was nearly 11,000, but because 10,000 voters had supported the Prohibition party's nominee, Marmaduke's majority over both candidates was only about 500 votes — less than the tally for the Democratic presidential candidate, Grover Cleveland, by more than 17,000 votes.[53] It is probable, from these returns, that some Union Democrats voted for Ford.

Frank James was intensely concerned about the outcome of this election, for it could determine whether a requisition from Minnesota would be honored. Edwards assured him in October, 1884, that even though he had no promise from Crittenden, he was sure Crittenden would deny a requisition.[54] When Crittenden left office there was very little praise for his administration. Many Democrats disliked him, and some stated openly that they were glad he was out.[55]

The final charge against James in Missouri, the robbery at Otterville, was dismissed on February 21, 1885, in a somewhat secret manner two days before the case was scheduled for trial. The explanation for dismissal was that the principal witness, R. P. Stapp, was dead.[56] Governor Marmaduke, it now appeared, would have to take a stand on the James issue, for rumors were circulating that a requisition from Minnesota would soon make its way to Missouri and that Democratic friends of James were endeavoring to persuade Marmaduke not to grant it, on the ground that Minnesota's action would constitute an attack on the Lost Cause.[57]

The Kansas City *Journal* intermittently attacked the element in the Democratic party that sought to protect Frank James from trial in Minnesota. It pointed out that three of James's lawyers in the Gallatin trial had advanced politically. Philips had been appointed judge of the Court of Appeals in Kansas City, Glover elected to Congress, and Slover appointed circuit judge in Jackson County.[58]

This last Republican assault upon the Missouri Democracy for its alleged friendship for Frank James was made needlessly, for there was no indictment against him in Minnesota, and no attempt was made to remove him there.[59] However, John N. Edwards was taking no chances, and on March 18, 1885, he wrote excitedly, on the stationery of the Missouri Senate, to Frank James:

At last I can write to you with the most perfect confidence and assurance. I have just five minutes ago left Governor Marmaduke, after a long, full, and perfect interview. This is almost exactly what he said: "Tell Frank James from me to go on a farm and go immediately to work. Tell him to keep away from every sort of display, like that Moberly business. Tell him to keep out of the newspapers. Keep away from fairs and fast horses, and to keep strictly out of sight for a year."

We talked further, and had a great deal of talk which I will not write, but will repeat to you in detail when I see you. Now, Frank, I think you have perfect confidence in my judgment and my knowledge of men, and I here say to you *that under no circumstances in life will Gov. Marmaduke ever surrender you to the Minnesota authorities, even should they demand you, which I am equally well satisfied, will never be done.* Now, you know all. You are as absolutely safe as if you were the Governor himself. Never mind what any alarmists or busy bodies say to you, trust *me*. I tell you that you are a free man, and can never be touched while Marmaduke is Governor.

Governor Marmaduke had commanded, as Colonel, the Confederate troops that co-operated with the forces of Shelby and Quantrill in northwest Arkansas in the winter of 1862–1863. If Ford had defeated him in the contest for the governor's chair in 1884, Frank James's future might have looked different.

Edwards' visit to Governor Marmaduke on Frank James's behalf was to be the last act that his devotion to the former guerrilla required of him, though had there been more that he could have done for Frank James, he would have undertaken it. A little over four years were to elapse before death would rescue Edwards from the torment of his long, losing fight with the bottle; it is not amiss to emphasize the words *torment* and *fight*. He died on May 4, 1889, in Jefferson City, where he was covering the session of the Missouri legislature for the Kansas City *Times*, to which he had returned in 1887. One of his last projects was the preparation of a petition for the release of the Youngers from prison in Minnesota.

His death evoked innumerable tributes. The legislature recessed, and the Missouri Pacific Railroad sent a special car to carry his body to Dover. According to a recent account, "Four hundred visitors flooded that hamlet to pay their last respects to a drunkard, an associate of outlaws, a traitor — and one of the finest gentlemen ever to grace Missouri's soil." [60]

Edwards, the James brothers' tireless champion in the press, was gone.

The surrender and trial of Frank James had not attracted as much attention throughout the country as had the death of Jesse, nor had it evoked as many pungent comments in the East about civilization — or the lack of it — in Missouri. But there were some expressions of the same contemptuous attitude toward the state.[61] Crittenden's alleged friendship for Frank James had not caused the East to change its opinion of the Governor. In the fall of 1885, Missouri's Democratic delegation in Congress recommended Crittenden for an appointment in the diplomatic service. When the Secretary of State failed to approve his nomination, Senators Vest and Cockrell called upon President Cleveland to press Crittenden's claims. The President curtly informed them that he could not consider Crittenden, for in the East the people believed he had "bargained with the Fords for the killing of Jesse James," and whether the basis for this belief was correct or not he could not "shoulder public opinion of the subject." [62]

The lawlessness attributed to the James-Younger band, the death of Jesse James, and the surrender and release of Frank James had lent color to Missouri politics for more than ten years. The force of the issue in Missouri's politics then subsided, but its effect on the growth of the James legend continued.

XIV

Jesse stole from the rich
And he gave to the poor,
He'd a hand and a heart and a brain.

COLLAPSE of the cases against Frank James did not end interest in the James band; even today, anything related, even in the remotest way, to the James story arouses attention. Through this concern old ingredients of the legend are retained and new added — some real, some imagined. These additions have altered very little the basic form that was shaped by the Civil War background, newspaper reports of banditry, conflicts in Missouri politics, and the other influences that played upon the events as they occurred. The crimes account for the notoriety attained by Frank and Jesse James, and the forces that have kept the legend alive are a significant part of the American cultural pattern.

The actors who played the parts and survived have never ceased to excite the popular fancy. This was as true of the Younger brothers as of Frank James. Their humility, penitent spirit, and gratitude for every kindness shown them after their capture remained characteristic of the Youngers through their years of imprisonment. Publicity given to their letters and frequent visits of Missouri friends and journalists kept them always before the public. Cole made astute use of his correspondence to cultivate sympathy. For instance, in a letter to an aunt, which was given to the press, he told how the sight of Fort Sumter, when he had visited Charleston Harbor, had reminded him of his youth. This observation led into a review of his life, in the course of which he commented: "But Sumter mostly interested me, for it was there that the first guns were fired of the dreadful war, that had been the cause of all my troubles — had robbed me of father, brothers, home and friends."[1]

The earliest attempt to obtain a pardon for the three brothers was made by Major Littleton P. Younger, their father's brother. In 1881 he returned to Missouri from Oregon, where he had lived since 1863, and after extensive inquiry among acquaintances of his nephews he went to St. Paul, Minnesota, to appeal to Governor John S. Pillsbury to pardon them. His plea was based on the argument that the circumstances under which the men became criminals extenuated their crimes to the degree that they had been sufficiently punished and should now be pardoned. It was the same sad plaint: The wrongs suffered by their family in war and the continuation of the battle against them by their enemies after Appomattox had driven them into banditry. Major Younger's visit to St. Paul in July and another in October, 1881, were fruitless,[2] but he had sung the refrain that was to be heard repeatedly.

In 1882 Warren Carter Bronaugh, during the war a Confederate soldier and now a prominent farmer of Clinton County, Missouri, visited Minnesota on his wedding trip. He went to view the three Missourians in the prison at Stillwater and to his astonishment recognized Cole Younger as the youthful picket who had, in August, 1862, saved his life by warning him of the presence of a large Federal force. Already sympathetic toward the Youngers, Bronaugh resolved to devote his life and fortune to obtain pardons for them.[3] For twenty years Bronaugh worked to fulfill his vow. The threat of political consequences influenced several governors to refuse pardons, for most Minnesotans believed the Youngers deserved hanging. This did not deter Bronaugh, who, while maintaining the Youngers were victims of circumstances connected with the Civil War, shifted his emphasis to the plea that they had been punished enough and should now be given an opportunity to prove their ability to live as good citizens. But Minnesotans doubted the sincerity of the Youngers' reform as long as they refused to name their accomplices.

Many well-placed Missourians, Minnesotans, and citizens from other parts of the country joined Bronaugh in his cause. Among those who appealed for the pardon of the Youngers were such Missouri leaders as Thomas T. Crittenden, William H. Wallace, George G. Vest, Lon V. Stephens, William J. Stone, Champ Clark, and William Warner. Warner, later United States Senator from Missouri, had served as commander-in-chief of the Grand Army of the Republic. Another Missourian, Major Emory S. Foster of St. Louis, with whom John N. Edwards had fought a bloodless duel in 1875 over Civil War issues, wrote the Governor of Minnesota in the Youngers' behalf, and former Governor William R. Marshall of Minnesota, Senator Cushman K. Davis, and Ignatius Donnelly, Minnesota Populist leader, wrote letters recommending pardon.

Senator Stephen B. Elkins of West Virginia, a Republican, also gave his assistance. When Elkins had taught school in Missouri before the war, one of his pupils was Cole Younger. In 1862 members of Quantrill's band arrested Elkins as a spy, but through the intercession of Cole Younger, the suspect's life was spared. This incident lent credence to the claim that many Union soldiers had been saved by this young guerrilla.

Before he died in 1889, John N. Edwards composed a petition for pardon that Bronaugh circulated among the members of the Missouri legislature. The petition set forth ten reasons for a pardon. These emphasized the Youngers' good behavior in prison, argued that the length of time already served was sufficient punishment, and asserted that the reform of the prisoners had been accomplished. The petition also explained that "their downfall and departure from the path of recitude" had resulted from "unfavorable conditions surrounding them during and following the late Civil War" and that "whatever may have been said to the contrary, the men were brave and honorable soldiers in battle, and merciful in victory." Almost every member of the Missouri legislature signed the petition, which asked that "in the spirit of Christian charity and mercy" these men be permitted to return to friends and relatives to spend their remaining years.[4] The petition did not convince the Governor of Minnesota, however, that he should pardon the Northfield robbers.

By this time Bob Younger was ill with tuberculosis. Appeals in the closing weeks of his life that he be released to die in freedom were unavailing, and on September 16, 1889, he died in prison. His body was returned to Missouri and interred at Lee's Summit.

The years went by, and in June, 1901, the Minnesota legislature passed the Deming Act, which granted the board of managers of the Minnesota state prison power to parole inmates with the approval of the governor and the chief justice of the state supreme court. On July 10, 1901, under provisions of the Deming Act, Jim and Cole Younger were granted paroles. Their paroles restored no legal rights and forbade their leaving the state of Minnesota. The released men found employment selling monuments for the P. N. Peterson Granite Company, but soon turned to other work.

Legal encumbrances due to their status as parolees made adjustment difficult for them. Jim had fallen in love with Alice J. Miller, a professional writer, but since efforts to obtain a pardon in 1902 failed, there was no legal way for them to marry. Jim became despondent and ended his life with a revolver. Throughout the years of imprisonment Jim had been able to take only liquid nourishment; he had lost most of his jaw as the result of a wound received at Northfield. His body, pitiably wasted, was returned to Missouri soil.[5]

The suicide of Jim Younger was soon followed by the granting of a full pardon to Cole, and in February, 1903, he returned to Missouri.[6] Throughout the years of his absence the James-Younger saga had been kept alive by the interest of people over the whole country in the events connected with the prison life of the captured bandits.[7] It may be assumed that the sympathy for the Youngers and the widespread acceptance of the explanation that they were driven to banditry extended to the Jameses as well.

From his final release in February, 1885, until his death in 1915, Frank James's conduct evidenced complete reform and won for him the friendship of many people. The effect of this change is difficult to estimate, but it surely did much to ameliorate the James band's reputation as robbers and murderers, so common in the 1870's and early 1880's. If James had accumulated money from his lawless career, his mode of living never revealed it. He worked irregularly until near the time of his death as a race starter, or timer, at county fairs and race tracks, but he also held regular jobs. Between 1885 and 1901 these yielded only a modest income. He sold shoes in a store at Nevada, Missouri, and for four years worked for the Mittenthal Clothing Company in Dallas, Texas. Between 1892 and 1894 he tended horses for Shep Williams, an importer of livestock, and lived at Paris, Texas; New Orleans, Louisiana; and Guttenberg, New Jersey. From 1894 to 1901 he was a doorman at Ed Butler's Standard Theatre, a burlesque house, in St. Louis, and he dropped the timer's flag at the Fair Grounds race track in racing season.[8]

During these years James declined offers for theatrical and circus appearances, for he had promised John F. Philips and Charles P. Johnson he would not exhibit himself in shows, but in 1901 he suffered a disappointment that turned him to the stage. It seems that some Democratic members of the Missouri legislature encouraged him to seek the position of doorkeeper of the lower house, and in the Democratic caucus he received 15 votes. However, the leaders who had encouraged him to apply decided that his selection would be too great a political liability for them to shoulder. Frank had hoped for the place seriously, for to him it would indicate that his conduct since surrender had vindicated him of the charges of other years.[9] The thwarting of this avenue to vindication was a factor in Frank's decision to accept offers for stage appearances. Surely he had kept his promise as long as those to whom he made it could expect. He would take no part in blood-and-thunder dramas; the roles he played were minor ones in traveling stock-company plays — apparently only two, "The Fatal Scar" and "Across the Desert." He was with these companies at intervals until 1905.[10]

In 1903 Frank joined Cole Younger in a tour of several months with the James-Younger Wild West Show. The terms of Cole's pardon did not permit him to perform in the show, but he sat in the reserved seat section and talked with those around him; after the performances he held impromptu receptions. Frank rode in the grand finale and was a passenger in a stagecoach that was robbed. The show started from Chicago in the spring and, after a tour of Illinois and a swing into the South, ended the season in Missouri.[11] When the James-Younger show visited Columbia, the *Missouri Herald* ran a long article reporting an interview with Frank James. It reviewed with some inaccuracies the careers of Frank and Cole and concluded with this statement:

This much can be said of the Youngers and the Jameses: They were not original crooks or outlaws. They were the product of the most vicious and terrible warfare of which history tells. For four years they were in constant carnival of blood and devastation. It was enough to turn men into demons. At the close of the war they found themselves outlawed. They kept on in the life they had led, justifying themselves on the ground that they were still in the enemy's country. Their crimes can not be excused, but they can be forgotten, now that they have been pardoned under the law, and can and should be covered with that Christian charity which hides a multitude of sins.[12]

Such an attitude was almost universal by this time.

The failure of Missouri Democrats to make him a doorkeeper of the legislature weakened Frank James's loyalty to his party. His disappointment, combined with admiration for Theodore Roosevelt, whom he considered a fighting man like himself, caused him to vote Republican in the presidential election of 1904. But he used poor judgment in selecting the place to announce his intention — a reunion of Quantrill's guerrillas at Independence. His announcement ruined the meeting, and he was lucky to escape without a fight. And there was a bit of paradox in the way the Republicans in Missouri welcomed his support.[13]

After 1901, Frank maintained his residence on the old James farm, except for the years 1907 to 1911, when he lived on a small farm near Fletcher, Oklahoma, which he bought and stocked. He died at the old home place on February 18, 1915;[14] his wife Annie continued to live in self-imposed seclusion on the Missouri farm until her death on July 6,

1944. In accordance with the wish of Frank James, who feared his body would be stolen from the grave, his ashes, which had been kept in a bank vault from the time of his passing, and hers were interred together in a Kansas City cemetery.[15]

Cole Younger lived at Lee's Summit, Missouri, until his death on March 21, 1916. At times he earned a livelihood on the lecture platform, speaking on the general theme, "Crime does not pay." In one series his subject was "What Life Has Taught Me." [16]

Through frugal living and aid from relatives, Jesse James's wife managed to give her two children Jesse Edwards and Mary the necessities of life. From his early teens "Young Jesse" worked to help maintain the family. They lived in Kansas City and Harlem (North Kansas City) until Mrs. James's death in 1900. The Crittenden family befriended them and helped Jesse find employment when he needed assistance.

"Young Jesse" was once accused, tried, and acquitted of train robbery. The holdup occurred on the Missouri Pacific Railroad at Leeds, near Kansas City, on the night of September 23, 1898. A few weeks later Jesse was arrested, and in February, 1899, he was tried in criminal court in Kansas City. Among his lawyers was Finis C. Farr, private secretary to Governor Crittenden at the time the James band broke up. The prosecuting attorney in the case, James A. Reed, later attained prominence as United States Senator from Missouri. Afterward, "Young Jesse" became a practicing attorney in Kansas City. The last years of his life were spent in California, where he died on March 27, 1951.[17]

Interest in the places connected with the lives of Frank and Jesse James has been no less significant in keeping the legend alive than the interest in the doings of the Youngers and the Jameses. In dozens of communities in Missouri the residents can and do tell of the relation of Jesse James or the James band to the community's past. Jesse may have slept at a farmhouse in the neighborhood, used a cave for a hideout or for storing his loot, befriended an unfortunate person, or have been suspected of a local robbery. These stories are dear to those who tell them. Other states, as well as Missouri, have their Jesse James locales at which they erect historical markers, and communities in Missouri and elsewhere commemorate his crimes with celebrations. The two places at which thousands have paid homage to the memory of Jesse James as at shrines are the house at St. Joseph in which he lived and was killed and the old James farm in Clay County, near Kearney.

Except for intervals when interest lagged, the house at St. Joseph has been open to the public for a small admission charge. The interest immediately after the killing has been noted. By 1884, it was reported, the list of registrants at the house included Jay Gould, Emma Abbott,

Eugene Field, Fanny Davenport, Governor Crittenden, and Senators Cockrell and Vest.[18] A time came, however, when townsmen of St. Joseph forgot their pride in Jesse's residence among them, and the commercial possibilities of the house were not exploited. Through default of taxes, it once became the property of the city, but in 1938 an enterprising businessman bought it and moved it from 1318 Lafayette Street to a more accessible location, at the edge of the city on U. S. Highway 71. Equipped with furniture and relics of Jesse's day, it is now operated by the Jesse James Enterprises, and hundreds of paying visitors go through it each year.[19]

Mrs. Samuel very early recognized the financial possibilities of making her farm a show place for the curious. Fearing grave robbers, she had Jesse's body buried in her own yard where she could keep the grave under surveillance. The grave, pictures, and family heirlooms were her main showpieces. The date at which she began charging an admission fee is not known, but by October, 1883, each visitor to the site paid twenty-five cents. Dr. Samuel reported at that time that enough flower seed to sow the whole farm in flowers had been sent to his wife by people in various states with the request that it be planted on the grave of her departed son.

Mrs. Samuel gave her customers their money's worth. She wept, told of the persecution of her sons, cursed detectives, and condemned the Ford boys to hell, and to the souvenir hunters she sold pebbles from Jesse's grave at a quarter each. According to common report the supply was frequently replenished from a nearby creek bed.

The farm continues to attract visitors. Located less than fifteen miles from Excelsior Springs, a widely known health resort, it is one of the resort city's major points of interest. No record of the number of visitors has been kept, but an estimate in 1910 placed the number who had visited it in the preceding ten years at 25,000.[20]

In 1902 Mrs. Samuel had Jesse's body removed from the grave in her yard and interred in the cemetery at Kearney. She wanted his grave near the place where she and other members of the family would be buried.[21] The marble shaft, over eight feet high, which had marked his resting place in the yard, was moved to the cemetery in Kearney. By the mid-1930's it was gone, carried away gradually by morbid curiosity-seekers from all over the country who had chipped off slivers until nothing was left.[22]

The interest that attaches to the places of importance in the James history is reflected also in the continuing flow of news stories and feature articles in newspapers and magazines. A compilation of these would fill many volumes. Their nature is indicated from the headings of a few of the innumerable clippings on the Jameses in the morgue of the Kansas City *Star*: "Jesse James bootmaker dies," "Frank Brooks recalls James boys," "Fought the James gang," "How a woman's pretty face caused the death of Jesse James," "She fed Jesse James," "Jesse James blacksmith dies," "He sat on Jesse James," and "He held Jesse James' horse." And they go on, seemingly without end. Only a slight prompting serves to bring forth these stories: the anniversary of an act of banditry, a happening in the life of a James or a Younger, a new James movie, an historical celebration, or simply the writer's need to produce a story. Most of these tales contribute no new knowledge, but occasional reminiscences of older men and women have cast new light on old events.[23]

Fantasy creates some of the tales. In 1939 it was claimed that there has long been a legend in the Devils Nest country of northern Nebraska that in 1869 Frank and Jesse James came to that area and established a trading post among the Indians. There, under the names of Frank and Jesse Chase, they met and married two beautiful Indian sisters, the daughters of Thomas Wabasha. In 1870 Jesse's Indian wife bore him a son, named Joe Jesse Chase, and Frank became the father of a daughter, Emma. On July 4, 1870, Frank and Jesse had a dispute with a French trader, killed him, and left for parts unknown. They wrote their wives, but the women's mother would not let them reply. Jesse's wife later married William Good Teacher, and Frank's wife went to Minnesota and was never heard of again. Emma and Joe Jesse were reared as brother and sister in the Good Teacher home. In 1939 Joe Jesse Chase told the story as he had heard it from his mother.[24]

Today, enthusiasts of the James history in Jackson and Clay counties of Missouri, who will not permit the use of their names, relate many tales of illegitimate offspring of Frank and Jesse James. On the other hand, legend has characterized the brothers as men of loving devotion to their wives and families.[25] Very few statements in conflict with this part of the legend that bear the semblance of credibility and are contemporary with the acts of banditry have been found. This lack does not, of course, rule out the possibility that others may be uncovered. For instance, one of the bits of evidence that Jesse was with the Youngers at Northfield was the statement made to a reporter for the St. Paul *Pioneer-Press* by the keeper of a "notorious house," who was known as Mollie Ellsworth, to the effect that Jesse James was one of three Northfield robbers who visited her brothel a few nights before the attempted robbery. She said she had known Jesse in St. Louis where, several years before, he had had a woman named Hattie Floyd.[26]

On April 11, 1882, the Kansas City *Times* published a long article on

Jesse, over the initials "H. C.," which characterized Jesse as "one of the most remarkable men that ever lived." He was brutal, and he never knew fear; his good actions in life were few:

There was nothing chivalrous in Jesse's nature. He lived for himself alone. Devoid of education, he had managed to become thoroughly posted on the affairs of the day. Licentious and cruel, yet there was something in his nature that led him to respect good women, and form liaisons with hundreds of others who were not pure. A natural child of his, a girl about 16 years of age, is now living in Howard County, this state. She is the daughter of a fascinating grass widow of Salt Creek bottom. Frank James also has an illegitimate boy, 10 years of age. The boy and his mother is now living in West Kansas. The country is well rid of Jesse, but having saved my life and spared a life for me, I was under eternal obligation to him, and I am glad to say his trust was never betrayed. Dick Little and the Ford boys I do not know, and am not sorry. What I have written may not prove satisfactory, but it is the truth unembellished. Let those deny who can.

The day before the *Times* printed the claims of "H.C." the Louisville *Courier-Journal* had been more specific in defaming Jesse's reputation for sexual morality. After the death of Jesse's aunt Nancy James Hite, her husband George married a seductively beautiful young widow of questionable character, Sarah Norris Peck. The *Courier-Journal* said that she had been in love with Jesse James and that his liaison with her caused disaffection between the Jameses and the Hites.

The Hites brought suit for libel against the *Courier-Journal* for this defamation of Mrs. Hite's character and asked for $25,000. The case was tried in March, 1883, and the testimony given by Governor Crittenden of Missouri helped the *Courier-Journal* to win the case. The Governor swore that George Hite, on a visit to his office in Jefferson City, had told him essentially the same story about Jesse James breaking up his home. Aside from this testimony, no proof of intimacy between Jesse and Mrs. Hite was shown. The bulk of the evidence presented by the *Courier-Journal* was used to show that Mrs. Hite's reputation was so bad that whatever was said about her would do no additional damage.[27]

Reasons for newspapers' and magazines' neglect of stories defiling Frank's and Jesse's reputations as devoted family men are understandable, but the news media have given full presentations of the most extreme expression of the James legend — the claim that Jesse James was not killed at St. Joseph, but that a hoax was perpetrated there. Such a ruse, of course, could hardly have been accomplished without the complicity of numerous persons, including officials of every rank up to the governor, who would keep their lips sealed ever afterward. Only eleven days after the St. Joseph killing, the Liberty *Tribune* commented:

Certain parties still aver that Jesse James is not dead, and intimate that the man killed and buried was not Jesse, but someone inveigled into Jesse's house and killed, to get the reward. Such a conclusion would implicate Mrs. James, Mrs. Samuel, Gov. Crittenden, Sheriff Timberlake, Police Com. Craig and others in a scheme of fraud and perjury. We believe nothing of the kind and have no doubt of Jesse's death.[28]

Scarcely a year had passed, however, before a Clay County farmer was reported to have seen Jesse James.[29]

The identification of the man who was shot in the Jameses' front room was positive enough to leave little doubt that the body buried in Mrs. Samuel's yard was Jesse James's. But numerous claimants have said, since, that they were Jesse. Nor are the pretenders limited to impersonation of Jesse. Even while Frank James was living, a berry picker in Washington "revealed" that he was Frank James.[30] Then there was the man who lived as Joe Vaughan in Wayton County, Arkansas. Vaughan died on February 26, 1925, and in the fall of 1926, Sarah E. Snow, who said she was a daughter of Frank James, alias Joe Vaughan, published what was allegedly a manuscript left by her father, telling the story of his life and setting forth his claims to being Frank James.[31] Burton Rascoe called the book "maudlin, illiterate, vague, confused, pathetic." [32] It is all of that.

Too many people knew Frank James from the time of his surrender to his death for these claims of pretenders to gain credence, but some claimants to the honor of being the notorious Jesse have obtained serious hearings, and persons with mysterious pasts have been credited posthumously with being Jesse James. An instance of this kind is the man who suddenly appeared in Brownwood, Texas, in the 1880's and, as a banker, lived respectably and prosperously under the name Henry Ford until thirty years after the killing of Jesse in St. Joseph.[33]

Another example of posthumous claim was that of a recluse who lived for over thirty years in the mountains near Wetmore, Colorado, under the name James Sears. Shortly after his death on July 2, 1931, it was made known that he had revealed to a friend, William White, that he was really Jesse James. The old fellow's reticence had aroused much curiosity during his lifetime. He had often asked people what they thought about Jesse James, and he was always pleased when the person he questioned defended the outlaw. Sears described the killing at St. Joseph as a hoax perpetrated to give Jesse an opportunity to escape punishment for the charges against him. He said the dead man at

St. Joseph was a member of the band who had died of typhoid fever and was then shot to give the impression that Bob Ford had murdered him. The physical characteristics of Jim Sears were enough like those of Jesse James to convince some Coloradans that his story was true.[34]

Soon after Jim Sears's claim made news another Jesse appeared upon the scene. If any honors were to crown Jesse James, this claimant intended to enjoy them, and he chose Excelsior Springs, Missouri, as the place to press his claims in January, 1932. Prominent citizens there attached enough likelihood to his story to cause the mayor, the chief of police, and three others to accompany him to Jefferson City, where he appeared before Governor Henry S. Caulfield and asked a pardon for all the crimes charged against him. The Governor refused.

This claimant, who did indeed resemble the real Jesse, was a parolee from the penitentiary at Menard, Illinois, where he had been serving a sentence for fatal assault on a man. He frequented Clay County for more than a year, posing as William Jesse James and representing himself to be a cousin of Frank and Jesse. He, too, described Jesse's death as a hoax carried out by Frank James, Bob Ford, and himself. His first story was that the body, resembling Jesse in physique and with similar scars, was obtained in a St. Louis morgue and hauled to St. Joseph in a covered wagon. Later, he modified his story to identify the body as that of another outlaw, Charles Bigelow, whom he (Jesse) had killed because Bigelow was committing crimes in Jesse's name.

The old man received nationwide attention. Citizens of Excelsior Springs checked his assertions and found many flaws in them, but in a most uncanny way he could recall, in conversations with older residents of Clay County, incidents that they believed only Jesse could have remembered. Opinion was divided as to the truth of "Jesse's" identity, but some believed him. His claims aroused the James family to the extent that the wife of Jesse Edwards James came from California to protest. She was able to embarrass him to the extent that most people around Excelsior Springs were convinced that he was a fake. One of Mrs. James's identifying devices was to show the old man one of Jesse's boots, size 6½, and ask him to try it on. Unlike Cinderella's slipper, it proved to be much too small for him.[35]

The old man was picked up by an enterprising showman and exhibited through the Southwest as the real Jesse James. In 1937 he was an attraction with Russell Brothers' circus and apparently exhibited himself on his own after that. He died in a hospital for the mentally ill at Little Rock, Arkansas, in December, 1947.[36]

The number of men who have claimed to be Jesse James is not definitely known. "Young Jesse" James once said he knew of twenty-six. Others have appeared since the younger Jesse summed them up, but surely the last has been heard. This latest and certainly last claimant was "discovered" by two newsmen at Lawton, Oklahoma, in May, 1948.[37] Until his death three years later, he was on exhibit at far-scattered points throughout the land. He had lived long under the name of J. Frank Dalton, and although his story was full of holes and sublimely ridiculous claims, there were those who would exploit him and the credulous and curious people with which the world abounds, so he went the rounds of the side shows.

All the attention paid to the living Jameses and Youngers after 1885, to places of their abode, to news and feature stories about them, and to these pretenders indicates less the significance of the James legend than the firm embedding of the Robin Hood tradition in American folklore. Robin Hood — the young man of good family and upright principles who risked an outlaw's fate in order to rob the exploitive rich and give to the deserving poor — is a figure that satisfies the discontented and fulfills the dreams of the disadvantaged, the poor, the adventure-hungry, the victims of vaguely understood injustices. The Jameses and Youngers, as interpreted by friends so determinedly biased as John Edwards and exploited by quick-return publishers, became native Robin Hoods and thus satisfied deep-seated needs in Americans of different age groups. To add to their appeal, these dashing figures were Americans of the familiar Midwest, contemporary — or nearly so — with their admirers.

Perhaps the apogee of the Robin Hood view is the crediting of Jesse James with the original widow's mortgage episode so often told of outlaws. It has many versions, but the essentials are these:

Jesse and his band have just made a haul — perhaps from a train, perhaps from a bank. They stop at the farm home of a widow and ask for a meal. Sometimes the widow is a young and attractive mother; often she is older; frequently she is the wife of a former Confederate comrade-in-arms. There is little food in the house, but she provides the visitors with the best she has. As Jesse is paying for the meal he sees tears on the widow's cheeks; inquiry reveals that a mortgage on her home and farm is to be foreclosed that afternoon by the banker of a nearby town. She has no money to meet the payment and no place to go after the inevitable foreclosure. The amount owed varies with the versions from three hundred to three thousand dollars. Whatever the sum, Jesse provides it, and the weeping widow, reluctantly accepting the money, is warned to recover the note and mortgage when she makes payment. The men depart.

In a few hours the pompous banker drives up, alights, and walks toward the door, greedily viewing the property that soon will be his. But to his astonishment, the money is ready for him, and he has no choice but to release the mortgage. This he does, and he starts the return trip to town a bit bewildered. As he jogs along in his buggy a mile or two away from the farm, Jesse suddenly steps from behind a tree and at gun point robs him of the money, plus his watch and chain for the trouble. The Robin Hood pattern has been fulfilled to perfection: A poor woman's property has been rescued from the clutches of the rich banker, with money stolen from a rich corporation — railroad company or bank — and the money recaptured for use in further illegal acts of justice.

Robertus Love, widely known St. Louis newspaperman, repeated this story in the mid-1920's and said, "I believe [it] most implicitly," adding, "I for one shall continue to applaud his achievement. . . . There was pathos in it, there was chivalric sentiment, there was simple human tenderness . . . and there was humor." [38] Mawkish though Love's appraisal is, he spoke for the multitude. The incident may have occurred, but certainly not repeatedly in all the locales attributed to it in Missouri, Tennessee, Arkansas, and elsewhere.[39] Yet not many years ago, one had only to mention Jesse James in rural Missouri for a native to begin a story with some phrase like, "My grandpa told me," "Back when I was a boy," "My grandma knew a man who," or "Over in Dry Creek holler." The tale would inevitably end with Jesse relieving the Shylock of the widow's mortgage money.

Most basic in the Robin Hood tradition is the hero's robbing the rich to give to the poor. The widow's mortgage story or some tale closely similar is as old as that of Robin Hood. As applied to Jesse James it is nebulous. The same is true of the stories about his gifts to the poor. In all the voluminous material that pertains to Jesse James and the James band, evidence of specific acts of generosity toward the poor, even with funds stolen from the vaults of banks and safes of express cars, is practically nonexistent, yet the impression that Jesse James robbed the rich and gave to the poor lives on.[40] Evidently, the band in its travels did often avail itself of the hospitality that characterized rural living, and its members usually compensated their hosts at least adequately. The gang made such stops, it is known, in their retreat from Gads Hill. Their liberality during this particular flight after a crime was of some importance no doubt in the growth of their reputation for generosity to the poor.

Although there is little evidence that Jesse was any more the leader of the band than Frank, except in the robberies by the reorganized band starting in 1879, Jesse has become the central figure in the legend. His alliterative name undoubtedly is partly responsible for his prominence in the annals of banditry. The fact that he was killed through treachery in his own band at the peak of his career, after the officers of the law had failed for fifteen years to apprehend him, contributed to his fame. Thus, the circumstance and the time of his death added stature to his reputation in the reverse world of crime. In the same view, Frank's quiet and peaceable life after his surrender damaged the halo that surrounded his head in his years as a bandit. Jesse escaped that decline of reputation, and it is he who holds permanent eminence in American folklore as The American Bandit.

Jesse James is indeed The American Bandit. No better evidence of this is needed than the importance of ballads about Jesse James in American folk songs. The list of regional and general collections in which they appear is long. Their authorship, like that of many ballads, is unknown. The ballad that seems to be the original from which most of the other versions have sprung is characterized by the refrain, "That dirty little coward that shot Mr. Howard/Has laid poor Jesse in his grave." No printed copies that can be dated before 1900 have been found, but evidently the ballad appeared soon after Jesse's death.[41] Vance Randolph, famed folklore authority, found six versions of the Jesse James ballad in the Arkansas and Missouri Ozarks, and one of these was sung to two tunes.[42]

The following version contains the most common stanzas of the many variations:

> Jesse James was a lad who killed many a man.
> He robbed the Glendale train.
> He stole from the rich and he gave to the poor,
> He'd a hand and a heart and a brain.
>
> *Chorus*:
> Jesse had a wife to mourn for his life,
> Three children, they were brave,
> But that dirty little coward that shot Mister Howard,
> Has laid Jesse James in his grave.
>
> It was Robert Ford, that dirty little coward,
> I wonder how he does feel,
> For he ate of Jesse's bread and he slept in Jesse's bed,
> Then he laid Jesse James in his grave.
>
> Jesse was a man, a friend to the poor.
> He'd never see a man suffer pain,
> And with his brother Frank he robbed the Chicago bank,
> And stopped the Glendale train.

It was on a Wednesday night, the moon was shining bright,
He stopped the Glendale train,
And the people all did say for many miles away,
It was robbed by Frank and Jesse James.

It was on a Saturday night, Jesse was at home,
Talking to his family brave,
Robert Ford came along like a thief in the night,
And laid Jesse James in his grave.

The people held their breath when they heard of Jesse's death,
And wondered how he ever came to die,
It was one of the gang called little Robert Ford,
That shot Jesse James on the sly.

Jesse went to his rest with his hand on his breast,
The devil will be upon his knee,
He was born one day in the county of Shea [43]
And he came from a solitary race.

This song was made by Billy Gashade,
As soon as the news did arrive,
He said there was no man with the law in his hand
Could take Jesse James when alive.[44]

H. M. Belden reported another song, not found by Randolph, which varies from the commonly accepted version.[45] Its first stanza is of interest:

Jesse James was one of his names,
Another it was Howard.
He robbed the rich of every stitch.
You bet, he was no coward.

The ballad continues by telling the story of the killing of Jesse and concludes with the fate of Bob Ford:

And then one day, the papers say,
Bob Ford got his rewarding:
A cowboy drunk his heart did plunk.
As you do you'll get according.

The widespread popularity of the ballads about Jesse James in American folk music has played a dual role in the James legend. It is both a result of and a factor in creating the figure of Jesse James as a modern Robin Hood.

All of America's media of entertainment have played, and continue to play, important roles in keeping alive the legend of Jesse James, with its many facets. The legend has been the subject of radio and television productions, but until September of 1965, when the ABC television network began weekly showings of a Jesse James series, neither of these media had exploited its possibilities as fully as have theatrical productions and the motion-picture industry. Both the latter have been influential in maintaining the Robin Hood features of the legend, even though the filmed versions have often distorted or completely misrepresented the facts.

Dramatizations of events in the life of Jesse James and of incidents pertaining to members of his band, including the Fords, date from immediately after the day Bob Ford shot Jesse. They continued to be stand-bys for traveling stock companies until competition from motion pictures and other factors brought the decline of such groups. In the week of Jesse's death a producer in New York announced he was preparing to stage a drama by J. J. McCloskey, *Jesse James, the Bandit King*. The announcement promised that the play would be "a sensational romance, founded upon the lives of the noted James boys, picturing their most daring exploits, and introducing the equine paradox, Nero and Bottle, the most educated horses in the country!" [46]

In May, 1883, Charles W. Chase's Mammoth James Boys' Combination appeared at Mosby's Grand Opera House in Richmond, Missouri. It advertised the following scenes:

> The Hanging of Dr. Samuels
> The Great Horse Racing Scene
> The Gains Place Stage Robbery
> The Wonderful Shell Explosion
> The Tragic End of Jesse James, shot by the Ford Boys, and the Surrender of Frank James [47]

A local newspaper reported that the cast played to a full house and that, while the show was a good representation of some of the band's acts of lawlessness and illustrated well how they defied the law with impunity, some of the audience were displeased with it. The negative reaction, the paper suggested, was to be expected so near to the James boys' home. [48]

A Jesse James troupe favored Tootle's Opera House in St. Joseph with a two-night engagement in November of 1883. The attraction featured a pair of horses that the company advertised as having belonged to Jesse. One, Roan Charger, was identified by a local man as a horse found in the outlaw's stable at the time of the assassination. The claim for the other, Bay Raider, was believed fraudulent. [49]

A play, *The James Boys in Missouri*, was presented for years by a stock company that traveled over the country. Reviews indicate that the plot emphasized the daring and bravery of the Jameses and the treachery of the Fords. Frank James sought a court order to prevent its showing in Kansas City in 1902, on the charge that the play portrayed him and the James family in a role he had been trying to live down for twenty years. In addition, he commented,

The dad-binged play glorifies these outlaws and makes heroes of them. That's the main thing I object to. It's injurious to the youth of the country. It's positively harmful. I am told the Gilliss Theater was packed to the doors last night, and that most of those there were boys and men. What will be the effect upon these young men to see the acts of a train robber and outlaw glorified? [50]

The court granted the injunction, subject to Frank's furnishing a bond of $4,000 to indemnify the company against loss, in case of appeal and reversal of the decision. These terms, Frank said, he could not fulfill without accepting the proffered help of friends, which he would not do. The show went on, but Frank thought the court had vindicated his position.[51] When the company returned to Kansas City with the play a year and a half later, Frank again voiced his disapproval of it. Billboards over the town, on which he was caricatured as a train robber, annoyed him especially, and he said they "humiliated and put [him] to shame." [52]

A critic who saw *The James Boys in Missouri* at the Imperial Theatre in St. Louis in 1907 described it as "packed full and running over with sensational climaxes [that] almost telescope one another," and, he said, "This drama affords to theater goers a fine opportunity to observe melodrama in its most primitive and not unattractive conditions." [53] In 1911, with the play again drawing large audiences in St. Louis, a reviewer called it "a real thriller which never fails to thrill." [54]

When *Missouri Legend* by Elizabeth Beall Ginty opened at the Empire Theatre in New York on September 19, 1938, Jesse James had come to Broadway. Into a time-span of two weeks preceding the death of Jesse and one day following, the author worked nearly all the ingredients of the Robin Hood tradition, including the widow's mortgage story. The portrayal of the hero as a man of strict morals and religious conviction, who is offended when a banker doubts his word, is so overdone that the intended comedy becomes a farce. The Broadway cast included Dorothy Gish, Mildred Natwick, José Ferrer, and Dean Jagger.[55] The run was moderately successful, and the play became a vehicle for amateur companies over the country.

It was to be expected that the James legend would provide themes for motion pictures as they developed, and by an interesting coincidence the first motion picture with a story line to be produced in the United States was entitled *The Great Train Robbery*, although it had nothing to do with the Jameses.

The first motion picture about Jesse James was produced by a company formed in 1920 for that purpose. Members of the James family were stockholders, as were several Kansas City businessmen. The filming was done in Jackson, Clay, and Clinton counties, with many local people playing parts; Jesse Edwards James starred in the role of his father. The premier showing of this production, *Under the Black Flag*, took place in March of 1921 at Plattsburg, Missouri. It pictured a young man from the East as having fallen in love with the granddaughter of Jesse James. To help the suitor decide whether her family was acceptable, the girl's father had him read an account of the career of Jesse James which, of course, was enacted on the screen. The story stressed the persecution that drove the young Jesse into guerrilla warfare and prevented his settling down after the war. The picture attracted considerable attention in western Missouri, but it was a financial failure.[56]

Since this beginning, no less than a score of motion pictures have been built around members of the James band. Frank and Jesse James are, as a reviewer of one of the films said, "among the most photographed characters of our folklore." In 1927 Paramount Pictures produced *Jesse James*, starring Fred Thompson and his famous horse, Silver King, with Jesse Edwards James — usually called Jesse James, Jr. — as technical adviser. Jesse was presented as a modern Robin Hood, and the company's advertising built up both Jesse and Thompson as Robin Hoods.[57]

Coincidental with Paramount's emphasis on Jesse's Robin Hood qualities, John H. Newman, a Kansas City lawyer, announced a movement among friends of the James family to erect a monument in Jesse's honor.[58] The wide publicity given Newman's proposal elicited comment pro and con. In the opinion of one writer, "The crimes with which he was charged, even if all true, are pale in comparison with those which society and posterity committed against him," [59] but another protested against "any such disgraceful and morbid proceeding as building a monument to the train robber, Jesse James." [60]

The widespread controversy over the monument [61] provided good publicity for Paramount's production, which, according to the Kansas City *Star*, "embellishes James with Robin Hood attributes — qualities that make a monument to him logical." The *Star* also ascribed to Thompson the statement that Jesse "was a strong, fearless man, without the trace of a mean trait. By the injustices that he suffered at the hands of his fellowmen he was driven from his hearth and home to become a hunted object outside the law — a hunted animal forced to prey upon others for his daily bread." Thompson stated that after the making of the picture was announced, his mail was flooded with letters from those who still cherished Jesse's memory for the kind deeds he had performed. When Jesse committed a robbery, Thompson commented, "It was always the bullion hoarded by some carpet-bagger that he and his boys were after. Never did they rob the poor and needy." [62]

The next motion picture about Jesse James did the Robin Hood tradition no harm. It, too, was titled *Jesse James* and was the most elaborate of all the pictures based on the James band's deeds. Filmed at Pineville, Missouri, by Twentieth Century-Fox in the summer of 1938 and released in January, 1939, its cast included Tyrone Power as Jesse James, Henry Fonda as Frank James, and Nancy Kelly as Jesse's wife Zee. The screenplay, written by Nunnally Johnson, resembled only slightly the real career of Jesse James. Supposedly, the killing of their mother by a bomb thrown into her house by representatives of the St. Louis-Midland Railroad who wanted to purchase her farm for a railroad right-of-way at two dollars per acre drove Frank and Jesse to robbing trains. Jesse's wooing of his wife, their separation which plunged him into robbing banks, their reconciliation, and the killing of Jesse by Bob Ford formed the core of the story. The widow's mortgage incident and the Northfield robbery were included, and a friendly newspaper editor was one of the characters. Excitement was added by Jesse's riding his horse through the glass window of a store and Frank's jumping his horse from a cliff into a river.[63] The huge box-office returns resulted in Twentieth Century-Fox's production of a sequel, *The Return of Frank James*. Almost entirely fictitious, it cast Frank James in the role of an avenger after the death of Jesse which, of course, was not true.[64]

More publicity attended the making and release, in February, 1957, of *The True Story of Jesse James* than of any other Jesse James movie since the one made at Pineville, Missouri, in 1938. The picture, starring Robert Wagner as Jesse James, was another Twentieth Century-Fox release, based again on a screen play by Nunnally Johnson, although the story was written by Walter Newman. This time Yankee injustice and persecutions, instead of a railroad's greed for land, set the Missourians on their career of crime, and many of the real events of the James history were worked into the script, even though at times considerably distorted. The story of the picture was also set forth in a Dell Movie Classic comic book that was widely available to readers of comic books.[65]

None of Hollywood's productions tarnished Jesse's reputation for boldness and daring. In the 1954 United Artists release, *Jesse James' Women*, however, four loose women vied for his favors, and in the film he became a most unsavory character despite his propensity for giving money away recklessly to worthy persons.[66] Inevitably, the film versions of banditry precipitated discussion of the question of whether Jesse James was a ruthless scoundrel by deliberate choice or a fine, brave young man driven by circumstance and injustice into a career of crime. The makers of motion pictures preferred the latter view, no doubt believing it promised richer box-office returns, regardless of which way lay truth. After all, their purpose was to entertain, but in giving the public what it wants, they have perpetuated the Robin Hood tradition of Jesse James.

This song was made
By Billy Gashade
As soon as the news did arrive.

T︎HE JAMES LEGEND took form early in books that were published while the outlaws still roved the Midwest. The first book dealing entirely with members of the James-Younger band came from the press in 1875. It is Augustus C. Appler's *The Guerrillas of the West; or the Life, Character, and Daring Exploits of the Younger Brothers.* Appler, editor of the Osceola, Missouri, *Democrat*, was, like John N. Edwards, a strong believer in the Confederate cause, and, as noted earlier, he had denied the guilt of the Youngers. He lived among their friends in St. Clair County, and his book, on the whole, was a defense of the Youngers, although he disavowed any intention of turning public opinion in their favor.

Appler's poorly organized and badly written account presents the traditional picture of the background and Civil War experiences of the Younger family. More than half the pages deal with Cole's war career; if only partially true, he was indeed a desperate character. Included is the story of Cole's testing his Enfield rifle on fifteen Jayhawkers, very much as Edwards had told it. Many times this story was to be repeated with flourishes and presented in color drawings on the cover of paperback books on the outlaws as the most characteristic illustration of this man Cole Younger.

Appler provided the reasons, as Edwards had done for the Jameses, for the Youngers' inability to settle down at home after the war. Cole had spent the time from the end of the war until the fall of 1866 in

Mexico and California. Upon his return to his mother's farm in Jackson County he worked at making rails to replace the fences destroyed during the war. John and Robert were at home when he arrived, and James returned shortly afterward from Kentucky, where he had gone with Quantrill. All the boys worked on the farm, but by the summer of 1866 the threats and activities of the "Vigilant Committees" organized by former Missouri militiamen and Kansas Jayhawkers made it unsafe for Cole to remain at home, so he left, going to Louisiana where he spent the summer of 1867. The other three boys continued to cultivate the family farm.

According to Appler, in the fall of 1867 Cole, believing the bitter feeling against him had subsided, came home and built a house for his mother. He "bore no ill-will against anyone." But it was different with his enemies, whose bitter hatred of Quantrill's men caused them to contrive to capture and kill Cole. Twice he narrowly escaped them. He saw that it was impossible for him to live at home in peace, and the other boys were so ill-treated that they, too, were afraid to stay. So Cole, Jim, and John went to Texas, and their mother, who remained in Missouri, died of consumption before they could return for her. Appler named some of the Youngers' alleged oppressors. His account is as specific as any on how Cole Younger was driven from home, and it became the standard version.

Appler's book includes Cole Younger's alibi letter to Lycurgus Jones, the proposed amnesty resolutions, reprints of several newspaper accounts of robberies charged to the James-Younger band, detailed accounts of John's and Jim's fight with the detectives at Monegaw Springs, John Younger's killing of the Texas sheriff, and statements by citizens of St. Clair County that verified some of the alibis offered by Cole. The book is full of implications and "evidence" that the Youngers did not commit the postwar depredations charged to them. Instead, they operated a cattle ranch in Texas that they called their home. They came to Missouri only to drive cattle to market, and then, quite naturally, they visited their friends in St. Clair and Jackson counties. The brothers indulged in but few of the lesser vices; they were often seen attending church.

Certainly, the Youngers' arrest at Northfield should have destroyed many of the book's claims, but it seems that this was not the case. Editions of it were published in 1876, 1878, 1893, and 1955.[1]

It is evident that Appler had access to the writings of Edwards or that both had access to the same sources, for in the matters both discussed there was little variation in their accounts. Edwards, called by one contemporary the "Victor Hugo of the West," had left his newspaper

181

work in St. Louis in 1876 and retired to the home of his father-in-law at Dover in Lafayette County to compose a history of the war on the border.

In March, 1877, Edwards' *Noted Guerrillas, or the Warfare of the Border* came from the press.[2] In the florid English that he favored, Edwards carried out his avowed purpose of giving the bushwhacker a respected place in history. Much of his information must have come from the former guerrillas, his own experience, and published accounts of war incidents, but his fertile imagination, nourished at times with alcohol, created a large portion of the book. The book came to be little less respected than the Bible by many guerrillas and their worshipers, although large portions of it have been shown by competent scholarship to be grossly in error.

Noted Guerrillas was intended to be a general history of guerrilla warfare, but evidently the notoriety that the Jameses and Youngers had achieved and Edwards' desire to solidify sympathy for them among former Confederates caused him to give Frank, Jesse, Cole, and Jim roles far out of proportion to their actual participation. In lurid language he told again of the persecutions that made them and others into desperate bushwhackers whom he presented as the heroic avengers during the war of all wrongs suffered by Confederate sympathizers. In narrating the acts of prowess of the Jameses and Youngers, Edwards stressed their human qualities and "sensitive natures." Even his account of the Lawrence raid emphasizes the acts of mercy and tenderness of Quantrill's men. Typical of Edwards' characterization of his heroes is a tale of Jesse James, who most surely was not at Lawrence, responding to the pleas of a beautiful girl:

Attracted by the boyishness of his face and a look in his blue eyes that seemed so innocent, a young girl came to Jesse James just as he was in the act of shooting a soldier in uniform who had been smoked out of a cellar. His pistol was against the Federal's head when an exceedingly soft and penetrating voice called out to him: "Don't kill him, for my sake. He has eight children who have no mother." James looked and saw a beautiful girl, probably just turned of sixteen, blushing at her boldness and trembling before him. In the presence of so much grace and loveliness he was a disarmed man. He remembered his own happy youth, his sister not older than the girl beside him, his mother who had always instilled into his mind lessons of mercy and charity, and he put away his pistol and spoke to the pleader: "Take him, he is yours. I would not harm a hair in his head for the State of Kansas."[3]

Several of the claims that are significant in the James legend and that made their way into print through the pen of Edwards are repeated in the book. These include ascribing to Jesse James the killing of Major Johnson at Centralia, the tale of Jesse's being shot near Lexington as guerrillas were surrendering at the war's end, the killing of Emmett Goss, plus numerous others. The memoirs of fellow guerrillas, written later, support many of Edwards' claims, but it is possible that reading *Noted Guerrillas* influenced their memories, however unwittingly, to conform to his version of events. The extent of this influence, if any, cannot be determined.

The specific events that allegedly made it impossible for Frank and Jesse James to live peaceably at home after the war were set forth again by Edwards, thus weaving them into the often repeated history of his heroes. These center around Frank's difficulties at Brandenburg, Kentucky, in 1866 and Jesse's fight with the militiamen who called that cold February night. This time Edwards has Jesse kill two of them. Near the conclusion of *Noted Guerrillas* Edwards made this statement:

To the great mass of the Guerrillas the end of the war also brought an end to their armed resistance. As an organization, they never fought again. The most of them kept their weapons; a few had great need to keep them. Some were killed because of the terrible renown won in the four years' war; some were forced to hide themselves in the unknown of the outlying territories; and some were mercilessly persecuted and driven into desperate defiance and resistance because they were human and intrepid. To this latter class the Jameses and Youngers belonged. No men ever strove harder to put the past behind them. . . . No men ever went to work with a heartier good will to keep good faith with society and make themselves amenable to the law. No men ever sacrificed more for peace, and for the bare privilege of going back again into the obscurity of civil life and becoming again a part of the enterprising economy of the commonwealth. They were not permitted so to do, try as they would, and as hard, and as patiently.[4]

The circulation of *Noted Guerrillas* probably was not more than a few thousand copies, but its effectiveness in creating opinion favorable to the former guerrillas was increased by the publication of portions of it in Missouri newspapers before and immediately after the book was issued. The sections selected for such presentation include accounts of the Lawrence raid, the Centralia massacre, and other events in which Frank and Jesse James were given prominent roles. Favorable comment and the continued printing of excerpts indicate they were well received.[5] The Chicago *Times* gave the book a very friendly and detailed review on publication.[6] Edwards, in *Noted Guerrillas*, expressed what many Confederate sympathizers already believed. His continued repetition of the claim that the James and Younger brothers were persecuted men and his connecting their careers so intimately with the Southern cause no doubt drew other partisans of the Confederacy to their defense.

No bank or train robberies were added in 1880 to the James band's list of crimes, but in that year at least three authors wrote "histories" of the band in full-length book form. These books unquestionably helped establish the James legend and sustain it for two or more generations. Evidently, the renewal of banditry at Glendale stimulated enough interest in the bandits to make such volumes profitable.

Early in 1880 W. S. Bryan published in St. Louis the *Life and Adventures of Frank and Jesse James and the Younger Brothers, The Noted Western Outlaws*. Its author was "Hon. J. A. Dacus, Ph.D.," credited on the title page with authorship of other books, including *Battling with the Demon* and *Guide to Success*. Dacus had also been an editorial writer on the St. Louis *Republican* and had served in the Missouri legislature. The publisher stated, in advertising for agents to sell the book, that 21,000 copies were sold in the first four months after publication.[7] This claim for the initial edition should be viewed with caution, but the book's success is a fact, and new editions were issued in both 1881 and 1882 as new happenings warranted additions. Sixteen different printings of these editions, no two of which were exactly alike, were owned in 1961 by one collector of Western Americana. After 1880 the copyrights were held by the N. D. Thompson Company of St. Louis, but other printings show Indianapolis and Cincinnati as places of publication and various companies as publisher. The points of variance are such details as illustrations, binding, number of pages, location of lists of illustrations, publisher, and place of publication.[8]

Dacus soon had a competitor, James William Buel, a Missouri newspaperman with experience on St. Louis and Kansas City papers. Buel took a double-barreled shot at the market with *The Border Outlaws*, described on the title page as "An Authentic and Thrilling History of the Most Noted Bandits of Ancient or Modern Times, The Younger Brothers, Jesse and Frank James, and their Comrades in Crime," and *The Border Bandits*, "An Authentic and Thrilling History of the Noted Outlaws, Jesse and Frank James, and their Bands of Highwaymen." The edition used in preparing this book bears the publication date 1882, and the two works are bound together in one volume. The original preface for both is dated December 15, 1880. On August 19, 1881, the Historical Publishing Company of St. Louis, Buel's publisher, advertised that in six months 65,000 copies of the volume containing both works had been sold at $1.50 each.[9] As did the Dacus work, the Buel books expanded in their later editions or printings as new robberies occurred.[10]

In his preface to *The Border Bandits*, Buel explained the need for a "correct history" of the James brothers:

So many improbable and romantic incidents have been credited to these noted brothers by sensational writers; so many dashing escapades and hair-breadth escapes attributed to them, which they never dreamed of, that thinking people, especially in the East, have begun, almost, to regard the James Boys as a myth, and their deeds as creations of sensational dreamers.

Both Dacus and Buel took their cues from the Jameses' background of guerrilla warfare and the rationale for their lawlessness, based on postwar persecution, which John N. Edwards, Augustus C. Appler, and oral tradition expressed. But whereas Appler and Edwards doubted the Jameses' and Youngers' guilt, the success of the Dacus and Buel books depended upon fully implicating the two sets of brothers in the crimes charged to them. Hence, the books named, without qualification, the participants in almost every robbery, and this practice became a characteristic of nearly every subsequent book on the James band.

The legend as known today attributes to Frank James the cool-headed planning for the band's robberies and to Jesse the qualities necessary for their daring execution. The truth of this assignment of roles would be difficult to determine, but similar beliefs were at times expressed in contemporary newspapers. Buel and writers like him may have merely reported popular belief, but in so doing they helped to make it an important part of the legend. In appraising the differences in his main characters, Buel wrote of Frank:

His cunning and coolness are remarkable, and to compare the two boys in this respect would be like comparing the boldest highwayman with the lowest sneak thief, so great is Frank's superiority. In the matter of education Frank . . . is a student, being a lover of books and familiar with different phases of life. He has murdered many men, and yet he is not destitute of mercy, and finds no gratification in deeds of blood. He has tried to imitate the traditions of Claude Duval, whose fictitious adventures Frank has read until he can repeat them like the written narrative.[11]

In contrast, Buel thus described Jesse:

His education is very limited, barely enabling him to read and write. He is revengeful in his nature, always sanguine, impetuous, almost heedless. It is due to Frank James' strategy and Jesse's desperate bravery that the latter has not long since been punished for his crimes. In deeds of violence Jesse finds especial delight, and in his nature there is not a trace of mercy.[12]

Buel also included the story, repeated still in hushed tones, of Jesse's questioned parentage:

It is asserted, by those who know them best, that Jesse and Frank are only half-brothers, having the same mother, but that Jesse's father is a physician in Clay County. What truth there is in this report the writer does not assume the responsibility of confirming, giving it only as the assertion of many prominent men of Clay County.[13]

At the time the Dacus and Buel books were published, the public had no authentic information on where Frank and Jesse and their families were living, and it is doubtful that these two authors knew. Lack of knowledge did not deter them, however, from filling in the years that had elapsed between the crimes at Northfield and at Glendale with fantastic stories of the Jameses' many dashing adventures in Texas and Mexico. No evidence has been found to confirm these splendid tales, and there is much to indicate that the brothers lived in an entirely different locale. Nevertheless, Dacus' and Buel's statements of their whereabouts continued to be repeated in books for years after the differing truth was known.

Another history of the Jameses and Youngers was "edited" by R. T. Bradley and published in one volume with John N. Edwards' *Noted Guerrillas* in 1880. An 1882 printing brought the story to October, 1881. Bradley's *The Outlaws of the Border or the Lives of Frank and Jesse James* is a sympathetic history of the Jameses and Youngers. He denied their participation in many of the robberies, especially in those where there was wanton bloodshed. The book begins with an eulogy to Frank and Jesse:

> In men whom men condemn as ill
> I find so much of goodness still:
> In men whom men deem half divine
> I find so much of sin and blot: —
> I hesitate to draw the line
> Between the two — where God has not.

Frank and Jesse James, outlaws as they are, and exiles under kindlier suns than their native land afforded them, have illustrated the American virtues of personal bravery and devotion to friends and to principle with such strong lights and with such gloomy shadows that their countrymen are patient with their follies and their faults. Their adventures and exploits when striplings during four years of savage border warfare, were such as brought grave looks and heightened color to the faces of bearded and determined men. Wild injustice roused them to resistance, and when roused they became devils to their enemies. There is nothing to show that they were cruel by nature, but it is not natural to suppose they would relent toward those who showed them no mercy.[14]

Except for its apologetic point of view, Bradley's book is little different from those of Dacus and Buel. Of the three, the Dacus work is far the superior in terms of thoroughness of treatment, literary style, and general attractiveness. All three were bound in hard covers and evidently sold for prices comparable to the $1.50 charged for Buel's book.

The earliest paperback history of the James band was anonymously written and published as No. 2 in the *Police Gazette Library* series of Richard K. Fox's *National Police Gazette of New York*. The Library of Congress copy is a revised edition, published January 13, 1883. The *Police Gazette* advertised No. 2 on September 24, 1881, as "The Most Thrilling Work Yet Published" and commented, "The career of these daring highwaymen, whose cruel murders and many crimes have made the mere mention of their names a terror to law-abiding citizens, is full of romance."

Another category of literature, known generally as the dime novel, also presented the James Story in 1881, apparently for the first time. In that year Frank Tousey's *Five Cent Wide Awake Library* began to publish a few stories about the James band, but the enormous output of dime novels about Jesse James was not to appear until later. It is from these dime novels that at least two generations of American youth obtained their image of Jesse James. Don Russell, well known as the editor of *The Westerners Brand Book*, Chicago, has commented that Buffalo Bill is probably the only actual person who figures as hero in more dime novels than Jesse James.[15] Ralph F. Cummings, former editor of the *Dime Novel Round-Up* and one of the country's best-known collectors and dealers in dime novels, reports that stories about the James brothers were published in the following: *Boys of New York, Golden Weekly, Young Men of America, Wide Awake Library, New York Detective Library, Boys of New York Pocket Library, Morrison's Sensational Series, American Weekly, Jesse James Stories, James Boys Weekly Adventure Series, New York Ledger, Bandit Stories*, and other papers.[16] Another collector and expert on dime novels related to the James band, J. Edward Leithead, has reported finding them in other series, including *Boys of America, Boy's Star Library, Secret Service Series, Bob Brooks Library*, and even in Westbrook's *American Indian Weekly*.[17]

The major publishers of the various series were Frank Tousey and Street & Smith. Tousey was first in the field with his *Five Cent Wide Awake Library*, in 1881. Although considered a weekly, the *Wide Awake Library* was issued irregularly.[18] It is typical of the literature popularly called dime novels in the 1870's, 1880's, and later. Like most "dime" novels in those years, its price was five cents. Each story is complete in an issue, which is printed in black and white, about 8½ x 11½ inches in size, and of varied lengths. Usually, an issue consists of about thirty pages, set in three columns. With very few exceptions, the stories are fiction.[19] While other topics make up the bulk of the *Wide Awake Library* issues, titles of seventeen about the James brothers, all crediting D. W. Stevens as author, were published between No. 440 and No. 550.[20]

Tousey printed some James stories in his *Boys of New York Pocket Library*. Titles of four, all by D. W. Stevens, have been found, and their numbers indicate that they were published in 1882.[21] However, Tousey's *New York Detective Library* published more stories about the Jameses than any other series. Between No. 342, of June, 1889, and No. 771, of September, 1897, 213 issues contain the names of members of the James band in their titles.[22] The series did not end with No. 771, and probably some issues concerned the James band even though the name of James did not appear in the title.

A few titles from the *New York Detective Library* will indicate the nature of the series: No. 364, *The Man From Nowhere, and His Adventures with the James Boys*; No. 428, *The James Boys at Bay*; or, *Sheriff Timberlake's Triumph*; No. 474, *The James Boys in Deadwood*; or *The Game Pair of Dakota*; No. 522, *Jesse James, the Midnight Horseman*; or, *The Silent Rider of the Ozarks*; No. 539, *The James Boys and the Dwarf*; or, *Carl Greene's Midget Detective*; and No. 730, *The James Boys and The Mad Sheriff*; or *The Midnight Run of "99"*.

Many of the later issues of the *New York Detective Library* are reprints of earlier issues, and all seventeen of the James items in the *Wide Awake Library* were used in the *New York Detective Library;* probably the most popular stories were reprinted or rewritten. Three years after termination of the *New York Detective Library*, Tousey reprinted at least 139 of the stories in *The James Boys Weekly* and issued them between 1901 and 1903. These were colored-cover weeklies.[23]

Practically all the Tousey publications on the James band were published under the name of D. W. Stevens, who is identified by authorities on the dime novel as John R. Musick.[24] That a Missourian originated so many fictional accounts of the James brothers is not surprising. Musick was born in St. Louis County, Missouri, in 1849. He graduated from the North Missouri Normal School, First District, at Kirksville in 1874, then studied law and engaged in its practice from 1877 to 1882, when he left it to devote his time fully to writing. In addition to dime novels, he wrote several historical novels and popular works of history.[25]

Tousey's chief competitor in the dime-novel field was the firm of

Street & Smith, which also published stories of the James band. However, Street & Smith was attracted to the subject considerably later than Tousey. Its first dime novels about the James boys are in the *Log Cabin Library*, which was issued weekly, starting in March, 1889. Between No. 4 and No. 344, fifty-nine titles have been found that carry the names of members of the James band. A few of these apparently deal with imitators of the Jameses. The *Log Cabin Library* (Pocket Edition), published in 1897 and 1898, contained at least twenty-two reprints from the original *Log Cabin Library*.[26] Street & Smith published a colored-cover "weekly" between 1901 and 1904, titled *Jesse James Stories* and totaling 138 issues. Many of these were reprints from the *Log Cabin Library*.[27]

Although there were some exceptions, the Street & Smith publications on the James band were published under a stock name, W. B. Lawson, which was used by several writers of dime novels on various subjects. Among those who are believed to have written the James materials published by Street & Smith were Prentiss Ingraham, Edward S. Ellis, Robert Russell, St. George Rathborne, H. P. Halsey, Captain Jake Shackleford, T. W. Hanshew, and Laurana Sheldon.[28] That Street & Smith stories were as fantastic as those published by Tousey is shown by the titles: No. 71, *Jesse James at Coney Island*; or, *The Wall Street Banker's Secret*; No. 74, *Jesse James in New York*; or, *A Plot to Kidnap Jay Gould*; and No. 138, *Jesse James Among the Mormons*, in the *Log Cabin Library*; and No. 58, *Jesse James at the Stake*; or *Doomed to Die by Fire*, in the *Jesse James Stories*.

These publications by Tousey and by Street & Smith represent by far the greater part of the dime-novel issues on the James band, but not the total.[29] The same subject matter has also been available in paper-back pulp books, usually selling for twenty-five cents. Examples of two series of this type may be noted. Between 1907 and 1910, the Arthur Westbrook Company of Cleveland, Ohio, published an Adventure Series containing thirty-six items on the Jameses and one on the Youngers. These credited authorship to William Ward, probably a stock name.[30] I. and M. Ottenheimer of Baltimore included eight titles dealing with the James band in their Bandit Series. The author was a "Capt. Kennedy," and three of the titles were *Jesse James, Man-Hunter*; *Jesse James' Wild Leap*; and *Jesse James' Mysterious Warning*.[31]

The *Log Cabin Library* had a weekly circulation of 25,000 to 30,000 copies.[32] No information on the circulation of the other publications has been found, but it is possible that some of them enjoyed equally high circulation.

A few of the dime novels are little different from the so-called histories of the band; they retell accounts of actual events, but most of them are works of fiction that merely took their cue from real persons and events. These imaginative tales that made Frank and Jesse James more mythical than real helped immeasurably in creating and perpetuating the Jesse James legend. A sampling of representative stories reveals that unusual shooting ability, courage in the face of danger, willingness to aid the unfortunate, deference to women, and ability to surmount all obstacles are common characteristics of the dime-novel James brothers. The theme of their being victims of persecution and injustice gets little attention. The Pinkertons and detectives in general did not fare well at the hands of these writers. Nothing was too mean for Jesse to do to an enemy, particularly a detective. One detective who refused to give Jesse information was tortured to madness by means of two rattlesnakes that were tied to lariats long enough to permit them to get within a few inches of the hapless operative's body.[33] Another story depicts Jesse and Frank as hunting down and finally killing every person involved in the bomb attack on the Samuel home in 1875.[34]

The portrayal of the James brothers by the dime novel is so many-sided that it is difficult to judge its effect on readers. However, in spite of the strange mixture of ingredients that make up the characters of the Frank and Jesse James of the dime novel, this portrayal is not greatly unlike the popular conception of them.

Naturally, the Jameses always triumphed in the end — except when traitorous Bob Ford fired his fateful shot — even if extricated from an improbable set of circumstances by only a sudden and unexpected turn of events in the last few pages. This pattern, in a sense, glorified law-lessness. By agreement Street & Smith and Frank Tousey finally discontinued publication of stories about the James band because they felt this tendency to glorify banditry was bad for business.[35] It is interesting that the famed House of Beadle and Adams carefully avoided the Jameses as subjects for their publications.

While the volume of the ephemeral fictional accounts is astounding, the impact of these so-called histories of the James band upon readers was probably greater. The publishers' increased interest would indicate this stronger effect.[36] The books by Dacus and Buel that were published during the life of their hero have been examined for their part in making Jesse notorious and shaping his public image. These were hurriedly expanded to include an account of his death and were again extended after Frank James's surrender. The *Police Gazette Library* No. 2 was also brought up to date. On April 20, 1882, seventeen days after Jesse's death, the Richmond *Democrat* reported that Dacus' book had been revised to include the events concerning the killing and was already on sale. By May 19 the Richmond *Conservator* had received a complimentary copy of the *Police Gazette's* volume. The *Conservator* called it "an abortive attempt at history writing" and declared that if "St. Jesse could read it he would not be able to recognize himself."

The upsurge of interest in the Jameses and the success of the first histories of their lives soon brought competing books. Jacob Spencer, owner of the St. Joseph *News* at the time of Jesse's death, wrote in 1922 that on the day of the murder he contracted with a printer to publish a book of about 200 pages, titled *The Life and Career of Frank and Jesse James*. His contract called for delivery of the book in less than a week, and it was necessary for him to write at night to supply copy. The book was ready on time, and before the last copy was bound, the entire edition of 5,000 was sold. Spencer thought he could have marketed 500,000 copies.[37] Spencer's statement, although made forty years after the event, represented well the spirit in which the life stories of the James brothers were written, following the assassination. The authors of the new books about the Jameses felt no qualms about plagiarism. Buel's and Dacus' works seem to have been their chief sources of information.

The Coburn & Newman Publishing Company of Chicago issued a 520-page book by Jay Donald, titled *Outlaws of the Border*, which was also published the same year by Douglas Brothers of Philadelphia.[38] In the preface the author proclaimed: "To faithfully portray the lives and characters of the boldest bandits that ever plagued the world; to strip from them the false garbs in which romancers have clothed them; to lay them bare in all their brutality, is the object of this book." The publishers, in a preface of their own, expressed fear that their motives in issuing the book might be misunderstood; they explained that their motive was higher than profits. Having observed the bad influence upon the minds of youth by books that made heroes of the outlaws and showed them "more sinned against than sinning," the publishers had "determined to issue a work that would reveal the true character of these brigands, and show to the youthful mind that an evil course of action is always sure to bring its own reward, and that the glamor of apparent success cannot compensate for the bad results of a vicious career." Despite these protestations, comparison of Donald's volume with that of Dacus indicates that Donald did little more than rewrite the Dacus book, omitting the theme that persecution had driven the Jameses and Youngers into banditry and adding only a few bits of information of his own.

Another volume, in two parts, was published by Belford, Clarke and Company of Chicago and St. Louis. The first part, *Train and Bank Robbers of the West*, is an anonymous account of the lives of the James boys; the second part is a reprint of Appler's book on the Youngers.[39] A third book, *Lives, Adventures and Exploits of Frank and Jesse James with an Account of the Tragic Death of Jesse James, April 3, 1882*, was evidently published soon after Jesse's death, since no mention is made of Frank's surrender, but the place and date of publication and name of publisher are omitted from the title page. The length of this book is only 96 pages, while the first part of the Belford, Clarke and Company work offers 351 pages of information on the James band.

A fourth narrative, by "One who dare not now disclose his identity," was published in both English and German editions by Barclay and Company of Philadelphia. The full title is *Jesse James: the Life and Daring Adventures of this Bold Highwayman and Bank Robber, and His No Less Celebrated Brother, Frank James. Together with the Thrilling Exploits of the Younger Boys.* The claim was made that this was "the only book containing the romantic life of Jesse James and his pretty wife, who clung to him to the last." The book hardly measures up to these claims in its 96 pages. The publication date of the edition in German is 1882, and the copy of the English edition examined gives 1886 as the copyright date.

A fifth post-Jesse addition to the literature of the James band claimed an advantage possessed by none of the others. Frank Triplett's *The Life, Times and Treacherous Death of Jesse James* was allegedly dictated by Jesse's widow Zee and his mother Mrs. Samuel, under contract with the publisher, J. H. Chambers Company of St. Louis.[40] Probably the two women did influence Triplett's presentation of some of the subject matter of the book and furnished information not readily available from other sources. However, the claim that they dictated the story is preposterous. The book's very massiveness and the speed with which it was produced contradict the claim. The book was reviewed in the St. Louis *Post-Dispatch* on May 26, 1882. In his haste, Triplett snatched material from a variety of sources and failed to fit it together into a narrative with a consistent pattern.

A more sympathetic account of the wrongs suffered by the James and Younger families during and after the war was never written, and not even John N. Edwards assailed Governor Crittenden so bitterly as did Triplett. Zee's love for and loyalty to her husband are praised, Pinkerton detectives are excoriated, Mrs. Samuel is treated with compassion, and all wanton murders charged to Frank and Jesse are denied in the book. The boys had not participated in any postwar crime before the bank robbery at Corydon in 1871. In discussing the holdup at Ste. Genevieve Triplett said:

The *staying* qualities of the band; their coolness in danger; their perfect nerve in the most trying situation; their rallying around a disabled comrade; a want of unnecessary brutality, and a desire to avoid the taking of human life, show it almost conclusively to be the work of the outlaws above referred to.[41]

By these standards Triplett measured each robbery to determine if Frank and Jesse had participated. In some instances the presence of Frank was left to conjecture even if Triplett was sure that Jesse participated; in others Frank was named. Since Frank was still at large when the book was published, it seemed unlikely that his sister-in-law and mother would brand him as guilty. Triplett attributed the robberies at Glendale in 1879 and at Winston and Blue Cut in 1881 to a band composed of Dick Liddil, Jim Cummings, the Ford brothers, and local talent, thus absolving Frank and Jesse.

In addition to a stinging criticism of Governor Crittenden for his alleged complicity in the killing of Jesse, Triplett included a long account of Crittenden's court-martial and execution of two "innocent" men of his command during the Civil War. The book did not sell well, and the view has been widely held that Crittenden suppressed it. Frank James is said also to have objected to it.[42] Certainly Frank should have been concerned that close kin were represented as admitting his guilt, but an accusation of moral misconduct also was made against him by inclusion of the long article that the Kansas City *Times* had published over the initials "H.C." on April 11, 1882. It will be recalled that "H.C." accused both Jesse and Frank of having fathered illegitimate children. This charge is believed to have aroused Frank's anger toward Triplett and Zee.

Zee's collaboration on the Triplett's book is indicated by the fact that on April 15, 1882, J. H. Chambers paid Zee and Mrs. Samuel $50 as advance royalty. On April 28 and 29, Attorney R. J. Haire, Zee, and a woman whose identity was a matter of speculation to newsmen were in St. Louis for conferences with J. H. Chambers and Triplett. A reporter from the St. Louis *Republican* interviewed Mrs. James and Chambers, the latter doing most of the talking. Everything seemed to be in order for publication of the book as planned, and Chambers exhibited the contract by which Zee and Mrs. Samuel committed themselves not to impart any information about the lives of Frank or Jesse James to anyone who would publish it, other than Chambers. He told of Zee's reading proofs and asking for changes in copy.[43]

A few days later Mrs. James was in Kansas City, and there she published a statement, verified by affidavit, that disowned and repudiated the claims of the Triplett book. She said she knew nothing of any crimes or unlawful acts imputed to Jesse or Frank and declared that any book purporting to be dictated by her would be a fraud.[44] Her denial of the book's contents has been attributed to demands made by Frank James, who, it is said, was so upset at the prospect of the publication that he, too, was in St. Louis, where he reached Mrs. James and ordered her to have nothing to do with the project.[45]

Whatever the reason for Zee's repudiation, it did not keep her and Mrs. Samuel from suing Chambers in 1884 for their royalties. They alleged a sale of 20,000 copies on which they said $2,150 was due. The jury found a sale of 4,500 copies and awarded the plaintiffs $942. They were represented by one of Frank James's lawyers, Charles P. Johnson.[46]

With the passing of the years publishers continued to print books, often of the paperback pulp kind, selling usually for twenty-five cents, and of the same type as the earlier accounts of robberies by the James band. Occasionally they were reprints of originals or deviated only slightly from them. By changing the order of chapters, adding some new illustrations, omitting a few chapters, or adding a chapter, a new book was produced.

J. W. Buel's *The Border Bandits* is a good example of the repeated use of material with slight change. In 1893, Donohue, Henneberry and Company of Chicago published an expanded edition of Buel's book. Buel had added to the original immediately after Jesse's death, and now he included an account of the killing of Bob Ford in Colorado in 1892. The same book, slightly abbreviated, was published by M. A. Donohue and Company, Chicago and New York, with the title, *The James Boys*, and without date of publication. The title page describes it as "A Complete and Accurate Recital of the Dare-Devil Criminal Career of the Famous Bandit Brothers Frank and Jesse James and Their Noted Band of Plunderers — Specially Compiled for the Publisher." The I. & M. Ottenheimer Company of Baltimore printed three other books under Buel's name. These are: *The Border Bandits* (Baltimore, n.d.), *The Border Outlaws* (Baltimore, n.d.), and *The Younger Brothers — The Notorious Border Outlaws* (Baltimore, n.d.). Two other Ottenheimer publications — *The James Boys* (Baltimore, n.d.) and *Frank James and His Brother Jesse* (Baltimore, 1915) — give no credit to Buel, but are obviously revisions of his books.

Other books of I. & M. Ottenheimer on the James band include: Thaddeus Thorndike, *Lives and Exploits of the Daring Frank and Jesse James* (Baltimore, 1909); Anonymous, *Jesse James: A Romance of Terror, Vividly Portraying the Daring Deeds of the Most Fearsome and*

Fearless Bandit Ever Known Within the Whole Range of Historical Out-lawry (Baltimore, 1910); Lige Mitchell, *Daring Exploits of Jesse James and His Band of Border Train Robbers — Containing Also Some Desperate Adventures of the Dalton Brothers* (Baltimore, n.d.) ; and Edgar James, *The Lives and Adventures, Daring Hold-ups, Train and Bank Robberies of the World's Most Desperate Bandits and Highwaymen — The Notorious James Brothers* (Baltimore, 1913). Superlatives in titles did not alter content, and all these books are like the early so-called histories although not as well done as some of them.

In 1891 Laird and Lee of Chicago published a new book on Jesse James: *Jesse James and His Band of Notorious Outlaws* by Welche Gordon. It was No. 42 in the company's Pinkerton Detective Series, issued monthly by subscription at three dollars a year. This company also reprinted the story of the James boys by an anonymous author, originally published in 1882 by Belford, Clarke and Company and bound with a reprint of Appler's work. Titled *The Wild Bandits of the Border* and expanded by additional chapters, it was published in at least two editions in 1892. The title pages of the two editions are exactly alike, but the cover illustrations and the last few pages differ. One book ends with a chapter titled "Fate of Ford Boys" and the other with "The Last of Bob Ford."

The Regan Publishing Corporation of Chicago published a Wild West Series that included six titles on the Jameses and Youngers, all credited to Clarence E. Ray. Dates of publication have not been determined. The six titles are: *The James Boys*; *Jesse James' Daring Raid*; *The Border Outlaws —Frank and Jesse James*; *The James Boys and Bob Ford*; *The Younger Brothers*; and *Bob and Cole Younger with Quantrell*. The first five of these twenty-five-cent paperback books have been examined. *Jesse James' Daring Raid* is entirely fiction, but the others are confined to discussion of events related to the bandits' career.

Members of the James and Younger families also contributed to outlaw literature: Jesse Edwards James wrote *Jesse James, My Father*, first printed at Independence, Missouri, in 1899 and later reprinted in a pulp edition under special contract with the Arthur Westbrook Company of Cleveland, Ohio; Cole Younger had been in Missouri scarcely a month in 1903 when *The Story of Cole Younger by Himself* came from the press of the Henneberry Company of Chicago. James's book offered nothing new about his father except a denial that he was a bandit, and he described the elder Jesse as merciful, charitable, and entirely misunderstood by all earlier biographers. An account of young Jesse's acquittal of participation in the train robbery at Leeds is a more important feature than the story of his father's life.

Younger's autobiography reviewed his Civil War career and the misfortunes suffered by his family. He denied connection with any crimes until he was driven by desperation to attempt the raid on the bank at Northfield. After describing the robbery at Northfield, the attempted escape, and his lengthy stay in prison, Cole concluded his account with emphasis on the moral, "Crime does not pay."

Like the dime novels, all the publications mentioned above are now collectors' items. While investigation of private collections might reveal others, enough have been found to indicate that their extent was considerable and that hundreds of thousands of people have had opportunity to read accounts of the lives of Frank and Jesse James. Certainly none of them reached the best-seller list, but some evidently sold several thousand copies.

All the histories of the James band follow much the same pattern. They are carelessly written accounts of the robberies charged to the band and of incidents in the lives of the Jameses and Youngers. Frequently in error, they still claim to be authentic. The reputation of the Jameses as highwaymen and robbers was enhanced by them, since they present the gang as both bad men and Robin Hoods. Two samples may be noted. Welche Gordon wrote in his preface:

And now an humble and impecunious scribbler wets his clumsy pen with thick ink to give a gaping and yawning world the history of one who, disdaining the glamour which envelops the romantic scoundrels of "ye olden days," stands the superior of all in audacity and rashness, courage and hellishness — Jesse James.

How can one begin the tale of this terrible man?

What language can furnish the vocabulary which contains enough lurid words, wild synonyms, ensanguinary adjectives, and murderous verbs, to do justice to this horrible monster; this insatiable vampire who has drank enough blood to print in red, an entire edition of this narrative?

Dead though he be, incapable of harming even a child; though he was at last overtaken by a tardy retribution, his memory alone still causes the strong man to look askance as he passes along the lonely Missouri roads which once echoed with the hoofbeats of Jesse James' wild horses, and makes the brave heart tremble at the sudden shadow cast by the waving tree limbs which once served to shelter this messenger of death.[47]

On the other hand, Edgar James wrote of Frank and Jesse:

They were unusual characters, these two Missouri desperadoes, who killed men and robbed trains and banks with almost the same easy grace that they manifested in protecting helpless women and children, to whom they were ever courteous and gentlemanly, or in aiding the poor and needy, to whom they were always royally generous and considerate.

They were not the ordinary rough-shod highwaymen typical in the Western country, but were more of the nature of modern Robin Hoods, who robbed the rich and gave to the poor; who took human life only when they deemed it necessary for the protection of their own and their liberty; who were addicted to none of the ordinary vices of the bad men; who used liquor, tobacco or bad language sparingly, and whom, in many particulars and traits, would have been model men had their vocations been honest and their lives unmarred by bloodshed and robbery . . . despite all the bad in their make-up, there were never two sons who loved their gray-haired mother more or who sought to show their love by constant kindness and devotion. . . . They were a queer combination of good traits and bad, a weird amalgamation of vice and virtue, the marvel being that any good traits ever found a place among the myriad evil ones in their natures.[48]

These passages are representative of the florid prose in which the dime novels and James histories were written, and they also show how writers, out of the same "facts," presented two interpretations of the James boys. It is clear that emphasis on Robin Hood characteristics materially weakened the bad-men concept.

With all the conflicting descriptions of, and opinions about, the James band and its lawlessness, both contemporary and posthumous, few writers have been concerned with attempting the difficult, if not impossible, task of distinguishing between fact and fiction. Nevertheless, many books contain summaries of the career of the James band.[49]

In 1926, Robertus Love, a St. Louis newspaperman, presented the first attempt at a factual study in his *Rise and Fall of Jesse James*. Before its publication in book form the Kansas City *Star*, St. Louis *Post-Dispatch*, and other papers printed it serially. As a reporter, Love covered some of the events connected with the later lives of Frank James, Cole Younger, and their friends. His book is the product of those experiences, his collection of newspaper articles, and his thorough knowledge of the earlier works dealing with the band. Long before he wrote the book, Love acquired a sympathetic view toward the James brothers. That sympathy he never lost. His book is largely a journalistic chronicle of the more colorful events in the lives of the Jameses, Youngers, and their associates.

Love frequently points out that his tales are not true or that their truth is highly doubtful, but if the story is interesting, he tells it. The reader's reaction could well be that of one reviewer, R. F. Dibble, who commented: "Mr. Love . . . habitually tries to differentiate between fact and fiction, with the result that the reader generally accepts the fiction and doubts the fact." [50]

Love's interpretation of the James brothers' careers is summarized early in the book:

They preferred the simple life, with its interest and prospective rewards comprising the sacred trinity of Mother, Home and Heaven; but having once got a-going in the wrong direction, they found it next to impossible to stop unless at a point immediately underneath a rope specifically noosed to fit their own necks with fatal tightness.[51]

To some extent Love debunks the legend by picturing Frank and Jesse James as ordinary men who were drawn into banditry by the prospect of adventure, but who were never happy in the profession. The book is a significant addition to the literature of the James band; its value is greater as such than as history. After staying in print for over fifteen years and going through several printings, it is still the best account of the James boys and their careers as outlaws.

Three other professional writers of note — Homer Croy, James D. Horan, and Paul I. Wellman — have been attracted to Jesse James as a subject, and their books have been published by well-established firms. They are significant, not because they have modified the legend in any appreciable way, but because they have helped to keep it alive.

Homer Croy's *Jesse James Was My Neighbor*[52] is an entertaining and refreshing telling of the tales in which Croy was steeped. A native of northwest Missouri, he had heard the stories about Jesse James from early childhood, but he made considerable effort to gather additional information, enabling him to present for the first time several good human-interest stories. Extensive notes at the back of the book discuss his sources of information for each chapter. No other writer on Jesse had done this, and the James enthusiasts liked it. Croy presented the James legend so convincingly that one is reminded of the native in the Ozarks who said, "A whopper ain't a lie unless you tell it for the truth." Croy must have had his tongue in his cheek at times, and he did no damage to the Robin Hood tradition.

James D. Horan noted that Croy left Jesse's somewhat tarnished halo intact, and Horan evidently intended to remove it when he devoted Book One of his *Desperate Men*[53] to the James band. The part concerning the Jameses fills 172 pages, over half of the first edition of the book. The work is based on the "historical files" of the Pinkerton National Detective Agency. These evidently are scrapbooks or a clipping collection and not the private records of the agency,[54] for practically everything Horan wrote about the Jameses can be found in some printed source. He views the outlaws as did the Pinkertons; they are not his heroes. Despite this view, the Pinkertons fail to emerge with any glory. Making the Jameses look bad does not make the detectives look good.

Readers of Horan's work get a good review of the Jesse James story, although the book is marred by several minor, but shocking, errors. Even the map provided to orient the reader is wildly inaccurate. Horan makes Frank, not Jesse, the writer of letters to editors, and he credits Frank with the letter of Cole Younger that was published in the Pleasant Hill *Review*. After reporting a favorable vote on the Amnesty Bill, he attributes the act's failure to pass to the presiding officer's ruling it out of order. He refers to the *Courier-Journal* as a St. Louis paper, when it was already in Jesse's time a distinguished voice for Louisville. Other errors as serious occur throughout the book.

The most sophisticated treatment of the James career is in *A Dynasty of Western Outlaws* by Paul I. Wellman.[55] It is the story of the outlaws of Missouri, Kansas, and Oklahoma, from Quantrill's raid on Lawrence to the Union Station Massacre in Kansas City on June 17, 1933, led by Pretty Boy Floyd. Wellman's thesis is that the American Civil War, as all wars, bred crime and criminals and that out of its dislocations grew a wave of lawlessness that through successive generations perpetuated itself in a dynasty of outlaws. In Pretty Boy Floyd, seeds sewn in war and kept alive through various bands of outlaws were harvested.

As a Kansas and Missouri newspaperman for many years before he moved to Los Angeles in 1944, Wellman was a student of the outlaws of the region. He knew personally many people who had firsthand information about them, and he gleaned from their supply. He was better qualified by background than Horan to wind his way through the multiplicity of conflicting claims, and his reasoned judgment is most often sound. When he gives credence, however, to Joe Vaughan's book, titled *The Only True History of Frank James, Written by Himself*, and when he says the James brothers and the Younger brothers were cousins, he is quite wrong. One can quarrel with some of his decisions concerning the James band's lawlessness and can find minor errors, but on the whole he has done a difficult job well.

Another writer who, however, does not have the reputation of a Croy, Horan, or Wellman has published two books on Jesse James and others on related subjects. Carl Breihan called his first book *The Complete and Authentic Life of Jesse James*.[56] Some readers may have accepted the book at face value, but not those who are informed on the subject. When Breihan described John N. Edwards as Frank James's lawyer and the condemnatory editorial Edwards wrote at the time of Jesse's death as his plea before the jury, he insulted the intelligence of those who know better. Besides, Edwards' admirers were irritated when Breihan spelled Edwards' middle name "Neumann." Breihan did a good job of exploding the claims of J. Frank Dalton, the last pretender, and the collection of photographs in the book is excellent. However, his photographic reproduction of Crittenden's reward proclamation must be phony, for it erroneously offers the reward for Frank and Jesse "Dead or Alive."

The historical part of Breihan's second book on Jesse, *The Day Jesse James Was Killed*,[57] is much improved over the first, though some errors, such as using the spelling "Neumann," persist. The beginning and some other sections are entirely imaginative, in order to create atmosphere for the flashbacks by which the story is told. Breihan avoids everything that might be interpreted as an attempt to perpetuate the Robin Hood version of Jesse's lawlessness.

A novel about Jesse James by Will Henry, which has been published under two titles, *Death of a Legend* and *The Raiders*,[58] is an avowed attempt to destroy the Robin Hood tradition. In a note at the beginning, Henry made clear his purpose:

Death of a Legend is an accounting, straightforward if sometimes sinister, of the "Robin Hood of the Little Blue." The real Jesse James will always remain part man, part myth. He lived that way, he died that way. It was the way he himself planned it and wanted it. But it is time for a long, hard look at Dr. Samuel's pale-eyed stepson — a look which peers beyond the popular fictions and stares flatly at the unpalatable facts. Jesse James was, in all truth, an incredibly wicked man.

By that token, readers from the home-state counties of Clay and Jackson . . . will now be warned that what follows is not another testimonial to the spotless memory of the sainted "Mr. Howard." Neither is it a further chanting of the threadbare recessional against the villainy of "the dirty little coward" who shot him, and thus, for two generations of weeping hero worshippers, "laid poor Jesse in his grave."

Death of a Legend is, basically, a true bill of indictment returned against the persistently misrepresented life of a cold-blooded murderer.

Having called his book a novel, Henry was under no obligation to stick to the facts, and at times he departed far from them. For his framework he seems to have leaned heavily on Horan's account. No matter how earnestly he tried to debunk the legend, he was not thorough, for he wove into the narrative a beautiful love story around the courtship and married life of Jesse and Zee. Of it he wrote:

This much remains to us of Jesse's love — he was as strange about it, as enigmatic, as contradictory and confusing as he was in any of his remembered traits.

Many damnations of Jesse James exist in cold fact. But upon one point of romantic record all accounts remain unanimous. Jesse looked once upon Zerelda Mimms, and never took his eyes away. Figuratively, she was the first woman he saw and, literally, she was the last.

And after comparing Jesse to other members of the band with regard to their relations with women, Henry concluded:

This much must stand upon the ledger of latter-day judgment, against any spelling of murder or inscription of social rapine, to the singular credit of Jesse James: he abode with his chosen woman, in sickness as in health, *until death did them part!* [59]

This emphasis compromises Henry's case, but even so, it is doubtful that he could have damaged the Robin Hood tradition, for it has been reinforced most effectively over the years by stage and screen productions.

Although there have been a few attempts, such as Henry's, to destroy the Robin Hood aspect of the James legend, it is apparent that it is too well rooted in American folklore to suffer serious damage. The forces that sustain it are far greater than any that would destroy it. Hence, the Jesse James legend will live on and continue to excite Americans with the exploits of their native Robin Hood. The legend's historical roots are easier to determine than those of the legends of many medieval outlaws: It is well established that the latter grew out of and were sustained by the injustices of a social system. People, frustrated in life's struggle and bored by its routine, will probably always be able to identify their situation with Jesse's and find satisfaction in his exploits, just as many of his contemporaries saw him as the unvanquished hero of the South's struggle against a tyrannical government.

Notes

NOTES TO CHAPTER I

1. Opie Read, *Mark Twain and I*, 11.
2. Carl Sandburg, *The American Songbag*, 420.
3. Welche Gordon, *Jesse James and His Band of Notorious Outlaws*, 8.
4. Edgar James, *The Lives and Adventures, Daring Hold-ups, Train and Bank Robberies of the World's Most Desperate Bandits and Highwaymen — The Notorious James Brothers*, 7–8.
5. Kansas City *Star*, September 11, 1927; "The Battle over a Jesse James Monument," *Literary Digest*, 95 (October 29, 1927), 44–50.

NOTES TO CHAPTER II

1. Records in James Family Bible.
2. Sworn statement of R. J. Waring, County Clerk of Scott County, Kentucky, given on November 20, 1944; records in James Family Bible; Liberty *Tribune*, October 25, 1850, April 14, 1882, February 26, 1915, and October 3, 1929; and interview with Robert James, July 6, 1950.
3. Clay County Probate Court Records, Liberty, Missouri.
4. Records in James Family Bible.
5. Kansas City *Daily Journal*, April 6, 1882.
6. Jesse Edwards James, *Jesse James, My Father*, 21–23.
7. I have heard this gossip many times. See J. W. Buel, *The Border Bandits*, 119.
8. In 1950 these letters were kept in the safety deposit box of Mr. and Mrs. Robert James, son and daughter-in-law of Frank James, at a bank in Kearney, Missouri.
9. Liberty *Tribune*, October 25, 1850, and February 14, 1851.
10. Kansas City *Daily Journal*, April 6, 1882; Robert F. James, interview, March 17, 1945.

11. Liberty *Tribune*, October 5, 1855; records in James Family Bible; Robert F. James, interview, March 17, 1945.
12. Anonymous, *The Wild Bandits of the Border*, 28–29.
13. Quoted in Floyd C. Shoemaker, *Missouri and Missourians*, I, 729.
14. William Frank Zornow, *Kansas, A History of the Jayhawk State*, 67–91; Richard S. Brownlee, *Gray Ghosts of the Confederacy: Guerrilla Warfare in the West, 1861–1865*, 8–10; William E. Parrish, *David Rice Atchison of Missouri: Border Politician*, 161–210; Paul Wallace Gates, *Fifty Million Acres: Conflicts over Kansas Land Policy, 1854–1890*, 1–4.

NOTES TO CHAPTER III

1. Brownlee, *Gray Ghosts of the Confederacy*, 10–15, provides a brief summation of these events. Other recent scholarship dealing with the start of the Civil War in Missouri includes William E. Parrish, *Turbulent Partnership: Missouri and the Union, 1861–1865*, 1–32, and Arthur Roy Kirkpatrick, "Missouri on the Eve of the Civil War," *Missouri Historical Review*, LV (January, 1961), 99–108, and "Missouri in the Early Months of the Civil War," *Missouri Historical Review*, LV (April, 1961), 235–66.
2. Kirkpatrick, "Missouri in the Early Months of the Civil War," 237.
3. Liberty *Tribune*, May 10, 1861.
4. Daniel O'Flaherty, *General Jo Shelby*, 33–45.
5. *Ibid.*, 53–54.
6. *Ibid.*, 48–49; Dan Saults, "Missouri's Forgotten Don Quixote," *Focus/ Midwest*, I (October, 1962), 20–23.
7. Brownlee, *Gray Ghosts of the Confederacy*, 23–25.
8. U. S., War Department, *The War of the Rebellion: A Compilation of the Official Records of the Union and Confederate Armies*, Series 1, Vol. VIII, 463–64. Hereafter cited as *O.R.*
9. *O.R.*, Series 1, Vol. VIII, 476–78.
10. Brownlee, *Gray Ghosts of the Confederacy*, 26.
11. *Ibid.*, 37–52.
12. *Ibid.*, 47–49; Albert Castel, *A Frontier State at War; Kansas, 1861–1865*, 50–64.
13. *O.R.*, Series 1, Vol. VIII, 818–19.
14. William Elsey Connelley, *Quantrill and the Border Wars*, 42, 54–235; Albert Castel, *William Clarke Quantrill: His Life and Times*, 1–69.
15. Liberty *Tribune*, February 21, 1862.
16. *O.R.*, Series 1, Vol. VIII, 506.
17. The Liberty *Tribune*, September 20, 1861, stated that Clay County had five companies in Price's army. In an interview on March 17, 1945, Robert F. James stated that his father Frank James said many times he was at Wilson's Creek.
18. *History of Clay and Platte Counties, Missouri*, 266.
19. *Ibid.*
20. Brownlee, *Gray Ghosts of the Confederacy*, 76–91.

21. *Ibid.*, 92–99; Castel, *William Clarke Quantrill*, 85–95.
22. Brownlee, *Gray Ghosts of the Confederacy*, 99–107; Castel, *William Clarke Quantrill*, 95–100.
23. Brownlee, *Gray Ghosts of the Confederacy*, 107–8.
24. *Ibid.*, 110–11; Castel, *William Clarke Quantrill*, 101–3.
25. O'Flaherty, *General Jo Shelby*, 153–56, 331–33; Jay Monaghan, *Civil War on the Western Border*, 264–65; Henry Huston Crittenden, compiler, *The Crittenden Memoirs*, 212–13; John Newman Edwards, *Shelby and His Men*, 117–18.
26. *History of Clay and Platte Counties*, 266.
27. John McCorkle, *Three Years with Quantrill: A True Story*, 46, 63–65.
28. Connelley, *Quantrill*, 251–52.
29. Brownlee, *Gray Ghosts of the Confederacy*, 43.
30. *O.R.*, Series 1, Vol. XXII, Part 2, 78–82. Brigadier General Benjamin Loan wrote Major General Samuel R. Curtis, under date of January 27, 1863, that Captain Walley confessed to the murder; Coleman Younger, *The Story of Cole Younger by Himself*, 9–31.
31. Brownlee, *Gray Ghosts of the Confederacy*, 110–21; Castel, *William Clarke Quantrill*, 116–23.
32. Brownlee, *Gray Ghosts of the Confederacy*, 121–27; Castel, *William Clarke Quantrill*, 123–43; Connelley, *Quantrill*, 284–420; John Newman Edwards, *Noted Guerrillas, or the Warfare of the Border*, 188–204.
33. Brownlee, *Gray Ghosts of the Confederacy*, 125–27; Castel, *William Clarke Quantrill*, 144–47; Albert Castel, "Order No. 11 and the Civil War on the Border," *Missouri Historical Review*, LVII (July, 1963), 357–68.
34. Castel, *William Clarke Quantrill*, 149–72; Brownlee, *Gray Ghosts of the Confederacy*, 128–41; Connelley, *Quantrill*, 420–50.
35. Connelley, *Quantrill*, 384–85.
36. Photograph of Fletcher Taylor, Frank James, and Jesse James, given to Charles Kemper of Independence, Missouri, by Cole Younger who said it was made at Bonham, Texas, in 1864; *History of Clay and Platte Counties*, 267; *Jim Cummins the Guerrilla*, 60, 68.
37. Robertus Love, *The Rise and Fall of Jesse James*, 37–47, and Edwards, *Noted Guerrillas*, 167–68, have statements of this tradition. See also *History of Clay and Platte Counties*, 267.
38. Castel, *William Clarke Quantrill*, 159.
39. Brownlee, *Gray Ghosts of the Confederacy*, 180–205.
40. *Ibid.*, 206–31.
41. *Ibid.*; Columbia *Missouri Herald*, September 24, 1897; Elmer L. Pigg, "Bloody Bill, Noted Guerrilla of the Civil War," *The Trail Guide*, I (December, 1956), 17–28; Edwards, *Noted Guerrillas*, 293–328.

NOTES TO CHAPTER IV

1. Connelley, *Quantrill*, 451–80. The parole papers issued to Frank James were in the possession of his son Robert F. James in 1945. Connelley

(p. 479) lists Bill Hulse, John Harris, John Ross, Ran Venable, Dave Hilton, Frank James, Bud Pence, Allen Parmer, Lee McMurtry, Ike Hall, Bob Hall, Payne Jones, Andy McGuire, and Jim Lilly as being paroled. He thinks two others were in the group.

2. Brownlee, *Gray Ghosts of the Confederacy*, 232–34; Edwards, *Noted Guerrillas*, 327–33.

3. Edwards, *Noted Guerrillas*, 327–33; Castel, *William Clarke Quantrill*, 217–18.

4. Brownlee, *Gray Ghosts of the Confederacy*, 234–35.

5. *O. R.*, Series 1, Vol. XLVIII, Part 2, 341–42.

6. *Ibid.*, 546, 552, 705–6; Richmond *North-West Conservator*, June 17, 1865; Liberty *Tribune*, May 26 and June 2, 1865.

7. Liberty *Tribune*, February 5, 1865; Robert F. James, interview, July 6, 1950.

8. St. Louis *Missouri Republican*, April 27, 1882; Boonville *Weekly Advertiser*, November 16, 1900; "Milestone Edition" of the Lexington *Advertiser*, October 30, 1930; Judge Thomas R. Shouse of Liberty, Missouri, interview, June 15, 1940. Jesse James told Shouse of the incident, and Shouse once saw both scars on Jesse's chest. Shouse in 1940 was past ninety years of age, but completely alert mentally. Before the James boys entered their career of banditry he knew them well, and he and Jesse for a time courted two sisters together. Judge Shouse, a resident of Clay County during the Civil War and the time of the James band's activities, was a respected authority on Clay County's history. Some accounts state that Jesse was shot on his way out of Lexington after he had surrendered. See John P. Burch, *Charles W. Quantrell*, 231.

9. Edwards, *Noted Guerrillas*, 338, 350; Henry F. Hoyt, *Frontier Doctor*, 112; Homer Croy, *Jesse James Was My Neighbor*, 30; Love, *Rise and Fall of Jesse James*, 100; North Todd Gentry, "General Odon Guitar," *Missouri Historical Review*, XXII (July, 1938), 425; Robert F. James, interview, July 6, 1950.

10. Boonville *Weekly Advertiser*, November 16, 1900, has a good statement of this tradition.

11. Judge Thomas R. Shouse, who knew the Jameses in the years immediately after the war, held firmly to the view that they could have lived in Clay County unmolested. *Texas Siftings*, May 13 and 27, 1882, named the Reverend Mr. M. Rodgers, then living in Austin, as the minister who baptized Jesse.

12. Liberty *Tribune*, February 16 and March 2, 1866, February 16, 1939, and February 15, 1943. An account of the robbery written by Greenup Bird for the bank's president, published in the *Tribune* on February 16, 1939, lists the funds taken.

13. Lexington *Caucasian*, October 31, 1866; Richmond *Conservator*, November 3, 1866; St. Louis *Daily Missouri Republican*, November 3, 1866.

14. Liberty *Tribune*, March 8, 1867.

15. Richmond *Conservator*, May 24, 1867.

16. St. Louis *Daily Missouri Republican*, March 23 and 26, 1868. Account of

the first date is from the Louisville *Democrat*, and the second is from the Louisville *Journal*.

17. Kansas City *Daily Journal of Commerce*, February 16, 1866; Lexington *Express*, in Liberty *Tribune*, March 2, 1866; Kansas City *Daily Journal of Commerce*, in Liberty *Tribune*, September 14, 1866.

18. Clay County Circuit Court Records, File Number 10.

19. St. Joseph *Morning Herald*, in the Liberty *Tribune*, March 29 and April 5, 1867.

20. Richmond *Conservator*, June 1, 1867.

21. Kansas City *Daily Journal of Commerce*, May 28, 1867; St. Louis *Tri-Weekly Missouri Democrat*, May 31, 1867.

22. Richmond *Conservator*, November 30, 1867.

23. Warrensburg *Weekly Journal*, June 5 and 19, 1867.

24. Richmond *Conservator*, January 4, February 29, and March 23, 1868; St. Louis *Daily Missouri Republican*, March 20, 1866; St. Louis *Tri-Weekly Missouri Democrat*, March 23, 1868.

25. Louisville *Courier*, in Liberty *Tribune*, July 24, 1868; St. Louis *Daily Missouri Republican*, July 13, 1868, in Richmond *Conservator*, July 18, 1868.

26. Independence *Sentinel*, in Jefferson City *Peoples' Tribune*, April 15, 1868; letter, D. G. Bligh to Governor of State of Missouri, March 3, 1875, in State Archives, State Historical Society of Missouri.

27. Love, *Rise and Fall of Jesse James*, 88–92.

28. St. Joseph *Gazette*, December 9, in Liberty *Tribune*, December 17, 1869; Kansas City *Times*, December 16, in St. Louis *Tri-Weekly Missouri Democrat*, December 18, 1869; Kansas City *Daily Journal of Commerce*, December 9, 1869; St. Louis *Globe-Democrat*, October 17, 1942.

29. St. Joseph *Gazette*, December 9, in Liberty *Tribune*, December 17, 1869.

30. St. Joseph *Morning Herald*, December 9, 1869.

31. Kansas City *Times*, December 16, in St. Louis *Tri-Weekly Missouri Democrat*, December 18, 1869. A sequel to this incident, told many times and in many ways, is that Jesse met Oscar Thomason years later in Texas and paid him for the horse. It is true that Jesse once met Oscar in Texas and gave him some money, but the horse was not mentioned. Love, *Rise and Fall of Jesse James*, 93–112, gives dramatic statements of both incidents. William H. Thomason, now deceased, in an interview on November 29, 1944, at Liberty, Missouri, said that his father was not on the horse when it was shot. He also said that Jesse James and a group of others, years later, came upon the camp of Oscar Thomason in Texas, and upon recognizing Thomason took position for battle. Greetings were then exchanged, and an agreement was reached that there would be no hostilities. The two parties then shared a meal. Jesse asked Oscar if he needed any money, and although Thomason replied that he did not, Jesse insisted that he accept $50. The horse was not mentioned. William H. Thomason was born in Clay County in 1855, the son of John S. Thomason and brother of Oscar.

32. See Croy, *Jesse James Was My Neighbor*, 55 and 56, and Robertus Love, *Rise and Fall of Jesse James*, 96–101.

33. Kansas City *Daily Journal of Commerce,* December 9, 1869; St. Joseph *Gazette,* in Liberty *Tribune,* December 17, 1869.
34. Kansas City *Times,* December 16, in the St. Louis *Tri-Weekly Missouri Democrat,* December 18, 1869. The horse on which Jesse James escaped from Deputy Sheriff Thomason's posse was believed to have been the one taken from Smoot outside Gallatin.

     Henry Clay McDougal, a lawyer whose home town was Gallatin, was approached by Smoot two days after the robbery to bring "an attachment suit for the race-mare, saddle, and bridle, which were there in a livery barn. The robbers had committed a felony and the right to an action was clear. . . . The fact came to me afterward that Smoot had been to all the older lawyers of the bar, and all had declined his case because of the defendants. Well, I brought his case in the old Common Pleas Court there, against Frank James and Jesse James, and attached this property early in 1870. . . . Then the opposition withdrew the answer, judgment was rendered, and the sheriff sold the attached property." Henry Clay McDougal, *Recollections, 1844–1909,* 29–30.
35. Liberty *Tribune,* December 17, 1869.
36. *Platte County Reveille,* in Liberty *Tribune,* January 14, 1870; Manuscript 557, State Historical Society of Missouri. This manuscript is a photostatic copy of a telegram from Governor McClurg to the Sheriff of Jackson County.
37. Kansas City *Times,* December 16, in St. Louis *Tri-Weekly Missouri Democrat,* December 18, 1869.
38. Kansas City *Times,* in Liberty *Tribune,* June 24, 1870.
39. Kansas City *Times,* in Liberty *Tribune,* July 15, 1870.
40. Kansas City *Times,* in Liberty *Tribune,* July 22, 1870.
41. Liberty *Tribune,* July 22, 1870.

NOTES TO CHAPTER V

1. The amount has been variously reported from $6,000 to $70,000. Most contemporary reports said $6,000.
2. Osceola (Iowa) *Republican,* June 8, 1871; Centerville (Iowa) *Weekly Citizen,* June 10, 1871; Cameron *Observer,* in Liberty *Tribune,* June 16, 1871; Hamilton *News Graphic,* in Richmond *Conservator,* June 17, 1871; Theodore M. Stuart, *Past and Present of Lucas and Wayne Counties, Iowa,* I, 274–76. Love, *Rise and Fall of Jesse James,* 115–18, states that the meeting was political and that Dean assured the crowd that the interruption was just an attempt to annoy him. Dean Davis, Kansas City, Missouri, grandson of the speaker, in an interview on March 23, 1945, said that his grandfather believed it was Frank James who interrupted him.
3. Kansas City *Times,* in Richmond *Conservator,* July 8, 1871. By Radical he meant Republican.
4. St. Joseph *Gazette,* in Liberty *Tribune,* March 8, 1872; Stuart, *Past and Present of Lucas and Wayne Counties, Iowa,* I, 274–76.

5. St. Louis *Daily Missouri Republican*, May 1, 1872; Evansville *Journal*, in St. Louis *Missouri Republican*, October 12, 1882; letter from D. G. Bligh to Governor of State of Missouri, March 3, 1875.

6. Evansville *Journal*, in St. Louis *Missouri Republican*, October 12, 1882.

7. Neosho *Times*, August 18, 1881.

8. Kansas City *Times*, September 27, 1872.

9. *Ibid.*

10. *Ibid.*, September 29, 1872.

11. Edwards was idolized by his friends of Southern sympathies, and, because of his personal qualities, he was loved and respected even by those contemporaries who opposed him most strongly. In the Boonville *Weekly Advertiser* of April 9, 1875, appeared this statement: "He always seems to be a stranger. . . . Walks alone and stands alone, seldom speaks to anybody, and does not smile three times a day. He is one of the oddest and best of men." At the time of the Kansas City Fair robbery, Edwards was fighting a personal battle with an antagonist that at times he thought, and his friends prayed, he had whipped — alcoholism — but in the end he lost the battle. In observing the end of the first century of journalism in Missouri in 1920, William Vincent Byars wrote that Major Edwards was "perhaps better known and better loved by his generation than any other newspaperman in any generation of the century. . . . Out of the maze of romance his genius substituted for realities, his eloquence expressed itself in dreams . . . and what he could not otherwise endure, he idealized." William Vincent Byars, "A Century of Journalism in Missouri," *Missouri Historical Review*, XV (October, 1920), 70–72.

12. Kansas City *Daily Journal of Commerce*, September 27, 1872.

13. Kansas City *Times*, October 15, 1872.

14. *Ibid.*, October 20, 1872.

15. *Ibid.*, October 25, 1872.

16. St. Louis *Missouri Republican*, May 28, 1873.

17. Kansas City *Daily Journal of Commerce*, May 30, 1873.

18. Alvin F. Harlow, *Old Waybills*, 326–43.

19. St. Joseph *Morning Herald*, July 23, 25, and 27 and September 4 and 7, 1873; Kansas City *Times*, July 23, 1873; Philip D. Jordan, "The Adair Train Robbery," *The Palimpsest*, XVII (February, 1936), 49–66.

20. St. Joseph *Morning Herald*, July 27, 1873.

21. Leavenworth *Times*, in Kansas City *Daily Journal of Commerce*, July 24, 1873.

22. Jefferson City *Peoples' Tribune*, January 7, 1874; Gallatin *North Missourian*, January 8, 1874; Liberty *Tribune*, January 9, 1874.

23. St. Louis *Republican*, February 2, 1874; St. Louis *Times*, February 2, 1874; Boonville *Weekly Advertiser*, February 6, 1874; Liberty *Tribune*, February 6, 1874.

24. St. Louis *Republican*, February 2, 1874.

25. *Ibid.*, February 11, 1874.

26. Grace Gardner Avery and Floyd C. Shoemaker, compilers and editors, *The Messages and Proclamations of the Governors of the State of*

Missouri, V, 350–51. Hereafter cited as *Messages and Proclamations of the Governors*.

27. Little Rock *Arkansas Gazette*, January 18, 1874.
28. St. Louis *Dispatch*, February 10, 1874.
29. Copy of telegram, in Walter B. Stevens' Scrap Book No. 61, in State Historical Society of Missouri.
30. St. Louis *Dispatch*, February 10, 1874.
31. Copy of the article, in Walter B. Stevens' Scrap Book No. 278, State Historical Society of Missouri.
32. *O. R.*, Series 1, Vol. XLI, Part 1, 589.
33. In some of the many accounts of this incident that are included in books on the James boys, the soldiers are said to have mistaken Frank for a horse thief and attempted to arrest him. Frank James's son Robert, in an interview March 17, 1945, said that he did not believe the incident occurred.
34. Many versions of this story were given in books written later, and this is the earliest and mildest account. Some statements have Jesse killing all five before they could fire a shot. Edwards wrote, in "The Terrible Quintette," that the incident actually occurred and that many Clay County residents were quite familiar with the circumstances. Contemporary newspapers of the area contain no mention of it. Robert James, in an interview on March 17, 1945, said it was his understanding that there was no basis for the story.

NOTES TO CHAPTER VI

1. Letter from H. S. Mosher, March 19, 1945. Mosher was then manager of Pinkerton's Department of Criminal Investigation.
2. Chicago *Times*, in Kansas City *Evening Star*, July 21, 1881; "Train Robberies, Train Robbers, and the 'Holdup' Men," address by William A. Pinkerton at Annual Convention of International Association Chiefs of Police, Jamestown, Virginia, 1907.
3. St. Louis *Democrat*, in St. Joseph *Morning Herald*, September 7, 1873.
4. Osceola (Missouri) *Democrat*, September 5, 1873.
5. Lexington *Caucasian*, August 30, in St. Joseph *Morning Herald*, September 3, 1873.
6. Liberty *Tribune*, September 12, 1873.
7. *Messages and Proclamations of the Governors*, V, 343–44.
8. The Chicago, Rock Island and Pacific Railroad Company had offered to pay $5,000 for the arrest and convictions of the Iowa train robbers; see St. Joseph *Morning Herald*, July 22, 1873. The *Herald* reported, on August 3, 1873, that a reward of $15,000 for the arrest of the James boys was hanging over their heads. Newspapers were inclined to exaggerate, or at least make statements of this kind carelessly. It is impossible to verify all such reports, but undoubtedly the total of the rewards offered was now high.
9. This name is also spelled *Wicher, Witcher, Wichel,* and *Whitcher* in the

various sources. The Liberty *Tribune*, published in the town where he gave his name to citizens, spelled it *Whicher*.

10. Kansas City *Times*, March 14, 1874; Jefferson City *Daily Tribune*, March 18, 1874; Liberty *Tribune*, March 20, 1874; St. Louis *Republican*, March 23, 1874.

11. St. Louis *Republican*, March 21, 1874; *Henry County Democrat*, in Richmond *Conservator*, March 28, 1874; Clinton *Democrat*, in Boonville *Weekly Advertiser*, March 27, 1874; Kansas City *Times*, March 22 and May 14, 1874; Augustus C. Appler, *The Guerrillas of the West or the Life, Character and Daring Exploits of the Younger Brothers*, 135–45.

12. St. Louis *Republican*, in Kansas City *Times*, May 7, 1874; letter, Sheriff Brown of Dallas, Texas, to Governor of Missouri, April 4, 1871, in letter book of Governor B. Gratz Brown, State Archives, State Historical Society of Missouri; Love, *Rise and Fall of Jesse James*, 141–43; Appler, *Guerrillas of the West*, 124–27.

13. Pleasant Hill *Review*, in St. Louis *Republican*, November 30, 1874.

14. Letter, Wm. A. Pinkerton to Don O. Conner, July 2, 1874, in State Archives, State Historical Society of Missouri.

15. St. Louis *Globe*, March 20, 1874; St. Louis *Republican*, March 21, 1874.

16. St. Louis *Republican*, March 23, 1874.

17. Kansas City *Times*, March 25, 1874.

18. Liberty *Tribune*, March 27, 1874.

19. St. Louis *Republican*, in Liberty *Tribune*, December 25, 1874.

20. *Messages and Proclamations of the Governors*, V, 326–28.

21. *Journal of the Senate, Twenty-seventh General Assembly of Missouri, Adjourned Session, 1874*, 741–42; *Journal of the House, Twenty-seventh General Assembly of Missouri, Adjourned Session, 1874*, 1610.

22. Jefferson City *Daily Tribune*, March 26, 1874; *Journal of the House, Twenty-seventh General Assembly of Missouri, Adjourned Session, 1874*, 1386.

23. Chicago *Tribune*, in the St. Louis *Times*, March 26, 1874.

24. New York *Herald*, in St. Joseph *Morning Herald*, March 27, 1874.

25. Pittsburgh *Commercial*, in St. Joseph *Morning Herald*, March 28, 1874.

26. Kansas City *Times*, May 24, 1874.

27. St. Louis *Missouri Democrat*, August 24, 1872.

28. Jefferson City *Daily Tribune*, March 25 and May 4 and 16, 1874; Richmond *Conservator*, May 4, 1874; Jefferson City *Peoples' Tribune*, July 15 and 22, 1874.

29. Columbia *Missouri Statesman*, September 11, 1874.

30. *Ibid.*, July 31, 1874.

31. Jefferson City *Peoples' Tribune*, September 30, 1874.

32. Columbia *Missouri Statesman*, June 5, 1874.

33. Jefferson City *Peoples' Tribune*, August 26, 1874; Columbia *Missouri Statesman*, September 4, 1874.

34. St. Louis *Republican*, September 24, 1874.

35. Kansas City *Times*, October 2 and 3, 1874.

36. *Ibid.*, September 24 and 29 and October 2, 1874; Jefferson City *Daily*

Tribune, September 28, 1874; Boonville *Weekly Advertiser*, September 18 and October 9, 16, and 23, 1874; Liberty *Tribune*, September 25 and October 23 and 30, 1874.

37. *Amerika*, in Liberty *Tribune*, September 25, 1874.

NOTES TO CHAPTER VII

1. Kansas City *Daily Journal of Commerce*, April 14, 1874.
2. Columbia *Missouri Statesman*, April 17, 1874; see also Kansas City *Daily Journal of Commerce*, April 16, 1874. That the Youngers had undoubtedly spent some time in Texas after the war lends support to the belief that Cole Younger was the father of a daughter born to Myra Belle Shirley, known as Belle Starr, the "Bandit Queen, or the Female Jesse James." Belle, whose first child went by the name of Pearl Younger, was living with her parents near Scyene, Texas, at a time Cole Younger was in the region. Cole admitted in later life that he had known her. See Burton Rascoe, *Belle Starr*, 115–23, and Homer Croy, *Last of the Great Outlaws*, 49–63, 82–94, and 133–57.
3. St. Louis *Dispatch*, June 7, 1874, in the Kansas City *Times*, June 11, 1874.
4. Love, *Rise and Fall of Jesse James*, 162–66.
5. Lexington *Caucasian* Extra, in Kansas City *Times*, September 1, 1874. The article was also reprinted in the St. Louis *Republican*, September 1, 1874, and in the Lexington *Caucasian*, September 5, 1874.
6. Lexington *Register* Extra, August 31, 1874, in *The Westerners Brand Book 1945–46* (Chicago, 1947), 151–55, and the part quoted in Kansas City *Times*, September 1, 1874.
7. Kansas City *Times*, September 9, 1874.
8. *Ibid.*
9. Lexington *Caucasian*, October 17, 1874.
10. *Ibid.*
11. Letters, J. W. Ragsdale to Silas Woodson, July 1, 1874; William A. Hall to Silas Woodson, November 24, 1874; J. W. Ragsdale to Silas Woodson, December 4, 1874; receipt from George W. Warren to Silas Woodson, July 9, 1874, for $350; receipt from George W. Warren to Silas Woodson, November 24, 1874, for $350 received on October 1, 1874, and for $20 received on November 24, 1874; memorandum signed by Silas Woodson, January 18, 1875, states that he paid J. W. Ragsdale $647.75 and William Warren $200 on December 19, 1874. The letters and receipts are in the State Archives, State Historical Society of Missouri.
12. Letters, C. C. Rainwater to Chas. P. Johnson, September 3, 1874; Jno. Reid to Chas. P. Johnson, September 8, 1874; L. Harrigan to Chas. P. Johnson, September 13, 1874; F. Yancey to Chas. P. Johnson, September 14, 1874; L. Harrigan to Chas. P. Johnson, September 16, 1874; F. Yancey to Chas. P. Johnson, September 19, 1874; telegrams, L. Harrigan to Chas. P. Johnson, September 4, 1874; L. Harrigan to Chas. P. Johnson, September 11, 1874; Thos. H. Bayliss to C. P. Johnson, September 14, 1874; F. Yancey to Governor of the State of Missouri, care

of Dr. Reddens, St. Joseph, Missouri, September 21, 1874, State Archives, State Historical Society of Missouri. St. Louis *Globe*, October 4, 1874, in Lexington *Caucasian*, October 10, 1874.

13. Lexington *Caucasian*, October 10, 1874.
14. Pleasant Hill *Review*, in St. Louis *Republican*, November 30, 1874.
15. St. Louis *Dispatch*, December 15, 1874.
16. St. Louis *Republican*, December 9, 1874; Liberty *Tribune*, December 11, 1874.
17. Letter, D. G. Bligh to the Governor of the State of Missouri, March 3, 1875, State Archives, State Historical Society of Missouri.
18. Kansas City *Daily Journal of Commerce*, December 9, 1874; Kansas City *Times*, in Liberty *Tribune*, December 11, 1874; Lexington *Caucasian*, December 12, 1874; St. Joseph *Morning Herald*, December 15, 1874.
19. Kansas City *Daily Journal of Commerce*, December 9, 1874; St. Louis *Republican*, December 12, 1874; New York *Sun* in St. Joseph *Morning Herald*, December 15, 1874.
20. Kansas City *Daily Journal of Commerce*, December 9, 1874.
21. *Ibid.*, December 12, 1874; St. Louis *Republican*, in Boonville *Weekly Advertiser*, July 9, 1875.
22. Lexington *Caucasian*, December 12, 1874.
23. Kansas City *Times*, January 27, 28, 29, 30, and 31, 1875; Sedalia *Daily Democrat*, January 29, 1875; St. Louis *Republican*, January 29 and 31, 1875; Boonville *Weekly Advertiser*, February 5, 1875; Liberty *Advance*, February 4 and 11, 1875; Liberty *Tribune*, February 5, 1875; Richmond *Conservator*, January 30, 1875; St. Joseph *Morning Herald*, in Richmond *Conservator*, April 3, 1875; E. P. Hall of Liberty, Missouri, interview, June 15, 1940.
24. E. P. Hall, interview, June 15, 1940; Kansas City *Times*, January 30, 1875; Liberty *Tribune*, February 5, 1875.
25. Kansas City *Times*, January 28, 1875.
26. Richmond *Conservator*, January 30, 1875.
27. Kansas City *Times*, January 28, 1875.
28. St. Louis *Dispatch*, January 27, 1875.
29. Jefferson City *Peoples' Tribune*, February 3, 1875.
30. *Journal of the House, Twenty-eighth General Assembly of Missouri, Regular Session, 1875*, 357–58.
31. *Journal of the Senate, Twenty-eighth General Assembly of Missouri, Regular Session, 1875*, 148; St. Louis *Republican*, February 3, 1875.
32. Kansas City *Daily Journal of Commerce*, January 29, 1875.
33. *Ibid.*, February 2, 1875.
34. Liberty *Tribune*, February 12, 1875. The newspapers printed the report Hardin submitted to the legislature. The original Bingham report has not been found.
35. Jefferson City *Peoples' Tribune*, February 10, 1875; *Journal of the House, Twenty-eighth General Assembly of Missouri, Regular Session, 1875*, 430–31.
36. Clay County Circuit Court Records, File No. 449; Richmond *Conservator*, March 27, 1875; St. Joseph *Morning Herald*, in Liberty *Tribune*, April 9, 1875.

37. Clay County Circuit Court Records, File No. 449; Chicago *Tribune*, in
   St. Louis *Republican*, February 4, 1875; Richmond *Conservator*,
   March 27, 1875; Kansas City *Times*, April 3, 1875; Liberty *Tribune*,
   September 22, 1875.
38. Clay County Circuit Court Records, Vol. 16, 459.
39. Clipping from Chicago *Times* in Walter B. Stevens' Scrap Book No. 278.
40. Jefferson City *Peoples' Tribune*, March 24, 1875; *Journal of the House,
   Twenty-eighth General Assembly of Missouri, Regular Session, 1875*,
   1084.
41. Kansas City *Times*, March 18, 1875.
42. Kansas City *Daily Journal of Commerce*, March 23, 1875.
43. Jefferson City *Daily Tribune*, March 19, 1875.
44. See, for example, the Sedalia *Daily Democrat*, March 19, 1875, and the
   Boonville *Weekly Advertiser*, March 26, 1875.
45. Kansas City *Daily Journal of Commerce*, March 19, 1875.
46. *Journal of the House, Twenty-eighth General Assembly of Missouri,
   Regular Session, 1875*, 1176; Kansas City *Times*, March 21, 1875; Jefferson City *Peoples' Tribune*, March 24, 1875; St. Louis *Republican*,
   March 26, 1875. No copy of the substitute resolution has been found.

NOTES TO CHAPTER VIII

1. Liberty *Tribune*, April 16 and 23, 1875; Richmond *Conservator*, April
   24, 1875; Kansas City *Daily Journal of Commerce*, April 15, 1875;
   Kansas City *Times*, April 18, 1875.
2. Liberty *Tribune*, April 16, 1875.
3. Letter, John S. Groom to Charles Harding, April 16, 1875, in State
   Archives, State Historical Society of Missouri. Groom misspelled Hardin's name.
4. Liberty *Tribune*, April 16 and 23, 1875.
5. Chicago *Times*, in Kansas City *Times*, May 5, 1875.
6. Kansas City *Times*, April 14, 1875; Kansas City *Daily Journal of Commerce*, April 15, 1875.
7. St. Louis *Republican*, April 20, 1875.
8. Liberty *Tribune*, April 23 and 30 and May 7 and 14, 1875; Liberty *Advance*, April 29 and May 6, 1875; Richmond *Conservator*, April 24,
   1875; St. Louis *Christian Advocate*, in Liberty *Tribune*, June 25, 1875;
   St. Louis *Dispatch*, May 1, 1875; Kansas City *Times*, April 30, 1875;
   Kansas City *Daily Journal of Commerce*, April 25 and May 2, 4, and 5,
   1875.
9. Liberty *Tribune*, May 28, 1875; Liberty *Advance*, June 3, 1875.
10. St. Louis *Republican*, May 16, 17, and 19, 1875; Kansas City *Times*, May
   15, 1875; letter, Mrs. N. A. Lambert and Bessie W. Sharp to Governor
   Hardin, May 15, 1875, in State Archives, State Historical Society of Missouri.
11. Kansas City *Times*, May 15, 1875.
12. St. Louis *Republican*, May 21, 1875; Louisville *Courier-Journal*, in Lib-

erty *Tribune*, June 25, 1875; Chicago *Journal*, in Liberty *Tribune*, July 30, 1875.

13. Kansas City *Times*, July 15, 1875.
14. Plattsburg *Lever*, in Richmond *Conservator*, August 27, 1875.
15. Kansas City *Daily Journal of Commerce*, in Sedalia *Daily Democrat*, May 20, 1882; Liberty *Tribune*, July 23, 1875; Nashville *Banner*, August 8, in Kansas City *Times*, August 12, 1875.
16. Love, *Rise and Fall of Jesse James*, 36.
17. Nashville *Banner*, August 8, in Kansas City *Times*, August 12, 1875.
18. Liberty *Tribune*, September 10 and 24 and October 1 and 15, 1875; St. Louis *Times*, in Boonville *Weekly Advertiser*, October 1, 1875; St. Louis *Republican*, September 16 and 19, 1875; Love, *Rise and Fall of Jesse James*, 169–75.
19. Liberty *Tribune*, April 7, 1876; Liberty *Advance*, April 13, 1876; Boonville *Daily Advertiser*, February 16, 1876; Kansas City *Times*, February 18, 1876.
20. Dallas *Herald*, in St. Louis *Republican*, May 22, 1876.
21. Boonville *Daily Advertiser*, July 8, 11, and 25, 1876; Boonville *Weekly Advertiser*, July 11 and 14, 1876; *Messages and Proclamations of the Governors*, V, 510–11.
22. Miller's first name was McClellan, but he was known familiarly as Clell, not Clem. Pitts's real name was Samuel Wells, and Chadwell's was William Stiles.
23. St. Louis *Republican*, August 13, 1876; letters, James McDonough to Governor C. H. Hardin, August 2, 6, and 19, and September 12, 1876, in State Archives, State Historical Society of Missouri.
24. Kansas City *Daily Journal of Commerce*, August 13, 1876.
25. Kansas City *Times*, August 18, 1876.
26. *Ibid.*
27. *Ibid.*, August 23, 1876.
28. *Ibid.*, August 25, 1876.
29. Kansas City *Daily Journal of Commerce*, August 30, 1876.
30. Kansas City *Times*, August 13, 1876; Kansas City *Evening Mail*, in Sedalia *Daily Democrat*, August 18, 1876.
31. Many accounts give 1874 as the correct date. Robert James, in an interview March 17, 1945, said his father and mother were married in 1874. The Kansas City *Times*, September 11, 1881, reported an interview with Ralston in which he said the marriage took place in June, 1874.
32. Kansas City *Times*, August 16, 1876.
33. George Huntington, *Robber and Hero*, is an account of the robbery and the subsequent chase. Love, *Rise and Fall of Jesse James*, 189–242, gives a good description of the robbery and of the capture of the Youngers. Contemporary newspaper accounts are similar. See the Liberty *Tribune*, September 15, 22, and 29, 1876. The St. Louis *Globe-Democrat*, St. Louis *Republican*, Kansas City *Times*, and Kansas City *Daily Journal of Commerce* for various dates in September, 1876, contain complete details of the developments in the pursuit.
34. Boonville *Daily Advertiser*, September 25, 1876; St. Paul *Pioneer Press*

and Tribune, in Boonville *Daily Advertiser,* September 27, 1876; Huntington, *Robber and Hero,* 73–75; Love, *Rise and Fall of Jesse James,* 241.

35. Letter, James McDonough to Governor C. H. Hardin, September 12, 1876.
36. Letter, James McDonough to Governor C. H. Hardin, September 22, 1876.
37. Letter, James McDonough to Governor C. H. Hardin, September 29, 1876.
38. Chicago *Times,* in Kansas City *Times,* October 6, 1876.
39. Chicago *Times,* November 17 and 20, 1876, in Liberty *Tribune,* November 24, 1876.
40. Boonville *Daily Advertiser,* October 17, 1876.
41. St. Louis *Republican,* October 22, 1876.
42. Younger, *The Story of Cole Younger by Himself,* 76–77. The first name of Ames was really Adelbert.
43. Love, *Rise and Fall of Jesse James,* 190–91.
44. Younger, *The Story of Cole Younger by Himself,* 80–81.
45. The Boston *Advertiser* suggested that the banks throughout the country contribute a fund for the benefit of the Heywood family. In less than a month, it was reported, over $11,000 had been raised. Ultimately, $17,602.06 was contributed. The First National Bank of Northfield gave $5,000. Although gifts came from banks all over the country, this was the only contribution from a bank that the Jameses and Youngers were accused of robbing. Chicago *Tribune,* in Liberty *Tribune,* September 22, 1876; Liberty *Tribune,* October 20, 1876; Huntington, *Robber and Hero,* 101–19.
46. St. Louis *Globe-Democrat,* September 25, 1876.
47. Kansas City *Daily Journal of Commerce,* September 27, 1876.
48. Boonville *Daily Advertiser,* October 17, 1876; St. Louis *Republican,* October 18, 1876.
49. Independence *News,* in Kansas City *Commercial Advertiser,* January 31, 1868. Clipping in Martin Ismert James Album No. 2.

NOTES TO CHAPTER IX

1. The name was also spelled *Goodwin* in the newspapers. *Goodin* was used most frequently after his identity was determined.
2. Letters, James McDonough to Governor C. H. Hardin, October 13, 19, and 25 and November 1, 1876; Kansas City *Times,* October 14 and 15, 1876. The expenses of McDonough's efforts to apprehend the James band, from about the middle of August until after the arrest of Goodin, were paid from the fund appropriated by the legislature and entrusted to the Governor for the suppression of banditry. This was not announced to the public. The cost, including expenses for McDonough's trip to Minnesota, was $688.12.
3. St. Louis *Missouri Republican,* November 17, 1879, and April 7, 1882.
4. St. Louis *Globe-Democrat,* October 16, 1876; Kansas City *Daily Journal of*

Commerce, October 18 and 20, 1876; St. Louis *Republican*, October 15, 1876. The *Republican* was a Democratic paper, but was at odds with the Democratic state administration.

5. Kansas City *Times*, October 19, 1876.
6. *Ibid.*, October 17, 1876.
7. Kansas City *Daily Journal of Commerce*, October 18, 1876.
8. Kansas City *Times*, October 19, 1876.
9. Kansas City *Daily Journal of Commerce*, October 20, 1876.
10. Kansas City *Times*, October 21, 1876.
11. Liberty *Advance*, November 30, 1876; Liberty *Tribune*, December 1, 1876; Richmond *Conservator*, November 24, 1876.
12. Kansas City *Times*, October 24, 1876; St. Louis *Globe-Democrat*, October 26, 1876; St. Louis *Republican*, in Boonville *Daily Advertiser*, November 27, 1876.
13. Sedalia *Daily Democrat*, August 14, 1877.
14. St. Louis *Republican*, August 6, 1878.
15. Sedalia *Daily Democrat*, August 9, 1878.
16. Notes on interview with Nolin Womack taken by Ovid Bell, Sr., Fulton, Missouri. Various parts of this story are repeated in Mokane *Missourian*, March 30, 1917; Fulton *Sun-Gazette*, February 26, 1938; and Auxvasse *Review*, February 15, 1939. In an interview, March 17, 1945, Robert F. James said that in the last years of her life, his mother Annie Ralston James frequently was amused at wild stories of the James boys. She thought stories of Jesse's conducting singing school particularly ridiculous, for she said Jesse could not "carry a tune."
17. See Belford, Clarke and Co., publishers, *Train and Bank Robbers of the West*, 239–63; Jay Donald, *Outlaws of the Border*, 319–57, 365–70; and J. A. Dacus, *Illustrated Lives and Adventures of Frank and Jesse James and the Younger Brothers*, 289–352.
18. John Lord, "Picturesque Road-Agents of Early Days," *Overland Monthly*, 70 (November, 1917), 492–94.
19. Denver *Tribune*, November 7, in St. Louis *Missouri Republican*, November 10, 1879.
20. Liberty *Tribune*, May 30, 1879.
21. Kansas City *Daily Journal*, October 10 and 11, 1879; Kansas City *Times*, October 9, 10, and 11, 1879; Liberty *Tribune*, October 10 and 17, 1879; Jefferson City *Peoples' Tribune*, October 15, 1879.
22. See Kansas City *Times*, October 11, 15, and 28, 1879; Kansas City *Daily Journal*, October 10 and 19, 1879; St. Louis *Post-Dispatch*, October 18, 1879; Richmond *Democrat*, October 16, 1879; Jefferson City *Peoples' Tribune*, October 15, 1879; Boonville *Weekly Advertiser*, October 17, 1879.
23. Sedalia *Daily Democrat*, October 29, 1879.
24. Kansas City *Times*, November 4, 1879; Kansas City *Daily Journal*, November 4, 1879.
25. St. Paul *Pioneer Press*, in Sedalia *Daily Democrat*, November 14, 1879.
26. Liberty *Tribune*, November 7, 1879.
27. Kansas City *Mail*, in Jefferson City *Peoples' Tribune*, November 19, 1879.
28. Richmond *Conservator*, in Liberty *Tribune*, December 5, 1879.

29. Kansas City *Times*, in Liberty *Tribune*, January 9 and May 21, 1880.
30. Sedalia *Daily Democrat*, November 20, 1879.
31. St. Louis *Missouri Republican*, November 21, 1879; Richmond *Democrat*, March 9, 1882.
32. Kansas City *Times*, in Richmond *Democrat*, November 20, 1879.
33. Kansas City *Daily Journal*, November 20, 1879.

NOTES TO CHAPTER X

1. Columbia *Missouri Statesman*, September 24, 1880.
2. Chicago *Commercial Advertiser*, August 28, 1879.
3. St. Louis *Post-Dispatch*, November 3, 1880.
4. Homer Clevenger, "Agrarian Politics in Missouri, 1880–1896," 22.
5. Kansas City *Times*, October 31 and November 1 and 10, 1880; William H. Wallace, *Speeches and Writings of William H. Wallace with Autobiography*, 273; Theodoric B. Wallace, Kansas City, Missouri, interview, March 20, 1945.
6. *Messages and Proclamations of the Governors*, VI, 275.
7. St. Louis *Chronicle*, July 12, 1881.
8. Liberty *Tribune*, August 5, 1881.
9. Kansas City *Times*, July 16, 17, and 18, 1881; Kansas City *Daily Journal*, July 16, 1881; St. Louis *Post-Dispatch*, July 16, 1881.
10. Kansas City *Times*, July 20, 1881.
11. Kansas City *Daily Journal*, July 19, 1881; Richmond *Conservator*, July 22, 1881.
12. Kansas City *Mail*, in Jefferson City *Peoples' Tribune*, August 3, 1881.
13. St. Louis *Globe-Democrat*, July 27 and 31, 1881; Kansas City *Daily Journal*, July 26, 1881; St. Louis *Chronicle*, July 29, 1881; Liberty *Tribune*, July 22, 1881.
14. Sedalia *Daily Democrat*, July 19, 22, 29, and 31, 1881.
15. Kansas City *Daily Journal*, July 19, 1881.
16. St. Louis *Missouri Republican*, July 30, 1881; Richmond *Democrat*, August 11, 1881; Jefferson City *Peoples' Tribune*, November 16, 1881.
17. Kansas City *Times*, July 28, 1881.
18. *Ibid.*, July 27, 1881.
19. Kansas City *Evening Star*, August 1, 1881.
20. Kansas City *Times*, August 11, 1881; St. Louis *Missouri Republican*, August 1, 1881; Liberty *Tribune*, August 5 and November 4, 1881, contain examples of these replies.
21. St. Louis *Globe-Democrat*, July 19, 1881; St. Louis *Missouri Republican*, July 22, 1881; Kansas City *Times*, July 17, 22, and 23, 1881; Kansas City *Evening Star*, July 27, 1881; St. Louis *Chronicle*, July 22, 1881.
22. The state constitution of 1875 limited the amount to $300.
23. St. Louis *Missouri Republican*, July 26 and 27, 1881; Kansas City *Daily Journal*, July 27, 1881; Crittenden, *The Crittenden Memoirs*, 60.
24. *Messages and Proclamations of the Governors*, VI, 494–96. The name *John McCulloch* should have been *Frank McMillan*, the passenger killed in the train robbery at Winston.

25. Sedalia *Daily Democrat*, September 10, 1881.
26. Kansas City *Times*, July 29 and August 1, 1881; Jefferson City *Peoples' Tribune*, August 10, 1881; St. Louis *Globe-Democrat*, August 2, 1881; St. Louis *Post-Dispatch*, July 26 and 27, 1881; and St. Louis *Chronicle*, July 27, 1881.
27. Thomas T. Crittenden, "Autobiography," in Crittenden, *The Crittenden Memoirs*, 59–60.
28. Kansas City *Times*, September 8, 9, and 10, 1881. Quotation is from September 8 issue.
29. Jefferson City *Peoples' Tribune*, September 14, 1881.
30. Kansas City *Daily Journal*, September 11, 1881; St. Louis *Missouri Republican*, September 12 and October 20, 1881; Richmond *Democrat*, October 20, 1881; Wallace, *Speeches and Writings*, 280–82.
31. St. Louis *Missouri Republican*, September 11, 1881; Jefferson City *Peoples' Tribune*, September 14, 1881; Liberty *Tribune*, September 16, 1881.
32. Boonville *Weekly Advertiser*, July 16, 1880; Liberty *Tribune*, December 3, 1880; Jefferson City *Peoples' Tribune*, September 28, 1881; Sedalia *Daily Democrat*, October 18, 1881; St. Louis *Missouri Republican*, September 28 and 29 and October 1, 2, 10, and 16, 1881; Sedalia *Daily Bazoo*, September 26, 1881; Wallace, *Speeches and Writings*, 274–83.
33. St. Louis *Missouri Republican*, October 1, 1881; Liberty *Tribune*, September 30 and November 25, 1881.
34. St. Louis *Missouri Republican*, September 28 and 29 and October 1 and 2, 1881.
35. Kansas City *Times*, September 29, 1881.
36. Wallace, *Speeches and Writings*, 239.
37. St. Louis *Missouri Republican*, September 30, 1881.

NOTES TO CHAPTER XI

1. Liberty *Tribune*, November 4, 1881.
2. St. Louis *Missouri Republican*, November 1 and 5, 1881; Russellville *Herald*, in St. Louis *Missouri Republican*, November 4, 1881; Louisville *Courier-Journal*, in St. Louis *Missouri Republican*, November 5, 1881.
3. Russellville *Herald*, in St. Louis *Missouri Republican*, November 4, 1881.
4. Richmond *Democrat*, March 2 and 9, 1882; Sedalia *Daily Democrat*, February 24, 1882; Liberty *Tribune*, February 24 and March 10, 1882.
5. Kansas City *Evening Star*, March 27, 28, 29, 30, and 31, 1882; Richmond *Democrat*, March 30, 1882; Kansas City *Times*, April 1 and 2, 1882.
6. Kansas City *Evening Star*, April 6, 1882; Wallace, *Speeches and Writings*, 280–82.
7. Kansas City *Evening Star*, March 31, 1881.
8. Kansas City *Evening Star*, March 31 and April 1 and 2, 1882; Kansas City *Times*, April 1 and 2, 1882; Kansas City *Daily Journal*, April 1 and 2, 1882; St. Louis *Missouri Republican*, April 1 and 2, 1882; Wallace, *Speeches and Writings*, 279–80.

9. St. Joseph *Herald,* April 4, 6, and 7, 1882; Kansas City *Times,* April 3, 4, 5, 6, 7, and 8, 1882; Kansas City *Evening Star,* April 3, 4, 5, 6, 7, and 8, 1882; St. Louis *Chronicle,* April 3, 4, and 5, 1882; St. Louis *Missouri Republican,* April 4, 5, 6, and 7, 1882; Liberty *Tribune,* April 7 and 14 and May 5, 1882; Boonville *Weekly Advertiser,* April 21 and 28 and June 23, 1882; Sedalia *Daily Democrat,* April 16, 1882.

10. St. Louis *Missouri Republican,* April 5, 1882.

11. Kansas City *Evening Star,* April 6, 1882.

12. St. Louis *Missouri Republican,* April 7 and 18, 1882; Sedalia *Daily Democrat,* May 5, 1882; Liberty *Tribune,* April 14, 1882.

13. Liberty *Tribune,* May 5, 1882.

14. St. Louis *Missouri Republican,* April 17 and 18, 1882; St. Joseph *Herald,* April 18, 1882; Buchanan County Circuit Court Records, Criminal Record 3, 554.

15. Crittenden, *The Crittenden Memoirs,* 60.

16. Love, *Rise and Fall of Jesse James,* 351, 361; E. P. Hall, interview, June 15, 1940.

17. St. Louis *Post-Dispatch,* April 4, 1882.

18. St. Louis *Missouri Republican,* April 7, 1882.

19. Sedalia *Daily Democrat,* April 13, 1882. The "brazen harlot" referred to either Mattie Collins or Martha Bolton, or to both; they had assisted in negotiations for Liddil's surrender. Both had bad reputations.

20. Sedalia *Daily Democrat,* April 13, 1882.

21. *Ibid.,* April 16 and 23 and May 7, 1882; St. Louis *Missouri Republican,* April 14 and 15, 1882.

22. Kansas City *Daily Journal,* April 23, 1882.

23. St. Louis *Chronicle,* April 14, 1882; Sedalia *Daily Democrat,* April 22, 1882; Boonville *Weekly Advertiser,* April 28, 1882; Kansas City *Times,* April 22 and May 4, 1882.

24. *Journal of the House, Thirty-first General Assembly of Missouri, Extra Session, 1882,* 20–21.

25. *Ibid.,* 20–22.

26. *Ibid.,* 28–30, 34.

27. *Ibid.,* 48–49.

28. *Ibid.,* 53.

29. Clevenger, "Agrarian Politics in Missouri, 1880–1896," 22.

30. St. Louis *Missouri Republican,* April 20, 1882.

31. Columbia *Missouri Statesman,* August 4, 1882.

32. St. Louis *Chronicle,* April 4, 1882.

33. *Howell County Journal,* in Sedalia *Daily Democrat,* April 19, 1882.

34. Richmond *Conservator,* July 28, 1882.

35. St. Louis *Missouri Republican,* April 17, 18, and 24, 1882; Sedalia *Daily Democrat,* April 13, 1882; Kansas City *Times,* April 25, 1882; Richmond *Conservator,* April 21, 1882.

36. New York *Illustrated Times,* April 22, 1882.

37. St. Louis *Missouri Republican,* April 7 and 17, 1882; Sedalia *Daily Democrat,* April 14, 1882.

38. Cincinnati *Enquirer,* April 10, 1882.

39. *Texas Siftings*, April 29, 1882.
40. *Ibid.*, May 27, 1882.
41. *The Judge*, July 15, 1882.
42. Richmond *Conservator*, April 21, 1882.

NOTES TO CHAPTER XII

1. Kansas City *Daily Journal*, April 4, 1882; St. Louis *Missouri Republican*, April 5, 1882.
2. Nashville *Banner*, in St. Louis *Missouri Republican*, April 21, 1882; Nashville *American*, in St. Louis *Missouri Republican*, April 22, 1882. Many feature articles dealing with Jesse James in Tennessee have been published. One of the best was written by F. A. Behymer of the St. Louis *Post-Dispatch* and published in that paper on June 24, 1923.
3. St. Louis *Chronicle*, April 7, 1882; Liberty *Tribune*, May 12 and July 28, 1882; Kansas City *Times*, April 8, 1882; Richmond *Democrat*, May 11 and 25, 1882; Boonville *Weekly Advertiser*, May 19, 1893.
4. St. Louis *Chronicle*, June 3, 1882; Sedalia *Daily Democrat*, May 31, 1882; Richmond *Democrat*, April 27 and June 1, 1882; Liberty *Tribune*, June 2 and 16, 1882; Boonville *Weekly Advertiser*, June 9, 1882.
5. Letter, August 1, 1882, to "My Dear Frank" from J. N. Edwards. This letter and all other letters from Edwards to Frank James hereinafter cited were in the possession of Mr. and Mrs. Robert James, Kearney, Missouri, in June, 1950.
6. St. Louis *Missouri Republican*, October 6, 1882.
7. *Ibid.*
8. *Ibid.*
9. *Ibid.*, October 7, 1882.
10. *Ibid.*, October 6, 1882.
11. Nashville *American*, in St. Louis *Missouri Republican*, October 14, 1882.
12. James Family Bible; interview with Robert F. James, March 17, 1945; St. Louis *Post-Dispatch*, June 24, 1923.
13. Kansas City *Times*, August 13, 1876.
14. *Ibid.*, September 11, 1881.
15. Interview with Robert F. James, March 17, 1945.
16. St. Louis *Missouri Republican*, September 9, 1883; John Winston Coleman, Jr., *Stage Coach Days in the Bluegrass*, 251–54.
17. Kansas City *Daily Journal*, October 9, 1882.
18. St. Louis *Globe-Democrat*, October 10, 1882.
19. St. Louis *Missouri Republican*, October 14, 1882.
20. St. Louis *Post-Dispatch*, October 6, 1882.
21. Boonville *Weekly Advertiser*, October 13, 1882.
22. Kansas City *Times*, October 6, 1882.
23. St. Louis *Post-Dispatch*, October 6, 1882.
24. Neosho *Times*, October 12, 1882.
25. Kansas City *Times*, October 8, 1882.
26. Sedalia *Weekly Democrat*, October 14, 1882. I have not had access to the Sedalia *Daily Democrat* for the latter half of 1882.

27. St. Louis *Globe-Democrat*, October 8, 1882.
28. Richmond *Conservator*, January 26, 1883; Liberty *Tribune*, January 26, 1883; St. Louis *Missouri Republican*, January 25, 1883; St. Joseph *Herald*, January 24, 1883.
29. Sedalia *Daily Democrat*, January 23, 1883; Richmond *Conservator*, January 26, 1883; Liberty *Tribune*, February 9, 1883; St. Joseph *Gazette*, March 10, 1885.
30. St. Joseph *Herald*, February 21, 1883; Richmond *Democrat*, February 15, 1883; Liberty *Tribune*, February 23, 1883. The indictments are in Criminal File No. 44, Daviess County Circuit Court Records.
31. Liberty *Tribune*, March 9, 1883; St. Joseph *Evening News*, in Richmond *Democrat*, March 22, 1883; Richmond *Democrat*, March 29, 1883.
32. Record J.227, filed December 23, 1883, U. S., Department of Justice Files; St. Louis *Missouri Republican*, November 2, 1882; Liberty *Tribune*, November 10, 1882.
33. Record J.227, Department of Justice Files.
34. St. Joseph *Gazette*, April 11, 1883.
35. St. Louis *Missouri Republican*, January 5, 1883; St. Joseph *Gazette*, January 6, 1883.
36. Wallace, *Speeches and Writings*, 268–70, 287–89.
37. All leading Missouri dailies had correspondents at the trial and gave it complete coverage. Except where otherwise stated, this account is based upon the St. Louis *Missouri Republican*, August 21-September 7, 1883. This paper was selected because its reports are as unbiased as any found and seem to be the result of capable reporting. I also read the reports published in the St. Joseph *Gazette* and the Kansas City *Times*. George Miller, Jr., editor and compiler, *The Trial of Frank James For Murder*, is a complete account of the trial. Miller, a cousin of W. H. Wallace, had the use of Wallace's papers in the production of the work. Also valuable is John D. Lawson, *American State Trials*, XI, 661–852. Lawson was for many years dean of the University of Missouri School of Law. Daviess County Circuit Court Record, Vol. M, 2–14, contains a record of the disposal of the case. No transcript of the evidence has been found.
38. Lawson, *American State Trials*, XI, 662–65, has brief biographical sketches of the lawyers in the case.
39. St. Joseph *Gazette*, August 24, 1883. Daviess County Circuit Court Records, Volume M, 4, list the jurors as Lonnzo W. Gilbrath, James J. Snyder, Oscar Chamberlin, Benjamin F. Feurt, Jason Winburn, William F. Richardson, Abisha H. Shellman, William L. Merritt, Richard E. Hale, Charles R. Nance, James W. Boggs, and James B. Smith. Richardson was the foreman.
40. St. Louis *Missouri Republican*, September 7, 1883; St. Joseph *Gazette*, September 8, 1883.
41. Wallace, *Speeches and Writings*, 287–89.
42. St. Joseph *Gazette*, September 7, 1883.

NOTES TO CHAPTER XIII

1. St. Louis *Missouri Republican*, September 7 and 8, 1883; St. Louis *Chronicle*, September 7, 1883; Jefferson City *Peoples' Tribune*, September 12, 1883; Richmond *Democrat*, September 13 and 20, 1883; Kansas City *Times*, September 7 and 13, 1883.
2. Commissioners of the supreme court sit with judges in hearing arguments and write opinions in cases assigned to them. The commissioners' opinions become decisions of the court only when approved by the judges.
3. St. Joseph *Gazette*, September 5, 1883.
4. Kansas City *Daily Journal*, September 7 and 8, 1883; St. Joseph *Herald*, September 7 and 8, 1883.
5. St. Louis *Post-Dispatch*, September 7, 1883.
6. *Ibid.*, September 11, 1883. This is different in tone from King's formal statement in the St. Joseph *Gazette*, September 11, 1883. There he praised Edwards as a gentleman and said nothing of the *Gazette*'s espousing the cause of Frank James.
7. St. Joseph *Herald*, September 12, 21, and 22, 1883.
8. St. Louis *Post-Dispatch*, September 12, 1883.
9. St. Louis *Missouri Republican*, September 9 and 12, 1883. Many other Missouri newspapers carried complete copies of the confessions.
10. St. Louis *Missouri Republican*, September 11, 1883; St. Louis *Post-Dispatch*, in St. Joseph *Gazette*, September 6, 1883.
11. St. Louis *Missouri Republican*, October 8, 1883.
12. Daviess County Circuit Court Records, Vol. M, 92; Liberty *Tribune*, November 9, 1883.
13. Daviess County Circuit Court Records, Vol. M, 102; Liberty *Tribune*, December 21, 1883.
14. St. Louis *Missouri Republican*, December 22 and 23, 1883, and January 3, 1884.
15. *Ibid.*, January 31, 1884.
16. State v. Grant, 79 Mo. 113; St. Louis *Missouri Republican*, December 18, 1883.
17. St. Louis *Missouri Republican*, February 6, 1884.
18. *Ibid.*, February 4, 1884.
19. *Ibid.*, February 12, 1884; Daviess County Circuit Court Records, Vol. M, 143.
20. St. Louis *Missouri Republican*, February 12, 1884.
21. *Ibid.*, February 15, 1884.
22. St. Louis *Post-Dispatch*, February 7, 1884.
23. *Ibid.*, February 12, 1884.
24. *Ibid.*, June 4, 1884.
25. St. Joseph *Herald*, February 15, 1884.
26. Kansas City *Daily Journal*, February 12, 1884.
27. St. Joseph *Gazette*, February 14, 1884.
28. Letter to Frank James from J. N. Edwards, March 1, 1884.

29. *Ibid.*, April 3 and 11, 1884.
30. St. Louis *Missouri Republican*, April 18, 19, 20, 22, 23, 24, and 26, 1884; Huntsville, Alabama, *Gazette*, April 19 and 26, 1884. W. Stanley Hoole, *The James Boys Rode South*, tells the story of the robbery and trial mainly from contemporary and later newspaper accounts.
31. Kansas City *Daily Journal*, April 27, 1884.
32. St. Louis *Missouri Republican*, April 26 and 27, 1884; Boonville *Weekly Advertiser*, May 2, 1884; letters, J. N. Edwards to Frank James, March 9 and 18 and April 3 and 11, 1884.
33. St. Joseph *Herald*, April 27, 1884.
34. Richmond *Conservator*, May 30, 1884.
35. St. Louis *Missouri Republican*, August 23 and September 7 and 13, 1884; Sedalia *Daily Democrat*, August 21, 1884.
36. St. Joseph *Herald*, September 13, 1884; Kansas City *Daily Journal*, September 12, 1884; A. J. D. Steward, ed., *The History of Bench and Bar in Missouri*, 641–45; letter, J. N. Edwards to Frank James, October 20, 1884.
37. Sedalia *Daily Democrat*, May 14, 1884.
38. St. Louis *Missouri Republican*, June 26, 1884.
39. Clevenger, "Agrarian Politics in Missouri, 1880–1896," 111, 114–15.
40. Richmond *Conservator*, July 11, 1884.
41. Clevenger, "Agrarian Politics in Missouri, 1880–1896," 121; Columbia *Missouri Statesman*, August 15 and 22, 1884.
42. Columbia *Missouri Statesman*, August 29, 1884.
43. St. Joseph *Herald*, August 14, 1884.
44. St. Louis *Missouri Republican*, September 3, 1884.
45. *Ibid.*, August 29, 1884.
46. Sedalia *Daily Democrat*, September 4, 1884.
47. St. Joseph *Gazette*, September 6, 1884.
48. *Official Directory of Missouri for 1885*, 97.
49. Jefferson City *Daily Tribune*, September 12, 1884.
50. Sedalia *Daily Democrat*, September 16, 1884.
51. Clevenger, "Agrarian Politics in Missouri, 1880–1896," 137.
52. St. Louis *Missouri Republican*, October 17, 1884.
53. *Official Directory of Missouri for 1885*, 18.
54. Letter to Frank James from J. N. Edwards, October 24, 1884.
55. Liberty *Tribune*, January 16, 1885.
56. Boonville *Weekly Advertiser*, February 27, 1885.
57. St. Louis *Globe-Democrat*, February 19, 20, and 23, 1885; St. Louis *Post-Dispatch*, February 19 and 23, 1885.
58. Kansas City *Daily Journal*, February 20, 23, 26, 27, and 28 and March 5, 1885.
59. St. Joseph *Gazette*, March 10, 1885.
60. Dan Saults, "Missouri's Forgotten Don Quixote," 23; Jennie Edwards, compiler, *John N. Edwards, Biography, Memoirs, Reminiscences and Recollections*, various pages.
61. New York *Daily Graphic*, September 8, 1883; St. Joseph *Herald*, September 20, 1883.

62. St. Louis *Missouri Republican*, January 23 and 25, 1886. Without obtaining Vest's permission, Crittenden released for publication their correspondence dealing with the matter.

NOTES TO CHAPTER XIV

1. *Cass County Times Courier*, in Liberty *Tribune*, August 26, 1880; also reprinted in Boonville *Weekly Advertiser*, August 27, 1880.
2. Liberty *Tribune*, March 4, June 17, July 29, and August 5, 1881; Kansas City *Times*, August 6 and 12, 1881; Kansas City *Daily Journal*, August 11, 1881; St. Louis *Globe-Democrat*, in Liberty *Tribune*, November 4, 1881.
3. W. C. Bronaugh, *The Youngers' Fight for Freedom*, is Bronaugh's story of his twenty-year fight for release of the Youngers from prison. The account here of his efforts is based on this work. Supplementary data are noted.
4. This petition with signatures is in the Western Historical Manuscript Collection at the University of Missouri.
5. Kansas City *Star*, October 20, 1902; Boonville *Weekly Advertiser*, October 24, 1902. The bone from Jim Younger's jaw was on display at the Minnesota State Historical Society in March, 1903. Kansas City *Times*, March 18, 1903.
6. Kansas City *Times*, February 4, 5, and 17, 1903; Kansas City *Star*, February 20, 1903.
7. See Cincinnati *Enquirer*, in Richmond *Conservator*, July 11, 1889; New York *World*, in Boonville *Weekly Advertiser*, June 25, 1897.
8. Interviews, E. P. Hall, June 15, 1940, and Robert F. James, November 30, 1944.
9. Jefferson City *State Journal*, January 3, 1901; Kansas City *Star*, in Boonville *Weekly Advertiser*, January 18, 1901; Robert F. James, interview, November 30, 1944.
10. St. Louis *Post-Dispatch*, November 10, 1901; Kansas City *Star*, February 10, 1902, and November 22, 1904; Kansas City *Times*, January 25, 1905; Robert F. James, interview, November 30, 1944.
11. Robert F. James, interview, November 30, 1944; Kansas City *Times*, February 18, 1903; Liberty *Tribune*, May 15, 1903; Boonville *Weekly Advertiser*, September 4, 1903; Liberty *Advance*, September 25, 1903.
12. Columbia *Missouri Herald*, August 28, 1903. Authorship has been attributed to Walter Williams, later dean of the School of Journalism and president of the University of Missouri.
13. Kansas City *Journal*, August 21, 1904; Columbia *Missouri Herald*, November 4, 1904.
14. Robert F. James, interview, November 30, 1944; Kansas City *Post*, July 2, 1907; Liberty *Tribune*, March 31 and April 28, 1911, and February 26, 1915; Liberty *Advance*, February 26, 1915; Kansas City *Times*, February 19, 1915.
15. Kansas City *Star*, July 6 and 16, 1944; Kansas City *Times*, July 7, 1944.

16. Liberty *Advance*, August 20, 1909, and February 10 and 17, 1911; Liberty *Tribune*, June 2, 1911; Kansas City *Times*, March 22, 1916; Lee's Summit *Journal*, March 23, 1916.
17. Kansas City *Star*, September 23, 1898, and February 23, 24, 25, 26, 27, and 28 and March 1, 1899; Boonville *Weekly Advertiser*, November 16 and 23, 1900; Kansas City *Times*, September 27, 1896; Howard Huselton, interview, March 19, 1945.
18. St. Louis *Chronicle*, in Richmond *Conservator*, May 8, 1884.
19. Kansas City *Star*, January 3, 1921, and August 4, 1922; Liberty *Advance*, November 16, 1925; St. Joseph *News-Press*, August 29, 1938, and July 10, 1939.
20. Albany *Sun*, in St. Joseph *Gazette*, October 17, 1883; Denver *News*, in Boonville *Weekly Advertiser*, January 24, 1890; Richmond *Conservator*, March 8, 1894; Kansas City *Star*, October 13, 1898; St. Louis *Post-Dispatch*, September 25, 1910; Excelsior Springs *Daily Standard*, November 5, 1931; Julian Street, *Abroad at Home*, 313–36; Howard Huselton, interview, March 19, 1945; Mr. and Mrs. Robert F. James, interview, March 17, 1945.
21. St. Louis *Post-Dispatch*, June 29 and 30, 1902.
22. Kansas City *Star*, March 17, 1936.
23. Thomas R. Shouse, "My Father's Part in Ending the Career of the James Boys," Kansas City *Star*, December 18, 1938, is an example of this type of article. His story was published in other papers, also. In the Kansas City Public Library clipping collection are long articles from the Louisville *Courier-Journal*, November 22, 1914; New York *Telegraph*, in Cincinnati *Enquirer*, December 25, 1915; and Washington *Post*, December 14, 1914, and February 28, 1915, that the fatal illness of Frank James motivated.
24. Omaha *World-Herald*, in Crofton, Nebraska, *Journal*, December 7, 1939; Lincoln *Sunday Journal and Star*, February 5, 1939; Excelsior Springs *Daily Standard*, January 29, 1939.
25. See Love, *Rise and Fall of Jesse James*, 269–81.
26. St. Paul *Pioneer-Press*, September 20, in Kansas City *Times*, September 24, 1876.
27. Louisville *Courier-Journal*, April 10, 1882, and March 20, 21, 22, 23, 24, and 25, 1883.
28. Liberty *Tribune*, April 14, 1882.
29. St. Joseph *Gazette*, April 20, 1883.
30. New York *World*, in Boonville *Weekly Advertiser*, August 21, 1914; Washington *Post*, July 28, 1914, in Kansas City Public Library clipping collection.
31. Joe Vaughan, *The Only True History of the Life of Frank James, Written by Himself.*
32. Rascoe, *Belle Starr*, 34.
33. Topeka *Capital*, March 8, 1914, in Kansas City Public Library clipping collection; H. D. Tucker, Columbia, Missouri, interview, July 9, 1945. Tucker lived in Brownwood several years and knew the son of Ford. The son said that his father would never reveal any information about his past.

34. Florence, Colorado, *Daily Citizen*, November 2, 3, 4, and 5, 1931; Wichita *Eagle*, November 22, 1931, in Kansas State Historical Society clipping collection; Kansas City *Star*, December 13, 1931.
35. Excelsior Springs *Daily Standard*, January 7, 8, 10, 11, 12, 13, 14, 15, 17, 21, 24, and 28, February 25, and April 6, 7, 17, and 18, 1932; Liberty *Tribune*, January 7, 1932; New York *Times*, April 24, 1932.
36. Kansas City *Star*, August 5, 1932, and July 5 and November 16, 1934; Denver *Post*, March 3, 1935; Marshall *Democrat-News*, April 28, 29, and 30, 1937; Lawton, Oklahoma, *Morning Press*, May 23, 1948.
37. Frank O. Hall and Lindsey H. Whitten, *Jesse James Rides Again*, presents his story.
38. Love, *Rise and Fall of Jesse James*, 282–83.
39. The earliest published version I am aware of was copied from the Hopkins, Missouri, *Journal* in the Boonville *Weekly Advertiser*, March 19, 1897. Hopkins is in northwest Missouri, and the *Journal* located the incident in "that part of the state." In 1899 Jesse Edwards James told the story in a book about his father, *Jesse James, My Father*, dating it one or two years after the Civil War and saying it occurred when his father and a guerrilla comrade visited the widow of a Quantrill man in Tennessee. A version published in the Liberty *Advance*, June 12, 1903, reported that Jesse killed the moneylender and recovered the money from his body. An account of the good deed in the Tipton, Missouri, *Times*, February 26, 1915, substitutes a very poor and aged couple for the widow. Love, *Rise and Fall of Jesse James*, 284, credits a St. Louis detective, Samuel E. Allender, with his version. Allender said that Frank James was his source of information and that James located the incident "somewhere in northern Missouri."
40. Liberty *Advance*, April 21, 1911; Paris *Mercury*, in Kansas City *Star*, March 2, 1915; Liberty *Tribune*, August 10, 1928; Omaha *World-Herald*, in Kansas City *Star*, April 14, 1938; Frank Condon, "Local Ghost Makes Good," *Colliers*, 102 (November 26, 1938), 14, 44, 46; Walter B. Stevens, "Missouri's Centennial," *Missouri Historical Review*, XI (April-July, 1917), 285–86.
41. Statement by Robert L. Kennedy in the Springfield, Missouri, *Leader*, October 18, 1933, quoted in Vance Randolph, ed., *Ozark Folksongs*, II, 17; E. R. Hamilton, insurance man at Columbia, Missouri, told me on May 29, 1945, that he remembers hearing an elderly Negro worker on his father's farm pick a banjo and sing the ballad during the 1880's.
42. Vance Randolph, *Ozark Folksongs*, II, 17–24.
43. In some versions *Shea* is *Clay*.
44. Margaret Larkin, *Singing Cowboy*, 156–59. Permission to quote has been granted by the holder of the copyright.
45. H. M. Belden, ed., *Ballads and Songs Collected by the Missouri Folklore Society*, 403.
46. Sedalia *Daily Democrat*, April 11, 1882.
47. Richmond *Democrat*, May 17, 1883.
48. *Ibid.*, May 24, 1883.
49. St. Joseph *Gazette*, November 11 and 13, 1883.

50. Kansas City *Star*, February 10, 1902; Kansas City *Times*, February 11, 1902.
51. Kansas City *Star*, February 12 and 13, 1902.
52. Kansas City *Times*, September 12, 1903.
53. *The Mirror*, April 18, 1907.
54. *Ibid.*, February 23, 1911.
55. St. Louis *Post-Dispatch*, September 25, 1938; Elizabeth Beall Ginty, *Missouri Legend*.
56. Robert F. James, interview, March 17, 1945; synopsis of "Under the Black Flag" filed with United States Copyright Office, Washington, D. C.; Liberty *Advance*, November 1, 1920, and March 21, 1921; Liberty *Tribune*, April 8, 1921; Richmond *Missourian*, April 8, 1921; Kansas City *Star*, July 25 and August 1, 1920.
57. Paramount press release on "Jesse James" starring Fred Thompson, filed with United States Copyright Office, Washington, D. C.; New York *Times*, July 31, 1927.
58. Kansas City *Star*, September 11, 1927.
59. New York *Times*, September 18, 1927.
60. *Ibid.*
61. *Literary Digest*, 95 (October 29, 1927), 44–50, summarized comments from the Boston *Globe*, the Dallas *Journal*, the Rochester *Democrat and Chronicle*, the New York *Times*, the New York *Sun*, and the New York *Herald-Tribune* and reproduced cartoons from the Detroit *News* and the Washington *Daily News*.
62. Kansas City *Star*, October 2, 1927.
63. C. A. Poindexter and Bracken Fitzpatrick, *The Historical Background, Setting and Synopsis of "Jesse James" Filmed at and Near Pineville, Missouri*; Frank Vreeland, *Foremost Films of 1938*, 341; "'Jesse James': Zanuck Makes a Hero of U.S.'s Greatest Outlaw," *Life*, VI (January 30, 1939), 41–43; Chicago *Daily News*, April 1, 1939.
64. New York *Times*, August 10 and 18, 1940.
65. Reviews of the picture were published in the Kansas City *Times*, March 5, 1957, and the New York *Times*, March 23, 1957. See also the Dell comic book, Number 757, A Movie Classic, *The True Story of Jesse James*.
66. The New York *Times*, September 29, 1954, has a review of "Jesse James' Women."

NOTES TO CHAPTER XV

1. I have not seen the 1875 edition of Appler's book; I used Augustus C. Appler, *The Guerrillas of the West or the Life, Character, and Daring Exploits of the Younger Brothers* (1876). See Raymon F. Adams, *Six-Guns and Saddle Leather*, for information on the 1875, 1876, 1878, and 1893 editions of Appler's book. The 1955 edition was published by Frederick Fell, Inc., New York. It contained a foreword by Burton Rascoe.
2. Edwards, *Noted Guerrillas*.

3. *Ibid.*, 194.
4. *Ibid.*, 448.
5. Richmond *Conservator*, February 23, 1877; Liberty *Tribune*, March 9 and 16 and April 6, 1877; Boonville *Daily Advertiser*, February 28 and March 1 and 24, 1877.
6. Chicago *Times*, February 25 and March 11, 1877, in Walter B. Stevens' Scrap Book No. 278.
7. Richmond *Democrat*, July 29, 1880.
8. This collector was Martin Ismert, now dead, who lived in 1961 at 51 West 53rd Street Terrace in Kansas City, Missouri.
9. Richmond *Conservator*, August 19, 1881.
10. *Ibid.*
11. James William Buel, *The Border Bandits*, 118.
12. *Ibid.*, 118–19.
13. *Ibid.*, 119.
14. R. T. Bradley, ed., *The Outlaws of the Border or the Lives of Frank and Jesse James*, and Edwards, *Noted Guerrillas*, 3.
15. Don Russell, *The Lives and Legends of Buffalo Bill*, 413.
16. Ralph F. Cummings, "The James Boys Stories," *Dime Novel Round-Up*, 10 (June, 1942).
17. J. Edward Leithead, "The Bandit Brothers of Old Missouri," *Dime Novel Round-Up*, 23 (September 15, 1955), 70–75.
18. No. 514 was issued August 9, 1882, and No. 539 was dated December 7, 1882, indicating twenty-five issues in seventeen weeks.
19. See Albert Johannsen, *The House of Beadle and Adams and Its Nickel and Dime Novels*, I, 3–4, for a discussion of what the dime novel was and what it was not.
20. The titles indicate the nature of the stories: No. 440, *The Train Robbers; or, A Story of the James Boys*; No. 457, *The James Boys as Guerrillas*; No. 462, *The James Boys and the Vigilantes*; No. 466, *The James Boys and the Ku Klux*; No. 469, *The James Boys in California*; No. 474, *The James Boys as Train Wreckers*; No. 482, *The James Boys as Highwaymen*; No. 488, *The James Boys' Longest Chase*; No. 490, *The James Boys in Mexico*; No. 492, *The James Boys at Cracker Neck*; No. 514, *The James Boys and Timberlake*; No. 521, *The James Boys in Court*; No. 527, *The James Boys' Cave*; No. 531, *The James Boys as Bank Robbers*; No. 538, *The James Boys' Brides*; No. 550, *The James Boys' Band*. Titles are from list on back of No. 538 and a letter from Albert Johannsen, March 16, 1945. Professor Johannsen, now dead, had in 1945 retired from the faculty of the University of Chicago, where he had been professor of petrology. He owned a collection of over 6,000 dime novels, mainly those published by Beadle and Adams. His published work on that firm is cited in the preceding note.
21. No. 76, *Life and Death of Jesse James*; No. 81, *Frank James, The Avenger*; No. 87, *Lives of the Ford Boys*; No. 105, *Frank James' Surrender*.
22. Titles obtained from backs of No. 373, D. W. Stevens, *Old Saddle-Bags, The Preacher Detective; or, The James Boys in a Fix*; No. 557, *Old*

King Brady and the James Boys Among the Choctaws; or, The Raid Into the Indian Nation in '81, by a New York Detective; No. 770, D. W. Stevens, *The James Boys and the Two Jims; or, The Fatal Run of the Fast Express.*

23. Charles Bragin, *Dime Novels, Bibliography, 1860–1928,* 21; J. Edward Leithead, "The Bandit Brothers of Old Missouri," 71–72. Bragin says there were 139 issues, and Leithead says he has a list of 142 titles.

24. Ralph Cummings and J. Edward Leithead both identify D. W. Stevens as John R. Musick in their articles cited earlier in this chapter.

25. *Who's Who in America, 1899–1900,* 518.

26. These figures are based on list of titles compiled from listings on backs of copies in the Library of Congress collection of dime novels.

27. Bragin, *Dime Novels, Bibliography,* 17; Leithead, "The Bandit Brothers of Old Missouri," 74.

28. Leithead, "The Bandit Brothers of Old Missouri," 73–75; Quentin Reynolds, *The Fiction Factory,* 115–16.

29. Leithead, "The Bandit Brothers of Old Missouri," gives information on several other, but less extensive, issues.

30. The Library of Congress holds most of these. The count was made from lists on the backs of the books in the Library of Congress collection.

31. From list on back of Capt. Kennedy, *Jesse James, Manhunter.*

32. Letter from Henry W. Ralston, June 15, 1945. Ralston was then vice-president of Street & Smith.

33. William Ward, *Jesse James' Midnight Attack,* No. 32 in the Arthur Westbrook Adventure Series.

34. D. W. Stevens, *The James Boys; or, The Bandit King's Last Shot,* No. 356, *New York Detective Library.*

35. Letter from Henry W. Ralston, June 15, 1945.

36. I have found a large number of them, but the survey given here should not be considered complete.

37. St. Joseph *Observer,* September 16, 1922. I have not been able to identify any book as Spencer's, but the St. Joseph *Herald* of April 13, 1882, reported: "The first book on the assassination, life and character of Jesse James was issued yesterday from the office of the Evening News. It meets with a ready sale, and Mr. Spencer, the author, is to be congratulated on the success of the book."

38. Jay Donald, *Outlaws of the Border;* see also Adams, *Six-Guns and Saddle Leather,* 124, 125.

39. Anonymous, *Train and Bank Robbers of the West,* and Appler, *The Life, Character and Daring Exploits of the Younger Brothers.*

40. Frank Triplett, *The Life, Times, and Treacherous Death of Jesse James.*

41. *Ibid.,* 99.

42. Adams, *Six-Guns and Saddle Leather,* 356.

43. St. Louis *Republican,* April 29, 1882.

44. St. Louis *Post-Dispatch,* May 1, 1882; Kansas City *Evening Star,* May 1, 1882; Richmond *Conservator,* May 19, 1882.

45. In August of 1961 the late Martin Ismert, lifelong student of the James story and acquaintance of many people with firsthand information, told me this story. The contemporary newspapers reported that Frank

James was in St. Louis and that he sent Mrs. James a letter. See Kansas City *Evening Star*, May 1, 1882.

46. St. Louis *Republican*, October 15, 16, and 18, 1884.
47. Gordon, *Jesse James and His Band of Notorious Outlaws*, 8.
48. James, *Lives and Adventures*, 7–8.
49. An example is Emerson Hough, *The Story of the Outlaw*, 340–70.
50. *The Nation*, 123 (July 14, 1926), 40–41.
51. Love, *Rise and Fall of Jesse James*, 7.
52. Croy, *Jesse James Was My Neighbor*.
53. James D. Horan, *Desperate Men* (1949). G. P. Putnam's Sons published this edition. A revised and expanded edition was issued in 1962 by Doubleday & Company, Inc., of Garden City, New York. Book One was published as a paperback under the title *Desperate Men* in 1951 by the Avon Publishing Company, New York.
54. On March 19, 1945, H. S. Mosher, who was then manager of Pinkerton's Department of Criminal Investigation, wrote me that the firm did not have records pertaining to its work directed toward apprehending the James band.
55. Paul I. Wellman, *A Dynasty of Western Outlaws*.
56. Carl Breihan, *The Complete and Authentic Life of Jesse James*.
57. Carl Breihan, *The Day Jesse James Was Killed*.
58. Will Henry, *Death of a Legend*; Will Henry, *The Raiders*. Random House, Inc., published the first title and Bantam Books the second. Permission to quote has been granted by the copyright owner.
59. Henry, *Death of a Legend*, 62.

Bibliography

PUBLIC DOCUMENTS OF THE UNITED STATES OF AMERICA

Copyright office. "Jesse James," a Paramount press release; "Under the Black Flag," synopsis of a motion picture.

Department of Justice. Files, Record J.227, filed December 23, 1883. Archives of the United States of America.

Historical Register and Dictionary of the United States Army, from its Organization, September 29, 1789, to March 2, 1903, Francis B. Heitman, ed. Washington, D. C., Government Printing Office, 1903. 2 vols. This is the unofficial work of a private compiler, purchased by direction of Congress.

Record and Pension Office. *Missouri Troops in Service during the Civil War*. Washington, D. C., Government Printing Office, 1902.

War Department. *The War of the Rebellion: A Compilation of the Official Records of the Union and Confederate Armies*. Washington, D. C., Government Printing Office, 1880–1902. 128 vols.

PUBLIC DOCUMENTS OF THE STATE OF MISSOURI

Journal of the House of Representatives of the State of Missouri. All sessions, 1867 through 1883. Jefferson City, 1867–1883.

Journal of the Senate of the State of Missouri. All sessions, 1867 through 1883. Jefferson City, 1867–1883.

The Messages and Proclamations of the Governors of the State of Missouri, Floyd C. Shoemaker and others, editors. Vols. III, IV, V, and VI. Columbia, State Historical Society of Missouri, 1922–1961. 19 vols.

Official Directory of Missouri, Michael K. McGrath, editor. St. Louis, John J. Daly and Company, 1881–1885.

Proceedings of the Missouri State Convention, March, 1861. St. Louis, George Knapp and Company, 1861.

Reports of Cases Argued and Determined in the Supreme Court of the State of Missouri. Vol. 79. Kansas City, Ramsey, Millett, and Hudson, 1884.

PUBLIC RECORDS

Buchanan County. Circuit Court Records. Criminal Record 3. St. Joseph, Missouri.

Clay County. Circuit Court Records. Files No. 10 and No. 449 and Volume 16. Liberty, Missouri.

Clay County. Probate Court Records. Estate of Rev. Robert James, James Harris, Administrator. Liberty, Missouri.

Daviess County. Circuit Court Records. Criminal Files No. 27 and No. 44 and Volume M. Gallatin, Missouri.

MANUSCRIPTS

Bronaugh-Bushnell Letters, 1852–1930. 550 items (19 letters, 1890–1925, regarding Younger brothers; 2 letters, Frank James to W. C. Bronaugh, January 14, 1891, and February 19, 1903). Western Historical Manuscripts Collection, University of Missouri, Columbia.

Brown, Governor B. Gratz, Miscellaneous Letter Book. State Archives, State Historical Society of Missouri, Columbia.

Croy, Homer, "Jesse James Still Rides." Manuscript 756, State Historical Society of Missouri, Columbia.

Edwards, John N., letters to Frank James. Twelve letters, August 1, 1882, to November 18, 1886. In possession of Mr. and Mrs. Robert James, Kearney, Missouri, in June, 1950.

Gregg, William H., manuscript. Gregg describes his experiences in the band of William C. Quantrill, 1861–1864. State Historical Society of Missouri, Columbia.

Hardin, Governor Charles H., "James Band of Outlaws." Forty letters and telegrams. State Archives, State Historical Society of Missouri, Columbia. The State Archives is a collection of approximately 115,000 items deposited with the State Historical Society. It is very incomplete.

Hawes, Harry B., "Frank and Jesse James *in Review*." Address delivered before The Missouri Society, Washington, D. C., February 25, 1939. Typescript in my possession.

James, Alex, parole papers. Issued by Captain R. W. Young by order of Major General J. M. Palmer, July 26, 1865, at Samuel's Depot, Kentucky. In possession of Robert F. James, Kearney, Missouri, in 1945.

James, Robert F., letters to Zerelda James, April 14, May 1, and July 19, 1850. In possession of Mr. and Mrs. Robert F. James, Kearney, Missouri, in June, 1950.

McClurg, Governor Joseph W., telegram to Sheriff of Jackson County, December 24, 1869. Photostat. Manuscript 557, State Historical Society of Missouri, Columbia.

Pinkerton, William A., "Train Robberies, Train Robbers, and the 'Holdup' Men." Address at Annual Convention of International Association of Chiefs of Police, Jamestown, Virginia, 1907.

Womack, Nowlin, interview by Ovid Bell, Sr., October 12, 1942. Notes in possession of Ovid Bell, Sr., Fulton, Missouri, in 1945.

Woodson, Governor Silas, "James Band of Outlaws." 28 letters and telegrams. State Archives, State Historical Society of Missouri, Columbia.

Younger, Cole, papers relating to the Civil War Service of Younger in connection with his application for a pension, May, 1915. Photostat. Manuscript 438, State Historical Society of Missouri, Columbia.

Younger brothers. Petition of members of Missouri legislature to the Minnesota Board of Pardons asking the pardon of the Younger brothers. Photostat. In my possession.

UNPUBLISHED THESES

Clevenger, Homer, "Agrarian Politics in Missouri, 1880–1896." Doctoral dissertation, University of Missouri, Columbia, 1940.

Donohue, Mae Florence, "The Democratic Party in Missouri, 1873–1880." Master's thesis, University of Missouri, Columbia, 1930.

Nowels, Ida Mae, "A Study of the Radical Party Movement in Missouri, 1873–1880." Master's thesis, University of Missouri, 1939.

Wilson, Donald Eugene, "The Republican Party in Missouri, 1860–1881." Master's thesis, University of Missouri, Columbia, 1930.

CLIPPING COLLECTIONS

Harry M. Fleenor, Jesse James Clipping Collection. Topeka, Kansas. Several hundred items dealing with the James band and related subjects. From newspapers, 1925–1945.

Martin Ismert, James Albums. Kansas City, Missouri. Four scrapbooks with pictures, clippings, and mementos relating to James band.

Kansas City Public Library, Miscellaneous Clipping Collection. Kansas City, Missouri. About one hundred items on James family and related subjects.

Kansas City Star Library, Miscellaneous Clipping Collection. Kansas City, Missouri. About four hundred items on James family and related subjects; covers period from 1897 to present.

Kansas State Historical Society, Miscellaneous Clipping Collection. Topeka, Kansas. Several hundred items on various subjects, including scattered items on James band.

Mrs. Charles McConn, Miscellaneous Clipping Collection. Liberty, Missouri. Clippings dating from about 1900, dealing with history of Clay County, Missouri. Contains about one hundred Jesse James items.

St. Louis Post-Dispatch Library, Miscellaneous Clipping Collection. St. Louis, Missouri. A few clippings on the James band, 1915 to the present.

St. Louis Public Library, Miscellaneous Clipping Collection. St. Louis, Missouri. About fifty clippings on James band, 1900 to present.

Walter B. Stevens' Scrap Books, Numbers 61, 66, 129, 278. State Historical Society of Missouri, Columbia.

CORRESPONDENCE

Walter H. Adams, Adams Lithographing Company, Chattanooga, Tennessee, February 1, 1945.

Albert Johannsen, 2203 West 111th Street, Chicago, Illinois, March 16, 1945.

Jay Monaghan, Illinois State Historical Library, Springfield, Illinois, January 6, 1945.

H. S. Mosher, Pinkerton Detective Agency, New York City, March 19, 1945.

Henry W. Ralston, Street & Smith, New York City, June 15, 1945.

INTERVIEWS

Edward Brining, Liberty, Missouri, June 15, 1940.

Dean Davis, Kansas City, Missouri, March 23, 1945.

John S. Frazier, Richmond, Missouri, November 24, 1944.

E. P. Hall, Liberty, Missouri, June 15, 1940.

E. R. Hamilton, Columbia, Missouri, May 29, 1945.

Howard Huselton, Kansas City, Missouri, March 19, 1945.

Martin E. Ismert, Kansas City, Missouri, August 16, 1961.

Robert F. and Mae James, Kearney, Missouri, November 30, 1944, March 17, 1945, and July 6, 1950.

James T. McGinnis, Richmond, Missouri, June 14, 1940.

Thomas R. Shouse, Liberty, Missouri, June 15, 1940.

William H. Thomason, Liberty, Missouri, November 29, 1944.

H. D. Tucker, Columbia, Missouri, July 9, 1945.

Theodoric B. Wallace, Kansas City, Missouri, March 20, 1945.

Purd B. Wright, Kansas City, Missouri, March 19, 1945.

NEWSPAPERS

Austin *Texas Siftings*, Austin, Texas, April and May, 1882.

Auxvasse Review, Auxvasse, Missouri, February 15, 1939.

Boonville Daily Advertiser, Boonville, Missouri, October 25, 1875–October 24, 1877.

Boonville Weekly Advertiser, Boonville, Missouri, October 24, 1873–1885; miscellaneous dates, 1886–1915.

Centerville Weekly Citizen, Centerville, Iowa, June 10 and 24, 1871.

Chicago Commercial Advertiser, Chicago, Illinois, August 28, 1879.

Chicago Daily News, Chicago, Illinois, April 1, 1939.

Chicago *Semi-Weekly Inter-Ocean*, Chicago, Illinois, March 27–December 29, 1879.

Chicago *Weekly Inter-Ocean*, Chicago, Illinois, March 12–December 31, 1874; January 22–December 28, 1876.

Cincinnati *Enquirer*, Cincinnati, Ohio, January, 1875; April and October, 1882; August and September, 1883; July 26, 1902.

Columbia Missouri Herald, Columbia, Missouri, September 24, 1897; August 28, 1903; November 4, 1904.

Columbia *Missouri Statesman*, Columbia, Missouri, 1862–1883.

Crofton Journal, Crofton, Nebraska, December 7, 1939.

Denver Post, Denver, Colorado, March 3, 1935.

Denver *Rocky Mountain News*, Denver, Colorado, April, 1882; August and September, 1883.

Excelsior Springs Daily Standard, Excelsior Springs, Missouri, September, 1931–April, 1932; January 29, 1939.

Florence Daily Citizen, Florence, Colorado, November 2, 3, 4, and 5, 1931.

Fulton Sun-Gazette, Fulton, Missouri, February 26, 1938.

Gallatin North Missourian, Gallatin, Missouri, January 8, 1874.

Huntsville Gazette, Huntsville, Alabama, April 19 and 26, 1884.

Jefferson City *Daily Tribune*, Jefferson City, Missouri, December 11, 1871–March 30, 1872; January–March, 1873; January 5, 1874–May 31, 1881; July 2, 1882–December 31, 1887; July, 1888–December 31, 1898.

Jefferson City *Peoples' Tribune*, Jefferson City, Missouri, October 4, 1865–December 26, 1883.

Missouri State Journal, Jefferson City, Missouri, January 3, 1901.

Kansas City Daily Journal, Kansas City, Missouri, 1866–1885; miscellaneous dates, 1885–1928. (Title varied: *Daily Journal of Commerce*, May, 1863–May 27, 1878; *Daily Journal*, May 28, 1878–February 8, 1897; *Journal*, February 9, 1897–October 3, 1928.)

Kansas City Evening Star, Kansas City, Missouri, September 23, 1880–September 6, 1881; September 28, 1881–September 8, 1882; October 3, 1882–September 14, 1883; September 23, 1883–September 3, 1884; miscellaneous dates, 1885–1963. (Became *Kansas City Star*.)

Kansas City Post, Kansas City, Missouri, July 2, 1907.

Kansas City Times, Kansas City, Missouri, August 20, 1871–November 13, 1874; 1875–1885; miscellaneous dates, 1886–1963.

Lawton *Constitution*, Lawton, Oklahoma, May–July, 1948.

Lawton Morning Press, Lawton, Oklahoma, May and June, 1948.

Lee's Summit Journal, Lee's Summit, Missouri, March 23, 1916.
Lexington Advertiser, Lexington, Missouri, "Milestone Edition," October 30, 1930.
Lexington *Caucasian*, Lexington, Missouri, April 25, 1866–1868; 1870–August, 1875.
Lexington Register, Lexington, Missouri, June and July, 1871.
Liberty Advance, Liberty, Missouri, February 4, 1875–February 1, 1877; January 11, 1884–December 26, 1884; January 9, 1885–April 17, 1885; 1901–1944.
Liberty Tribune, Liberty, Missouri, 1846–March, 1885; 1903–1943.
Lincoln *Sunday Journal and Star*, Lincoln, Nebraska, February 5, 1939.
Little Rock *Arkansas Gazette*, Little Rock, Arkansas, 1874–1875.
Louisville *Courier-Journal*, Louisville, Kentucky, April and October, 1882; March, August, and September, 1883.
Marshall *Democrat-News*, Marshall, Missouri, April 28, 29, and 30, 1937.
Mokane Missourian, Mokane, Missouri, March 30, 1917.
Neosho Times, Neosho, Missouri, August 18, 1881; October 12, 1882.
New York *Daily Graphic*, New York, April and October, 1882; August and September, 1883.
New York Times, New York, miscellaneous dates, 1927–1964.
New York *World*, New York, May 6, 1874.
Norborne Democrat and Leader, Norborne, Missouri, October–December, 1938.
Osceola Democrat, Osceola, Missouri, August and September, 1873; April, 1874; July and August, 1875.
Osceola Republican, Osceola, Iowa, June 8, 1871.
Richmond *Conservator*, Richmond, Missouri, 1865–1885; September 16, 1886–1897. (*North-West Conservator*, 1865–March, 1866.)
Richmond Democrat, Richmond, Missouri, 1879–1885.
Richmond Missourian, Richmond, Missouri, 1919–1944.
St. Joseph Gazette, St. Joseph, Missouri, January, 1883–March, 1886.
St. Joseph Herald, St. Joseph, Missouri, February 12, 1862–February 11, 1865; September 1, 1865–February 16, 1875; 1882–1885. (*Morning Herald* to October 10, 1876.)
St. Joseph News-Press, St. Joseph, Missouri, August 29, 1938, and July 10, 1939.
St. Joseph Observer, St. Joseph, Missouri, November 1, 1919, and September 16, 1922.
St. Louis Democrat, St. Louis, Missouri, 1873–1875. (*Missouri Democrat*, 1852–1872.)
St. Louis Dispatch, St. Louis, Missouri, November 22, 1873; 1874–1878.
St. Louis Evening Chronicle, St. Louis, Missouri, July 31, 1880–1885.
St. Louis *Globe*, St. Louis, Missouri, March 20, 1874, and March 17, 1875.
St. Louis Globe-Democrat, St. Louis, Missouri, January 26, 1876–Febru-

ary, 1878; June–August, 1879; October, 1880–March, 1881; July and August, 1881; August–December, 1882; January 4–February 28, 1885; miscellaneous dates, 1885–1953.

St. Louis *Missouri Republican*, St. Louis, Missouri, November 3, 1866; May 16, 1867–1869; January 18–April 18, 1870; May, 1870–July, 1872; November, 1874–March, 1885; miscellaneous dates, 1885–1919. (Title varied: *Daily Missouri Republican* to November 3, 1873; *Republican*, November 4, 1873–December 15, 1876; *Missouri Republican*, December 16, 1876–May 30, 1888; *Republic* after 1888.)

St. Louis Post-Dispatch, St. Louis, Missouri, 1878–June, 1881; 1882–1884; miscellaneous dates, 1885–1953.

St. Louis Times, St. Louis, Missouri, 1874–1876.

St. Louis *Tri-Weekly Missouri Democrat*, St. Louis, Missouri, 1866–1867; February 28, 1868–June, 1870; 1871–1872.

Sedalia *Daily Bazoo*, Sedalia, Missouri, September 26, 1881.

Sedalia Daily Democrat, Sedalia, Missouri, 1875–June 30, 1882; 1883–1885.

Sedalia Weekly Democrat, Sedalia, Missouri, 1882.

Tipton Times, Tipton, Missouri, February 26, 1915.

Union *Franklin County Tribune*, Union, Missouri, March 17, 1950.

Warrensburg *Weekly Journal*, Warrensburg, Missouri, May–July, 1867.

DIME NOVEL WEEKLIES

The dates listed are not inclusive for the entire series, but for only the numbers cited. All the dime novel weeklies listed are in the Library of Congress.

Boys of New York Pocket Library. New York: Frank Tousey, 1882–1883. Numbers 76, 81, 87, 105.

Five Cent Wide Awake Library. New York: Frank Tousey, 1881–1883. Numbers 440, 457, 462, 466, 469, 474, 482, 488, 490, 492, 514, 521, 527, 531, 538, 550.

Log Cabin Library. New York: Street & Smith, 1889–1896. Numbers 4, 49, 50, 54, 61, 71, 74, 90, 94, 101, 104, 110, 113, 117, 126, 131, 148, 165, 167, 171, 174, 175, 195, 196, 342, 344.

Log Cabin Library (Pocket Edition). New York: Street & Smith, 1897–1898. Numbers 2, 6, 10, 14, 15, 18, 19, 20, 22, 26, 28, 34, 38, 66, 68, 69, 72, 75, 78, 80, 84.

New York Detective Library. New York: Frank Tousey, 1889–1897. Numbers 356, 358, 359, 364, 368, 373, 377, 382, 386, 387, 389, 393, 416, 420, 421, 425, 426, 428, 430, 433, 436, 438, 441, 442, 444, 446, 450, 453, 461, 464, 466, 467, 470, 474, 484, 491, 492, 557, 630, 635, 636, 637, 649, 673, 674, 675, 676, 677, 678, 683, 707, 734, 736, 742, 750, 754, 762, 766, 770.

ILLUSTRATED WEEKLIES

Frank Leslie's Illustrated Weekly Newspaper. New York, 1882–1883. University of Missouri Library, Columbia.

Illustrated Times. New York, April and May, 1882. Library of Congress, Washington, D. C.

The Judge. New York, October 29, 1881–October 21, 1882, St. Louis Public Library, St. Louis; October 28, 1882–April 18, 1885, Library of Congress, Washington, D. C.

The Mirror. St. Louis, 1899–1912. State Historical Society of Missouri, Columbia.

National Police Gazette. New York, 1878–1885. Library of Congress, Washington, D. C.

ARTICLES

Barry, Phillips, "Native Balladry in America." *Journal of American Folk-Lore*, XXII (July–September, 1909), 305–73.

Bascom, Louise Rand, "Ballads and Songs of Western North Carolina." *Journal of American Folk-Lore*, XXII (April–June, 1909), 238–350.

"The Battle Over A Jesse James Monument." *Literary Digest*, 95 (October 29, 1927), 44–50.

Belden, H. M., "Balladry in America." *Journal of American Folk-Lore*, XXV (January–March, 1912), 1–23.

Boder, Bartlett, "Jesse James Was a Vaquero." *Museum Graphic*, VI (Fall, 1954), 9.

———, "Mrs. Quantrill and Zerelda James Samuel, Two Mothers." *Museum Graphic*, VII (Fall, 1955), 7–9.

———, "Jesse James, The Dingus," "The Brothers' War in Missouri," "Susan James," "County Jail at Saint Joseph," "Daviess County," "The Sterling Price Raid," "Harlem, Clay County," "For Some the War Ended, But Not for Jesse James," "Jesse James of St. Joseph," "Jesse James as He Looked the Day He was Killed," "Jesse By Jehovah!" "Marshal Enos Craig," "The Station Agent Said: 'Gentlemen, Gentlemen, Don't Pull Your Pops in Here.'" *Museum Graphic*, IX (Spring, 1957), 3–30.

———, "Following Up on Jesse James." *Museum Graphic*, IX (Summer, 1957), 6–11.

———, "Rose Marie and Thomas Howard." *Museum Graphic*, XIII (Winter, 1961), 8.

Byars, William Vincent, "A Century of Journalism in Missouri." *Missouri Historical Review*, XV (October, 1920), 70–72.

Castel, Albert, "Order No. 11 and the Civil War on the Border." *Missouri Historical Review*, LVII (July, 1963), 357–68.

Chilcote, Merrill, "Jesse James: A Scoundrel and a Martyr." *Museum Graphic*, II (Spring, 1950), 6 and 9.

Condon, Frank, "Local Ghost Makes Good." *Colliers,* 102 (November 26, 1938), 14, 44, 46.

Cooper, Courtney Ryley, "Draw, Stranger!" *Saturday Evening Post,* 198 (January 2, 1926), 28–36.

Cummings, Ralph F., "The James Boys Stories." *Dime Novel Round-Up,* 10, No. 117 (June, 1942).

Currie, Barton W., "American Bandits: Lone and Otherwise." *Harper's Weekly,* 52 (September 12, 1908), 15, 35.

De Casseres, Benjamin, "The Complete American." *American Mercury,* 10 (February, 1927), 143–47.

Dibble, R. F., "'Sblood!" *The Nation,* 123 (July 14, 1926), 40–41.

Fletcher, John Gould, "Some Folk-Ballads and the Background of History." *Missouri Historical Review,* XLV (January, 1951), 113–23.

Gentry, North Todd, "General Odon Guitar." *Missouri Historical Review,* XXII (July, 1938), 419–51.

Grinnell, Charles E., "Crime as a Political Power in the East and the West." *American Law Review,* 16 (May, 1882), 400–403.

Holbrook, Stewart H., "The Bank the James Boys Didn't Rob." *American Mercury,* LXVI (January, 1948), 25–28.

Ismert, Martin E., "Quantrill: Man and Myth—An Examination of W. E. Connelley's Historianship." *The Trail Guide,* VI (June, 1961), 1–12.

"The James Boys Jesse and Frank." *Scholastic,* 33 (January 21, 1939), 30–31.

"'Jesse James': Zanuck Makes a Hero of U.S.'s Greatest Outlaw." *Life,* VI (January 30, 1939), 40–43.

Jordan, Philip D., "The Adair Train Robbery." *The Palimpsest,* XVII (February, 1936), 49–66.

Kellar, Herbert A., ed., "Lexington *Register* Extra." *The Westerners Brand Book 1945–46* (Chicago, Illinois, 1947), 151–55.

Kirkpatrick, Arthur Roy, "Missouri in the Early Months of the Civil War." *Missouri Historical Review,* LV (April, 1961), 235–66.

———, "Missouri on the Eve of the Civil War." *Missouri Historical Review,* LV (January, 1961), 99–108.

Lavery, Ray, "The Man Who Made a Folk-God out of Jo Shelby and Created a Legend for Jesse James." *The Trail Guide,* VI (December, 1961), 1–15.

Leithead, J. Edward, "The Bandit Brothers of Old Missouri." *Dime Novel Round-Up,* 23 (September, 1955), 70–75.

Lomax, John A., "Some Types of American Folk-Song." *Journal of American Folk-Lore,* XXVIII (January–March, 1915), 1–17.

Lord, John, "Picturesque Road-Agents of Early Days." *Overland Monthly,* 70 (November, 1917), 492–94.

Nolan, Warren, and Owen P. White, "The Bad Man From Missouri."

Colliers, 81 (January 14, 1928), 5–6; (January 21, 1928), 17; (January 28, 1928), 13–14.

"Notes and Queries." *Journal of American Folk-Lore*, XXXIV (January–March, 1921), 124.

Odum, Howard W., "Folk-Song and Folk-Poetry as Found in the Secular Songs of Southern Negroes." *The Journal of American Folk-Lore*, XXIV (July–September, 1911), 255–94; (October–December, 1911), 351–96.

Perrow, E. C., "Songs and Rhymes From the South." *Journal of American Folk-Lore*, XXV (April–June, 1912), 137–55.

Pigg, Elmer L., "Bloody Bill, Noted Guerrilla of the Civil War." *The Trail Guide*, I (December, 1956), 17–28.

Pound, Louise, "Traditional Ballads in Nebraska." *Journal of American Folk-Lore*, XXVI (October–December, 1913), 351–66.

Rasch, Philip J., "Jesse James in New Mexico Folklore." *The Westerners Brand Book, New York Posse*, 4 (1957), 62–63.

Russell, Don, "Jesse James — Postwar Bandit." *The Westerners Brand Book 1944* (Chicago, Illinois, 1946), 23–33.

Saults, Dan, "Missouri's Forgotten Don Quixote." *Focus/Midwest*, I (October, 1962), 20–23.

Settle, William A., Jr., "The James Boys and Missouri Politics." *Missouri Historical Review*, XXXVI (July, 1942), 412–29.

Shouse, Thomas R., "My Father's Part in Ending the Career of the James Boys." *Kansas City Star*, December 18, 1938.

Starnes, Lee, "The Legend of Jesse James." *Museum Graphic*, IV (Spring, 1952), 3–4.

Stevens, Walter B., "Missouri's Centennial." *Missouri Historical Review*, XI (April–July, 1917), 249–88.

Tolman, Albert H., "Some Songs Traditional in the United States." *Journal of American Folk-Lore*, XXIX (April–June, 1916), 155–202.

"Unvarnishing Jesse James," *Literary Digest*, 50 (March 20, 1915), 653–54.

White, Owen P., "Belle Starr, Bandit." *Colliers*, 89 (February 6, 1932), 21, 51, 52.

BOOKS

Adams, Raymon F., *Six-Guns and Saddle Leather*. Norman, University of Oklahoma Press, 1954.

Allsopp, Frederick William, *Folklore of Romantic Arkansas*. New York, The Grolier Society, 1931. 2 vols.

Alvarez, N., *The James Boys in Missouri*. Clyde, Ohio, Ames Publishing Co., 1907.

Appler, Augustus C., *The Guerrillas of the West or the Life, Character and Daring Exploits of the Younger Brothers*. St. Louis, Eureka Publishing Company, 1876.

————, *The Younger Brothers*. With a Foreword by Burton Rascoe. New York, Frederick Fell, Inc., 1955.

Argall, Phyllis, *The Truth About Jesse James*. Sullivan, Missouri, Lester B. Dill and Rudy Turilli, 1953.

Arthur, George Clinton, *Bushwhacker*. Rolla, Missouri, Rolla Printing Company, 1938.

Barclay, Thomas Swain, *The Liberal Republican Movement in Missouri, 1865–1871*. Columbia, State Historical Society of Missouri, 1926.

Belden, H. M., ed., *Ballads and Songs Collected by the Missouri Folk-Lore Society*. University of Missouri Studies, Vol. XV, No. 1. Columbia, University of Missouri, 1940, 1955.

Benet, William Rose, *Golden Fleece*. New York, Dodd, Mead & Company, Inc., 1935.

Biographical and Historical Record of Wayne and Appanoose Counties, Iowa. Chicago, Inter-State Publishing Co., 1886.

Botkin, Benjamin A., *The Treasury of American Folklore*. New York, Crown Publishers, 1944.

————, *A Treasury of Western Folklore*. New York, Crown Publishers, 1951.

Bradley, R. T., ed., *The Outlaws of the Border or The Lives of Frank and Jesse James*, and Edwards, John Newman, *Noted Guerrillas*. St. Louis, J. W. Marsh, 1882.

Bragin, Charles, *Dime Novels, Bibliography, 1860–1928*. Brooklyn, Charles Bragin, 1938.

Breihan, Carl W., *The Complete and Authentic Life of Jesse James*. New York, Frederick Fell, Inc., 1953.

————, *The Day Jesse James was Killed*. New York, Frederick Fell, Inc., 1961.

————, *The Outlaw Brothers: The True Story of Missouri's Younger Brothers*. San Antonio, The Naylor Company, 1961.

————, *Quantrill and his Civil War Guerrillas*. Denver, Sage Books, 1959.

Bronaugh, Warren C., *The Youngers' Fight for Freedom*. Columbia, Missouri, E. W. Stephens Publishing Company, 1906.

Brownlee, Richard S., *Gray Ghosts of the Confederacy: Guerrilla Warfare in the West, 1861–1865*. Baton Rouge, Louisiana State University Press, 1958.

Buel, James William, *The Border Bandits*. Baltimore, I. & M. Ottenheimer, n.d.

————, *The Border Bandits*. Chicago, Donohue, Henneberry and Company, 1893.

————, *The Border Outlaws*. Baltimore, I. & M. Ottenheimer, n.d.

————, *The Border Outlaws*, and *The Border Bandits*. St. Louis, Historical Publishing Company, 1882.

————, *The James Boys*. Chicago, M. A. Donohue and Company, n.d.

———, *The Younger Brothers — The Notorious Border Outlaws*. Baltimore, I. & M. Ottenheimer, n.d.

Burch, John P., *Charles W. Quantrell, A True History of Guerrilla Warfare on the Missouri and Kansas Border during the Civil War of 1861–1865 as told by Capt. Harrison Trow*. Vegas, Texas, privately printed, 1923.

Burt, Olive Woolley, *American Murder Ballads*. New York, Oxford University Press, 1958.

Cambriare, Celestin Pierre, *East Tennessee and Western Virginia Mountain Ballads*. London, The Mitre Press, n.d.

Castel, Albert, *A Frontier State at War: Kansas, 1861–1865*. Ithaca, New York, Cornell University Press, 1958.

———, *William Clarke Quantrill: His Life and Times*. New York, Frederick Fell, Inc., 1962.

Coleman, John Winston, Jr., *Stage Coach Days in the Bluegrass*. Louisville, Kentucky, The Standard Press, 1935.

Conard, Howard L., ed., *Encyclopedia of the History of Missouri, a Compendium of History and Biography for Ready Reference*. Vol. II. New York, Haldeman, Conard and Company, 1901. 6 vols.

Connelley, William Elsey, *Quantrill and the Border Wars*. Cedar Rapids, Iowa, The Torch Press, 1910.

———, *Quantrill and the Border Wars*. With an Introduction by Homer Croy. New York, Pageant Book Company, 1956.

Cox, John Harrington, *Folk-Songs of the South*. Cambridge, Harvard University Press, 1925.

Crittenden, Henry Huston, compiler, *The Crittenden Memoirs*. New York, G. P. Putnam's Sons, 1936.

Croy, Homer, *Jesse James Was My Neighbor*. New York, Duell, Sloan and Pearce, 1949.

———, *Last of the Great Outlaws*. New York, Duell, Sloan and Pearce, 1956.

Cummins, Jim, *Jim Cummins' Book*. Denver, The Reed Publishing Co., 1903.

Jim Cummins the Guerrilla. Excelsior Springs, Missouri, The Daily Journal, 1908.

Dacus, Joseph A., *Illustrated Lives and Adventures of Frank and Jesse James and the Younger Brothers, The Noted Western Outlaws*. St. Louis, N. D. Thompson and Company, 1882.

Dale, Henry, *Adventures and Exploits of the Younger Brothers, Missouri's Most Daring Outlaws, and Companions of the James Boys*. New York, Street & Smith, 1890.

Dalton, Kitt, *Under the Black Flag*. Memphis, Lockard Publishing Company, 1914.

Davis, Edwin Adams, *Fallen Guidon*. Santa Fe, Stagecoach Press, 1962.

Dibble, Roy Floyd, *Strenuous Americans*. New York, Boni and Liveright, 1923.

Dobie, James Frank, *Coronado's Children*. Garden City, New York, Garden City Publishing Company, 1930.

Donald, Jay, *Outlaws of the Border*. Philadelphia, Douglas Brothers, 1882.

Drago, Harry Sinclair, *Outlaws on Horseback*. New York, Dodd, Mead & Company, Inc., 1964.

Drury, John, *Historic Midwest Houses*. Minneapolis, University of Minnesota Press, 1947.

Edwards, Jennie, compiler, *John N. Edwards, Biography, Memoirs, Reminiscences and Recollections,* including a print of *Shelby's Expedition To Mexico*. Kansas City, privately printed, 1889.

Edwards, John Newman, *Noted Guerrillas, or the Warfare of the Border*. St. Louis, Bryan, Brand and Company, 1877.

———, *Shelby and His Men*. Cincinnati, Miami Printing and Publishing Company, 1867.

———, *Shelby's Expedition to Mexico*. Kansas City, Kansas City Times, 1872.

Evans, Clyde, ed., *Adventures of Great Crime Busters*. New York, New Power Publications, 1943.

Federal Writers' Project, *Arkansas, A Guide to the State*. New York, Hastings House, 1941.

———, *Cincinnati; A Guide to the Queen City and Its Neighbors*. Cincinnati, The Weiesen-Hart Press, 1943.

———, *Iowa; A Guide to the Hawkeye State*. New York, The Viking Press, 1938.

———, *Kansas; A Guide to the Sunflower State*. New York, The Viking Press, 1939.

———, *Kentucky; A Guide to the Bluegrass State*. New York, Harcourt, Brace & Company, Inc., 1939.

———, *Louisiana; A Guide to the State*. New York, Hastings House, 1941.

———, *Minnesota; A State Guide*. New York, The Viking Press, 1938.

———, *Missouri; A Guide to the "Show Me" State*. New York, Duell, Sloan and Pearce, 1941.

———, *Nebraska; A Guide to the Cornhusker State*. New York, The Viking Press, 1939.

———, *The Oregon Trail*. New York, Hastings House, 1939.

———, *Tennessee; A Guide to the State*. New York, The Viking Press, 1939.

———, *Texas; A Guide to the Lone Star State*. New York, Hastings House, 1940.

———, *Vermont; A Guide to the Green Mountain State*. Boston, Houghton Mifflin Company, 1937.

———, *West Virginia; A Guide to the Mountain State*. New York, Oxford University Press, 1941.

———, *Wyoming; A Guide to Its History, Highways, and People*. New York, Oxford University Press, 1941.

Finger, Charles J., *Frontier Ballads*. Garden City, New York, Double-day, Page and Company, 1927.

Frank James and His Brother Jesse. Baltimore, I. & M. Ottenheimer, 1915.

Gardner, Raymond Hatfield, *The Old West*. San Antonio, The Naylor Company, 1944.

Garwood, Darrel, *Crossroads of America, The Story of Kansas City*. New York, W. W. Norton & Company, Inc., 1948.

Gates, Paul Wallace, *Fifty Million Acres: Conflicts over Kansas Land Policy, 1854–1890*. Ithaca, New York, Cornell University Press, 1954.

George, Todd Menzies, *Just Memories, and Twelve Years with Cole Younger*. Kansas City, Quality Hill Printing Co., 1959.

Ginty, Elizabeth Beall, *Missouri Legend*. New York, Random House, Inc., 1938.

Gish, Anthony, *American Bandits*. Girard, Kansas, Haldeman-Julius, 1938.

Good Bye, Jesse! With an Introduction by Martin E. Ismert. Facsimile of the article that appeared in the Kansas City *Daily Journal* announcing the death of Jesse James. Special Publication No. 1, Kansas City Posse, The Westerners, Kansas City, 1959.

Gordon, Welche, *Jesse James and His Band of Notorious Outlaws*. Chicago, Laird and Lee, 1891.

Hall, Frank O., and Lindsey H. Whitten, *Jesse James Rides Again*. Lawton, Oklahoma, LaHoma Publishing Company, 1948.

Harlow, Alvin F., *Old Waybills*. New York, D. Appleton-Century Company, 1934.

——, *"Weep No More My Lady."* New York, McGraw-Hill Book Company, Inc., 1942.

Heilbron, W. C., *Convict Life at the Minnesota State Prison*. St. Paul, W. C. Heilbron, 1909.

Hendricks, George D., *The Bad Man of the West*. San Antonio, The Naylor Company, 1950.

Henry, Mellinger Edward, *Folk-Songs from the Southern Highlands*. New York, J. J. Augustin, 1938.

Henry, Will, *Death of a Legend*. New York, Random House, Inc., 1954.

——, *The Raiders*. New York, Bantam Books, 1956.

Hicks, Edwin P., *Belle Starr and her Pearl*. Little Rock, C. Armitage Harper, 1963.

Hicks, John Edward, *Adventures of a Tramp Printer 1880–1890*. Kansas City, Midamericana Press, 1950.

History of Clay and Platte Counties, Missouri. St. Louis, National Historical Company, 1885.

The History of Daviess County, Missouri. Kansas City, Birdsall and Dean, 1882.

Holbrook, Stewart H., *Little Annie Oakley and Other Rugged People*. New York, The Macmillan Company, 1948.

———, *The Story of American Railroads*. New York, Crown Publishers, 1947.

Hoole, W. Stanley, *The James Boys Rode South*. Tuscaloosa, Alabama, privately printed, 1955.

Horan, James D., *Desperate Men*. Garden City, New York, Doubleday & Company, Inc., 1962.

———, *Desperate Men*. New York, Avon Publishing Company, 1951.

———, *Desperate Men*. New York, G. P. Putnam's Sons, 1949.

Horan, James D., and Paul Sann, *Pictorial History of the Old West*. New York, Crown Publishers, 1954.

Hough, Emerson, *The Story of the Outlaw*. New York, Outing Publishing Company, 1907.

Hoyt, Henry F., *Frontier Doctor*. Boston, Houghton Mifflin Company, 1929.

Hubbard, Freeman H., *Railroad Avenue*. New York, McGraw-Hill Book Company, Inc., 1945.

Huntington, George, *Robber and Hero*. Northfield, Minnesota, Christian Way Company, 1895.

James, Edgar, *The Lives and Adventures, Daring Hold-ups, Train and Bank Robberies of the World's Most Desperate Bandits and Highwaymen — The Notorious James Brothers*. Baltimore, I. & M. Ottenheimer, 1913.

James, Jesse Edwards, *Jesse James, My Father*. Independence, Missouri, Sentinel Publishing Company, 1899.

James, Jesse Lee, *Jesse James and the Lost Cause*. New York, Pageant Press, 1961.

The James Boys. Baltimore, I. & M. Ottenheimer, n.d.

The James Boys: A Thrilling Story of the Adventures and Exploits of Frank and Jesse James. St. Joseph, Missouri, Luhn's Stamp and Book Shop, 1947.

Jesse James. Philadelphia, Barclay and Company, n.d.

Jesse James. A Romance of Terror, Vividly Portraying the Daring Deeds of the Most Fearsome and Fearless Bandit Ever Known Within the Whole Range of Historical Outlawry. Baltimore: I. & M. Ottenheimer, 1910.

Jesse James. Das Leben und die verwegenen Abenteuer dieses kühnen Räuberhauptmanns und seines nicht weniger berühmten Bruders Frank James nebst den kecken Thaten der Gebrüder Younger. Versasst von ***** (Welcher sich für jetzt nicht nennen darf.) Das einzige Buch, welches enthält das romantische Leben des Jesse James und seiner hübschen Frau, welche ihm bis in den Tod freu blieb. Philadelphia, Verlag von Barclay & Co., n.d.

Johannsen, Albert, *The House of Beadle and Adams and Its Nickel and Dime Novels.* Norman, University of Oklahoma Press, 1950. 2 vols.

Johnson, Allen, and Dumas Malone, eds., *Dictionary of American Biography.* IX. New York, Charles Scribner's Sons, 1928–1936. 20 vols.

Jones, Virgil Carrington, *The Hatfields and the McCoys.* Chapel Hill, University of North Carolina Press, 1948.

Kelly, Thomas P., *Jesse James, His Life and Death.* Toronto, London, New York, Export Publishing Enterprises, Ltd., 1950.

Kennedy, Capt., *Jesse James, Manhunter.* Baltimore, I. & M. Ottenheimer, 1917.

Lambert, Oscar Doane, *Stephen B. Elkins.* Pittsburgh, University of Pittsburgh Press, 1955.

Larkin, Margaret, *Singing Cowboy.* New York, Alfred A. Knopf, Inc., 1931.

Lavine, Sigmund A., *Allan Pinkerton, America's First Private Eye.* New York, Dodd, Mead & Company, Inc., 1963.

Lawson, John D., *American State Trials.* XI. St. Louis, F. H. Thomas Law Book Company, 1914. 14 vols.

Leonard, John W., ed., *Who's Who in America, 1899–1900.* Chicago, A. N. Marquis and Company, 1899.

Lewis, Lloyd, and Henry Justin Smith, *Oscar Wilde Discovers America.* New York, Harcourt, Brace & Company, Inc., 1936.

Lives, Adventures and Exploits of Frank and Jesse James with an Account of the Tragic Death of Jesse James, April 3, 1882. n.p., n.p., n.d.

Lomax, John A., and Alan Lomax, *American Ballads and Folk Songs.* New York, The Macmillan Company, 1935.

———, *Cowboy Songs and Other Frontier Ballads.* New York, The Macmillan Company, 1938.

Lord, John, *Frontier Dust.* Hartford, Edwin Valentine Mitchell, 1926.

Love, Robertus, *The Rise and Fall of Jesse James.* New York, G. P. Putnam's Sons, 1926.

McCorkle, John, *Three Years with Quantrill: A True Story.* Armstrong, Missouri, Armstrong Herald, n.d.

McDougal, Henry Clay, *Recollections, 1844–1909.* Kansas City, Franklin Hudson Publishing Co., 1910.

McNeil, Cora, *Mizzoura.* Minneapolis, Mizzoura Publishing Company, 1898.

Marshall, James, *Santa Fe, The Railroad that Built an Empire.* New York, Random House, Inc., 1945.

Miller, George, *Missouri's Memorable Decade.* Columbia, Missouri, E. W. Stephens Publishing Company, 1898.

Miller, George, Jr., editor and compiler, *The Trial of Frank James For Murder.* Columbia, Missouri, E. W. Stephens Publishing Company, 1898.

Monaghan, Jay, *Civil War on the Western Border.* Boston, Little, Brown & Company, 1955.

Mott, Frank Luther, *History of American Magazines*. Volume I, *1741–1850*, New York, D. Appleton-Century, 1930; Volume II, *1850–1865*, and Volume III, *1865–1885*, Cambridge, Harvard University Press, 1938; Volume IV, *1885–1905*, Cambridge, Harvard University Press, 1947. 4 vols.

Musick, John R., *Mysterious Mr. Howard*. New York, G. W. Dillingham Co., 1896.

Oates, Stephen, *Confederate Cavalry West of the River*. Austin, University of Texas Press, 1961.

Odum, Howard W., and Guy B. Johnson, *The Negro and His Songs*. Chapel Hill, University of North Carolina Press, 1925.

O'Flaherty, Daniel, *General Jo Shelby*. Chapel Hill, University of North Carolina Press, 1954.

Otero, Miguel Antonio, *My Life on the Frontier, 1864–1882*. New York, The Press of the Pioneers, Inc., 1935.

The Outlaw Brothers Frank and Jesse James or Lives and Adventures of the Scourges of the Plains. New York, National Police Gazette, 1883.

Parrish, William E., *David Rice Atchison of Missouri: Border Politician*. Columbia, University of Missouri Press, 1961.

———, *Turbulent Partnership: Missouri and the Union, 1861–1865*. Columbia, University of Missouri Press, 1963.

Paxton, W. M., *Annals of Platte County*. Kansas City, Hudson Kimberly Publishing Company, 1897.

Poindexter, C. A., and Bracken Fitzpatrick, *The Historical Background, Setting and Synopsis of "Jesse James" Filmed at and Near Pineville, Missouri*. Pineville, Pineville Democrat, n.d.

Randolph, Vance, *Ozark Folksongs*. Columbia, State Historical Society of Missouri, 1946–1950. 4 vols.

Rascoe, Burton, *Belle Starr*. New York, Random House, Inc., 1941.

Ray, Clarence E., *The Border Outlaws — Frank and Jesse James*. Chicago, Regan Publishing Corporation, n.d.

———, *The James Boys*. Chicago, Regan Publishing Corporation, n.d.

———, *The James Boys and Bob Ford*. Chicago, Regan Publishing Corporation, n.d.

———, *Jesse James' Daring Raid*. Chicago, Regan Publishing Corporation, n.d.

———, *The Younger Brothers*. Chicago, Regan Publishing Corporation, n.d.

Read, Opie, *Mark Twain and I*. Chicago, Reilly & Lee Co., 1940.

Redmond, Frank, *The Younger Brothers*. St. Louis, Dramatic Company, 1901.

Reynolds, Quentin, *The Fiction Factory*. New York, Random House, Inc., 1955.

Roe, Edward Thomas, *The James Boys*. Chicago, E. A. Weeks & Co., 1893.

Roe, G. M., *Our Police*. Cincinnati, n.p., 1890.

Rogers, John William, *The Lusty Texans of Dallas*. New York, E. P. Dutton & Co., Inc., 1951.

Rowan, Richard Wilmer, *The Pinkertons — A Detective Dynasty*. Boston, Little, Brown & Company, 1931.

Russell, Don, *The Lives and Legends of Buffalo Bill*. Norman, University of Oklahoma Press, 1960.

Russell, Jesse Lewis, *Behind the Ozark Hills*. New York, The Hobson Book Press, 1947.

Sandburg, Carl, *The American Songbag*. New York, Harcourt, Brace & Company, Inc., 1927.

Schrantz, Ward L., *Jasper County, Missouri, in the Civil War*. Carthage, Missouri, Carthage Press, 1923.

Shoemaker, Floyd C., *Missouri and Missourians: Land of Contrasts and People of Achievements*. I. Chicago, The Lewis Publishing Company, 1943. 5 vols.

Spring, Agnes Wright, *The Cheyenne and Black Hills Stage and Express Routes*. Glendale, California, Arthur H. Clark Company, 1949.

Steward, A. J. D., ed., *The History of Bench and Bar of Missouri*. St. Louis, The Legal Publishing Company, 1898.

Stout, Ernest, *The Younger Brothers*. Chicago, Dramatic Company, 1902.

———, *The Younger Brothers' Last Raid*. Chicago, Dramatic Company, 1902.

———, *The Youngers' Last Stand*. Chicago, Dramatic Company, 1902.

———, *The Youngers Out West*. Chicago, Dramatic Company, 1902.

Street, Julian, *Abroad At Home*. New York, The Century Company, 1914.

Stuart, Theodore M., *Past and Present of Lucas and Wayne Counties, Iowa*. Chicago, S. J. Clarke Publishing Co., 1913. 2 vols.

Sutley, Zack T., *The Last Frontier*. New York, The Macmillan Company, 1930.

Sutton, Fred E., *Hands Up!* Indianapolis, The Bobbs-Merrill Company, 1927.

[Switzler, William F.], *History of Boone County, Missouri*. St. Louis, Western Historical Company, 1882.

Switzler, William F., *Switzler's Illustrated History of Missouri, from 1541 to 1877*. St. Louis, C. R. Barns, 1879.

Thorndike, Thaddeus, *Lives and Exploits of the Daring Frank and Jesse James*. Baltimore, I. & M. Ottenheimer, 1909.

Townsend, Robert S., ed., *Decade of Decision 1855–1865*. Kansas City, Kansas City Life Insurance Company, 1960.

Train and Bank Robbers of the West, and Appler, Augustus C., *The Life, Character and Daring Exploits of the Younger Brothers*. Chicago, Belford, Clarke and Company, 1882.

Triplett, Frank, *The Life, Times, and Treacherous Death of Jesse James*. St. Louis, J. H. Chambers and Company, 1882.

The True Story of Jesse James. Dell Comic Book, No. 757, a movie classic. New York, 1957.

Van Every, Edward, *Sins of America as "Exposed" by the Police Gazette*. New York, Frederick A. Stokes Company, 1931.

Van Nada, M. L., ed., *The Book of Missourians*. Chicago, T. J. Steele and Company, 1906.

Vaughan, Joe, *The Only True History of Frank James, Written by Himself*. Pine Bluff, Arkansas, Sarah E. Snow, 1926.

Vestal, Stanley, *The Missouri*. New York, Farrar and Rinehart, 1945.

Violette, Eugene Morrow, *A History of Missouri*. New York, D. C. Heath & Company, 1918.

Vreeland, Frank, *Foremost Films of 1938*. New York and Chicago, Pitman Publishing Corporation, 1939.

Walker, Henry J., *Jesse James "the Outlaw," Jesse Woodson James alias J. Frank Dalton 1848–1951*. Des Moines, Iowa, Wallace Homestead Company, 1961.

Wallace, William H., *Speeches and Writings of William H. Wallace with Autobiography*. Kansas City, Western Baptist Publishing Company, 1914.

Ward, William, *Jesse James' Blackest Crime*. Cleveland, Arthur Westbrook Company, 1909.

———, *Jesse James' Midnight Attack*. Cleveland, Arthur Westbrook Company, 1910.

———, *Jesse James' Mid-Winter Lark*. Cleveland, Arthur Westbrook Company, n.d.

———, *Jesse James' Race for Life*. Cleveland, Arthur Westbrook Company, n.d.

Watts, Hamp B., *The Babe of the Company*. Fayette, Missouri, Democrat Leader Press, 1913.

Wellman, Paul I., *A Dynasty of Western Outlaws*. Garden City, New York, Doubleday & Company, Inc., 1961.

The Wild Bandits of the Border. Chicago, Laird and Lee, 1892.

Winch, Frank, *Thrilling Lives of Buffalo Bill*. New York, S. L. Parsons and Company, 1911.

Younger, Coleman, *The Story of Cole Younger by Himself*. Chicago, The Henneberry Company, 1903.

Zornow, William Frank, *Kansas, A History of the Jayhawk State*. Norman, University of Oklahoma Press, 1957.

Index

detective raid, 78; failure of Republican resolutions in, 79; consideration of amnesty resolution, 80–84; consideration of resolutions resulting from death of Jesse James, 122–23; recess of, in respect for J. N. Edwards, 158; petition for release of the Youngers, 162

Leithead, J. Edward, 187

Lexington, Missouri: bank robbery at, 34, 36; omnibus robbery at, 70–72

Lexington, Missouri, *Caucasian*, 59, 71–74

Lexington, Missouri, *Expositor*, 16

Lexington, Missouri, *Register*, 72, 73

Liberty, Missouri: location, 9; Federal arsenal seized, 14; bank robbery at, 33–36, 50, 101

Liberty, Missouri, *Advance*, 100

Liberty, Missouri, *Democratic Platform*, 10

Liberty, Missouri, *Tribune*, 14, 20, 22, 23, 35, 40, 42, 85, 102, 115

Liddil, Dick: presidential pardon sought for, 137–38; witness in Gallatin trial of Frank James, 140, 141, 143; confession published, 148; controversy over pardon for, 150–52; witness in Alabama trial of Frank James, 152; mention of, 108, 114, 116–19, 132–34, 193

Liggett, James: and Shepherd "killing" of Jesse James, 103–5

Lilly, Jim, 206

Lindsay, James M., 6

Little, Thomas, 36–37, 41

Logan County, Kentucky: and rumors of James band, 115; mention of, 54

Lone Jack, Battle of, 21

Long, Nimrod, 35

Loot from robberies, 33–35, 39, 43–45, 47, 49, 50, 70, 71, 75, 87, 88, 103, 108, 111, 112, 114, 118, 133, 137, 208

Louisville, Kentucky, *Courier*, 37

Louisville, Kentucky, *Courier-Journal*: libel suit against, 168

Love, Robertus: quoted, 172; book on Jesse James, 197–98

Low, Marcus A., 139

Lull, Louis J.: killed by John Younger, 60–62; mention of, 68

Lyon, Nathaniel P., 13, 14, 15

McClain, Judge John: resistance of bandits by, 34

McClurg, Governor Joseph W., 41

McCorkle, Jabez, 23

McCorkle, John, 22–23

McCoy, Arthur: in "A Terrible Quintette," 51, 53; mention of, 38, 50, 60, 71

McCulloch, Benjamin, 14, 15

McDaniel, Bud, 75, 87

McDaniel, Thompson, 87

McDaniels, R., 36

McDonough, James: and arrest of John Goodin, 98–99; mention of, 88–89, 94

McDougall, Henry C.: and suit to attach horse lost by bandits at Gallatin, 208; mention of, 139

McDowell, William A., 38–40

McGinnis, Alfred R., 42

McGuire, Andy, 36, 37, 50, 206

Machette, Reverend Jamin, 141

McMillan, Frank: killed in train robbery, 108; Frank James's trial for murder of, 139–41

McMurtry, Lee, 206

Malvern, Arkansas: stage robbery at, 49–50

Mammoth Cave, Kentucky: robbery of sightseers' stage at, 133

Manning, A. B., 92

Marmaduke, Governor John S.: election as governor, 1884, 155–57; visit by J. N. Edwards, 157–58; mention of, 22, 27

Marshall, Governor William R., 161-62

Martin, R. A. C.: killed by bandits, 44

Martin, Reverend J. M., 119, 126

Merritt, William L., 222

Miller, Alice J., 162

Miller, Clell: death of, at Northfield, 93, 94; mention of, 43, 44, 57, 89, 104, 113

Miller, Ed, 104, 108, 113, 114, 116, 148

Miller, Robert H., 14

Mimms, John, 31

Mimms, Zerelda (Zee). *See* James, Zerelda.

Miserez, P. J., 36

Missouri, State of: Constitution of 1865, 31, 32; criticism of, by Eastern press, 124–26

Missouri City: raided by Fernando Scott, 22

Missouri-Kansas border welfare, 10

Missouri, Kansas and Texas Railroad, 58

Missouri Legend, 176

Missouri Pacific Railroad: trains robbed, 88–90, 165; and Edwards, 158

"Missouri Roundelay, A," 127

Missouri State Convention, 13, 15

Mitchell, David, 23

Mittenthal Clothing Company, 163

Monegaw Springs, Missouri, 59, 60